DUMBARTON OAKS
MEDIEVAL LIBRARY

Jan M. Ziolkowski, General Editor

ON MORALS OR
CONCERNING EDUCATION

THEODORE METOCHITES

DOML 61

On Morals or
Concerning Education

THEODORE
METOCHITES

Translated by

SOPHIA XENOPHONTOS

DUMBARTON OAKS
MEDIEVAL LIBRARY

HARVARD UNIVERSITY PRESS
CAMBRIDGE, MASSACHUSETTS
LONDON, ENGLAND
2020

Theodore Metochites Greek text reprinted by permission from *Ēthikos ē Peri Paideias* by Ioannis Polemes, Revised Edition (Athens: Ekdoseis Kanake, 2002).

First Printing

Library of Congress Cataloging-in-Publication Data
Names: Metochites, Theodoros, 1270–1332, author. | Xenophontos, Sophia A., 1985– translator. | Metochites, Theodoros, 1270–1332. Ēthikos ē Peri paideias. Greek (Modern Greek) | Metochites, Theodoros, 1270–1332. Ēthikos ē Peri paideias. English
Title: On morals, or, Concerning education / Theodore Metochites ; translated by Sophia Xenophontos.
Other titles: Concerning education | Dumbarton Oaks medieval library ; 61.
Description: Cambridge, Massachusetts : Harvard University Press, 2020. | Series: Dumbarton Oaks medieval library ; 61 | Includes bibliographical references and index. | This is a facing-page volume: Greek on the versos; English translation on the rectos.
Identifiers: LCCN 2019038763 | ISBN 9780674244634 (cloth)
Subjects: LCSH: Moral exhortation—Early works to 1800. | Moral education—Early works to 1800. | Ethics, Medieval—Early works to 1800.
Classification: LCC BJ255.M482 P47 2020 | DDC 170—dc23
LC record available at https://lccn.loc.gov/2019038763

Contents

Introduction

Theodore Metochites, a distinguished figure in the intellectual and political landscape of the early Palaiologan period (1261–1341), was born in Constantinople in 1270. From a middle-class background, he rose to the very top of early Palaiologan society and established the Metochites family among the late Byzantine aristocracy. He was the son of the leading advocate of union with the Latin Church, George Metochites, whom he had to follow into temporary exile in Asia Minor around 1283 owing to the anti-unionism of the new emperor, Andronikos II (r. 1282–1328). But thanks to the depth and breadth of his scholarly interests, Theodore soon attracted the attention of Andronikos II (most likely during the latter's tour of the Anatolian provinces in 1290) and became one of his most trusted associates. From that point onward, he held various offices (*logothetes ton agelon, logothetes ton oikeiakon, logothetes tou genikou*) and in 1321 was invested as *megas logothetes,* although his most important function was perhaps the more informal office of *mesazon* (prime minister).[1]

Metochites's rapid advancement, coupled with his participation in diplomatic missions to Cyprus, Cilicia, and

Serbia (often involving marriage negotiations), helped him amass considerable wealth. His connections with the imperial family were further strengthened by the marriage of his daughter, Irene, to the emperor's nephew, the Caesar John Palaiologos. At the emperor's invitation Metochites assumed responsibility for the restoration of the imperial monastery of the Chora (modern day Kariye Camii) between 1316 and 1321. One of the most spectacular mosaics he commissioned as a donor, at which any modern visitor can still marvel in the church's inner narthex, portrays Metochites as a supplicant, kneeling before the figure of Christ enthroned and offering him a model of the renovated Chora church.[2] Moreover, at the height of his powers Metochites assembled the library of the Chora, which most probably remained one of the largest monastic libraries in Constantinople up to 1453.[3] He was quite despised, since he was seen as responsible for Andronikos II's rapacious fiscal policies, and when Andronikos II was deposed in 1328, Metochites fell into disfavor; his palace was plundered, he was imprisoned, stripped of his fortune, and eventually exiled to Didymoteichon in Thrace. In 1330 he was allowed to return to Constantinople and retire to the Chora monastery, where he died as the monk Theoleptos in 1332.[4]

METOCHITES'S MILIEU

Metochites lived in a period of turmoil that witnessed the gradual shrinking of the empire's frontiers in the Balkans and Asia Minor, especially in the face of the encroaching Ottoman Turks. The internal calamities of the civil war between Andronikos II and his grandson, Andronikos III

(r. 1328–1341), exacerbated the foreign threat.[5] Corruption, fiscal pressure as a result of territorial losses and the consequent disruption of tax revenue, as well as the impoverishment that plagued the cities of Thrace and more especially Constantinople and Thessalonike (where the influx of refugees increased in the first decade of the fourteenth century) were the main causes for pessimism on a day-to-day basis.[6]

Despite the enfeebled fabric of Byzantine politics and the economy, a new age emerged in terms of culture, initially as part of an imperial attempt to recreate former glories due to Michael VIII's (r. 1259–1282) policies of restoration in 1261. Through a sustained revival of classical Greek scholarship, Palaiologan literati infused their works with overt links to their Hellenic heritage, providing impressive evidence of intellectual activity.[7] They hunted for manuscripts preserving ancient texts and produced a large number of editions and commentaries, often reviving knowledge of authors who had been neglected or indeed unknown in earlier centuries. Demetrios Triklinios edited anew the Athenian tragedians, while Maximos Planoudes rediscovered Ptolemy's *Geography* and brought together for the first time Plutarch's miscellaneous essays forming the collection of the *Moralia* (Ἠθικά), a label he gave it himself. Other polymaths, most notably Manuel Moschopoulos and Thomas Magistros, composed grammars and dictionaries in order to facilitate the learning of impeccable Attic Greek, and they and others provided scholia, for instance to Pindar and Aristophanes, as another tool for studying antique literature. Last but not least, a group of late Byzantine writers devoted much of their energy to the production of new scientific handbooks, especially on mathematics, astronomy, and medi-

cine, in which they engaged with their predecessors through creative emulation and to some extent originality. George Pachymeres not only wrote on history and theology but also penned a huge mathematical compendium; John Zacharias Aktouarios, a practicing physician and medical author, made significant contributions in the fields of uroscopy and pharmacology; Nikephoros Gregoras was both a historian and a keen musicologist and astronomer.

Knowledge of Latin literature, resulting from cultural contacts between the Byzantines and the West from as early as the twelfth century, increased. That points to another feature peculiar to the late Byzantine period, the translations of Latin works into Greek, such as those enthusiastically undertaken by Maximos Planoudes (including works of Cicero, Caesar, and Ovid) or those by Demetrios Kydones some time later (for example, of tracts by Augustine and Thomas Aquinas), all of which testify to the introduction of Latin and scholastic thought into the Palaiologan world. Translations also became a functional medium in the dialogue with non-Western ideas. George-Gregory Chioniades and George Chrysokokkes gravitated toward Persian scientific material, which they rendered in Greek. By the late thirteenth century, Byzantine culture had become dynamic, diverse, and receptive to outside influence.

We should see the scholarly activity of Theodore Metochites as being at the very heart of the Palaiologan revival. His interests seem to have been informed by some of the key trends of his time, such as the strong influence of the authors of the so-called "Second Sophistic" period (roughly the first through third centuries CE) or the composition of rhetorical works intended to be performed in the various

late Byzantine *theatra,* salons of the intelligentsia hosted by imperial or elite patrons.[8]

METOCHITES AND HIS WORKS

In his enormous output, Metochites engaged with a wide range of genres: he wrote paraphrases of Aristotle's treatises on natural philosophy, twenty poems in approximately 9,200 dactylic hexameters on various subjects entailing some fascinating pieces of personal confession, and eighteen orations to the emperor, various saints, and contemporary friends, as well as encomia in praise of Nicaea and Constantinople. He was particularly acclaimed for his achievements in astronomy, which he considered a noble science, intended only for elite adepts. His *Elements of Astronomy (Stoicheiosis astronomike),* a three-part introduction to Ptolemaic astronomy, triggered a resurgence of interest in ancient science in Byzantium. Furthermore, he produced a collection of letters, preserved in a fifteenth-century manuscript that was later destroyed in the fire of 1671 at the Real Biblioteca del Monasterio de El Escorial.[9] The most characteristic testimony to Metochites's antiquarianism is his *Sententious Remarks (Semeioseis gnomikai,* also known as *Miscellanea),* which is a collection of 120 essays bringing together encyclopedic material from physics, logic, history, politics, religion, and ethics, comprising extracts from more than eighty pagan authors.[10]

Metochites's multilayered production reflects both a passion for mining the books of antiquity and a recurrent tone of complaint, arising out of his frustration that his eagerness to dedicate himself to intellectual pursuits was often

thwarted by his overloaded schedule of private and public duties.[11] Some of his works have educational aspirations too—often very grand ones, especially in relation to his protégé and the addressee of some of his pieces, Nikephoros Gregoras. Metochites scholars tend to draw evaluative conclusions about the quality of his corpus based on one particular work or set of works, at times carried away by his elaborate, high-flown style, which was criticized in Metochites's own day by his adversaries.[12] This restricted perspective, together with the fact that a significant part of Metochites's writings remains unpublished, hinders any comprehensive assessment of his thought and output.

The *On Morals or Concerning Education*

Topic and Date of Composition

The *On Morals or Concerning Education* (*Ethikos,* henceforth abbreviated as *On Morals*) is an extensive disquisition about the significance and status of cultural education (*paideia*) in the context of Palaiologan society. The oration might also be seen at least partly as an autobiographical narrative exposing Metochites's inner reflections and anxieties.

On the basis of Metochites's reference to his very young children in the *On Morals* (chapter 47.3), 1305 has been suggested as a possible date for the composition of the work.[13] A recent study has proposed moving the *terminus post quem* to 1307, arguing that Metochites's complaints about his lack of time for intellectual endeavors in all likelihood result from his busy political schedule in a period when Andronikos II was trying to combat the Catalan mercenaries after the famine of 1306–1307 in Constantinople.[14] Given that Metochites

refers to his *On Morals* in his poem addressed to Nikephoros Kallistos Xanthopoulos (Poem 12) of the late 1320s (perhaps not long before 1328),[15] what can be deduced with certainty is that the work must have been composed before that date. Moreover, taking into account that the contents of Vindobonensis phil. gr. 95 (the only manuscript preserving Metochites's orations) are placed in chronological order, and that the *On Morals* comes just before the *Byzantios* for which the *terminus ante quem* is the year 1317 or 1320,[16] we can narrow the time period for its composition down to somewhere between 1307 and 1317 or 1320; or indeed closer to 1307 if we accept Ihor Ševčenko's hypothesis that Metochites's son, Demetrios, mentioned in the *On Morals* as a baby, was between twenty and twenty-five years old when Andronikos III assumed power in 1328.[17]

STRUCTURE AND SUMMARY

The structure of the work is obscured primarily by the author's rhetorical extravagance and partly by a number of lacunae in the codex, which disrupt certain passages. The text can be divided into sections, as follows.[18]

Chapters 1–5 (Preface): Metochites addresses an anonymous young man, who may well represent a generic addressee rather than a specific individual, with the objective of persuading him of the importance of education. He refers to his difficulties in composing the *On Morals,* a work that he hopes will benefit both himself and his reader. In his encomium of learning, he strongly opposes detractors of education and those who underestimate the power of the intellect.

Chapters 6–9: The foundation of education is the acqui-

sition of true knowledge about the nature and providence of God. People must show unquestioning faith in God's Trinitarian and unified nature and never distrust traditional Christian principles.

Chapters 10–14: Virtue is the second most important requirement for good living, because it endures despite the general mutability of human life. The author praises the contemplative life, seeing it as a path toward tranquility and bliss.

Chapters 15–24: Education is a requirement for a virtuous life. Unlike wealth, fame, and other external blessings, education never ceases; it helps people combat the misfortunes of life with equanimity. Books are mines of philosophical and historical information, while the cultural underpinnings of ancient Greece (with special reference to Plato, Socrates, and Diogenes) and Rome are put forward as a model for Metochites's contemporaries to imitate.

Chapters 25–33: Intellectual pleasure stemming from the study of past events is highlighted. According to Metochites, unlike Epicurean hedonism that animates the lower part of the soul (that is, the part dealing with emotions and desires), intellectual hedonism can assist the rational faculty of the soul to regulate one's bewildering passions.

Chapters 34–37: In order to corroborate his impartiality in examining the value of education, Metochites challenges the widely held claim that education alone provides immortality. In Metochites's opinion, this holds for other arts too, for instance sculpture or painting. He also emphasizes that education and philosophy are not the only blessings in life, and that, as Plato argued, political virtue is also important.

Chapters 38–44: Rivalries among scholars provoke suspi-

cion of education. Metochites delves into the dark side of human behavior, dealing with the role played by gossip, calumny, and malicious abuse.

Chapters 45–48: The author confesses that he has abandoned education for the sake of his daily duties and is frustrated to realize that it is challenging to combine the active and the contemplative life.

Chapters 49–59: Metochites refutes the accusations leveled against education; he argues that the most effective way of facing up to the changeability of human affairs is by rationalizing misfortunes, given that certain circumstances are outside our control.

Chapters 60–64: Another accusation aimed at education is that knowledge is often the cause of sorrow and distress. For Metochites, however, ignorance would reduce men to the level of animals.

Chapter 65 (Conclusion): Metochites exhorts his addressee to get involved in education on the grounds that this will enhance his relationship with God and the saints, who in turn will assist him with his concerns.

Genre

The *On Morals* belongs to the genre of the *protreptikos,* a hortatory speech designed to encourage its readers to study philosophy and attain virtue. Typical protreptics in classical literature include Plato's *Phaedo* and *Euthydemus,* Isocrates's *Antidosis,* Aristotle's fragmentary *Protreptic,* and the later *Protreptic* by Iamblichos, although the origins of the genre may go back to the writings of the Sophists of the fifth century BCE. Besides seeking to persuade through a sequence of ra-

tional arguments, the protreptic also uses various strategies to arouse the audience's emotional responses in the process of reading.

In referring to specific typological distinctions between works of ethical philosophy, Philo of Larisa, once head of the Platonic Academy, suggested a threefold categorization: 1) protreptic works that guide the reader toward morally appropriate courses of behavior, 2) therapy that offers philosophical guidelines for the treatment of particular emotions, and 3) advice, which proposes lifestyles through which to achieve happiness by means of the therapy that has already been applied.[19] The thematic backdrop, content, and language of the *On Morals* attest to its dependence on the protreptic, yet this would not preclude its having also been influenced by the subgenres of therapy and advice: at times Metochites widens the scope of his work to discuss the treatment of destructive emotions such as grief and distress (chapters 58–62), whereas he ends by recommending general behavioral patterns and a philosophical attitude to life.

SOURCES AND MODELS

The protreptic is also related to the genre of the diatribe, used and developed by the Stoic philosophers, notably Seneca, Epictetus, and Marcus Aurelius. The two genres are not always distinguishable from one another, especially in terms of content. Topics such as the changeability of human fortune *(tyche)* as a contrast to the stability of philosophy, virtue, and wisdom; the role of self-exploration and self-reformation; and the management of disturbing passions through the practice of reason *(askesis)* are perennial fea-

tures of Stoic psychotherapy informing the work of Metochites. Furthermore, the employment of medical terminology with reference to the healing of the soul, the doctrine that we should not be aggrieved about situations that we cannot control ("what is up to us and what is not up to us"), the idea that happiness is the only thing that matters in life, while everything else including wealth and fame are moral "indifferents," and the need to anticipate negative experiences as a way of mitigating their emotional impact (the well-known *praemeditatio futurorum malorum*) are all traditional topoi of late Stoicism that Metochites adopts.

These Stoic tenets, however, were critically transformed by some philosophers of middle Platonism, for instance Plutarch. Metochites's emphasis on psychic equanimity or, in close connection with this, the mastery of the rational over the irrational faculty of the soul, echoes Plutarch's *On Tranquility of the Soul* and others of his moral essays, which Metochites quotes, for instance, *On Listening to Poetry* and *On Progress in Virtue*. The fact of the matter is that Metochites's dependence on Plutarch goes beyond the limits of the *On Morals;* the Byzantine scholar devotes a separate essay in his *Sententious Remarks* (no. 71) exclusively to the philosopher of Chaeronea, whom he uses as a rhetorical persona for his self-presentation.[20] Additional philosophical influences on the *On Morals* encompass Philo of Alexandria (ontological theory, isolation of the intellectual man) and Synesios (intellectual pleasure as described in the *Dion*).[21]

The vast range of citations (explicit or allusive) from many other antique authorities testify to Metochites's immersion in the Greek classical legacy: Pythagoras *(Golden Words),* Plato *(Republic, Charmides, Timaeus, Meno,* etc.), and

Aristotle *(Nicomachean Ethics)*, anecdotal material on Socrates and Diogenes, Homeric lines especially from the *Iliad,* historical events from classical Greece, such as the Persian wars, and snippets from the tragic poets and Sappho all feature predominantly throughout the *On Morals.*

Context, Readership, and Influence

The composition of the *On Morals* situates Metochites in the tradition introduced a generation before him by the emperor Theodore II Laskaris (r. 1254–1258), whose *Ethical Epitomes* show the special emphasis he laid on moral didacticism.[22] It is highly probable in this respect, especially if one considers Metochites's heightened degree of self-consciousness, that with the *On Morals* he sought to establish himself as a continuator of ancient moral philosophy in late Byzantium. This suggestion is corroborated primarily by the exceedingly moral character of the *Sententious Remarks.* At the same time the features of his exhortation itself align it with traditional protreptics from the classical period onward, with Metochites's engagement with the conventions of the genre moving beyond mere imitation and faithful reproduction. The work is "modernized" to exert a strong appeal on the educated elite, who would have been inspired and presumably fascinated by the exemplar of the cultivated man *(pepaideumenos)* that Metochites revives. After all, late Byzantine literati held notions such as *paideia,* virtue, and power very dear, so Metochites must have been playing with his audience's sense of honor and social ambition *(philotimia)* too. Although there is no obvious attempt to Christianize the work by infusing it with scriptural quo-

tations or sections from homiletics, for example (which is consistent with Metochites's working method in his poems), some overarching features of the Christian community of later Byzantium punctuate the discussion (see the following section on Scholarly Significance), thereby making the text meaningful to contemporary readers. Consequently, although written in the vein of ancient protreptics, the *On Morals* is a starkly Byzantine piece, with this interconnectedness between pagan philosophy and religiosity reflecting one of Metochites's most characteristic signatures.

Despite the author's grandiose aspirations, the *On Morals* does not seem to have been circulated widely among his contemporaries (it is preserved only in Vindobonensis phil. gr. 95, as seen above), and although it might have been occasionally performed in a *theatron,* it enjoyed only limited reception in later times.[23] The only direct reference to the later circulation of the *On Morals* of which we are aware is connected with the sixteenth-century monk and orator Theophanes Eleavoulkos,[24] who revised the original text to make it a better fit for his own ideological and pedagogical conflict with his rival Hermodoros in imitation of Metochites's polemics with Nikephoros Choumnos.[25]

SCHOLARLY SIGNIFICANCE

The text provides much information about the critical role of philosophy (and to some extent rhetoric) in an age of intensified sophistic revival (chapters 18 and 20). It is also useful for examining the social and cultural history of the early Palaiologan era, for instance the distinction between the active and the contemplative life or the social position of schol-

ars (chapter 17). Furthermore, in chapter 6 the work deals with the nature of Christian faith (with special discussion of ontology) and could contribute to modern scholarly debates over the philosophy of religion or the precise nature of the interplay between religious and secular learning *(thyrathen paideia)*.

More important, as its name suggests, the *On Morals* was expected to function as an ethical *vade mecum,* a manual of proper behavior in leading the good life. In it Metochites explores human psychology, for instance, the bipartition of the soul (chapter 30), offering numerous insights into discussions on ethical (re-)formation. Furthermore, the text is rich in material concerning Metochites's views on emotions, highlighting some intriguing components of affective discourse: for instance, definition and theorization of emotions, the role of sensation in normative psychological operations (chapter 30), antecedent conditions of emotional arousal (17), symptomatology of passions (10), their physiological etiology (12), metaphors used to convey unpleasant emotions, such as disgust (8–9), the passivity of the subject experiencing an emotion (43), analysis of envy as a social passion (8, 45), and many others.[26]

Since the *On Morals* draws heavily on a number of ancient philosophical sources, its study not only promotes the vibrant field of Byzantine philosophy but also casts new light on the reception of the classical philosophical tradition in the early fourteenth century, in particular the dialogue Byzantine scholars maintained with (Neo-)Platonic, Aristotelian, Stoic, and Epicurean concepts. The *On Morals* is also important for studying the reception of the *protreptikos/ ethikos* genre in Metochites's day, an issue with wider impli-

cations, given that the exhortative-style orations of antiquity became less common in the early and middle Byzantine periods, often taking on a Christian guise (Ambrose, Chrysostom, Origen) and therefore serving religious rather than secular purposes.

The *On Morals* includes authorial self-references (for example, to Metochites's anxieties and family commitments), offering a way of penetrating the darker sides of Metochites's idiosyncratic personality and investigating—by means of careful contextualization—how he wanted his worldview and character to appear to others. Finally, the text provides some insights into issues of mystical theology, natural philosophy, astronomy, and metaphysics, and forms part of the ideological background to the Hesychastic controversy that arose some years later.

Note on the Translation

Metochites's prose is convoluted and unorthodox, often defying translation, and is also obscured by the use of abstract terminology and intricate sentence structures, making navigation through the syntax a daunting task. This translation is a compromise between an attempt to provide a readable English text but at the same time reflect the original Greek locutions as closely as possible, thereby retaining Metochites's individual diction where appropriate. I provide here the main translation principles I have followed to facilitate interpretation of the text.

Some longer sentences have been broken up into two or more shorter units. Metochites is fond of *prothysteron,* a rhetorical trope that transposes what would naturally come first

to later in the sentence. In such cases, I reorder the terms to streamline the English narrative. Some necessary reordering has been applied in other instances as well, as syntax requires. Many synonyms are often added in a row; although the text therefore reads in a repetitive and stilted manner, I normally translate all of them, in order to remain faithful to the author's stylistic intricacies. When two nouns are given in parataxis, I occasionally adjectivize the first when context requires. Readers can consult the Greek at their own discretion to track the original terms. Superfluous lexical items (often adverbs that do not affect the meaning) are not translated for the sake of clarity. Long periods are often interrupted with verbal asides such as "I think" (οἶμαι) or "as it seems" (ὡς ἔοικε); in cases in which the already complex wording needs to be simplified, I refrain from translating these. The text abounds in proverbs, whose literal meaning I always render either in the main text or in the notes to make it intelligible to the reader. I treat proverbs as direct quotations and therefore italicize them (except in cases in which I was unable to identify them). Another colloquial feature of the text is the use of the locution "how shall one put/say it?" (πῶς ἂν εἴπῃ τις;) in the form of an indirect aside included in parentheses and normally designed to convey doubt or astonishment. A complex term within the *On Morals* is *logos,* which I generally translate as "education" or "learning" in its broader sense. At other times, *logos* might refer to rational discourse as a constitutive element of philosophy, and I accordingly translate as "the faculty of reason" contrasted to passions. Alternatively, *logos* can be the written manifestation of reasoning, hence a literary work, a treatise or a rhetorical speech, and by extension "litera-

ture" as well. Finally, the term may simply refer to a "word" or a "statement." In religious contexts, it denotes Christ or "divine Word." Metochites's style is rather dense, as a consequence of which implied terms often need to be supplied to render passages comprehensible. This occurs more frequently at the beginning of periods or semiperiods. Translator's insertions for the purpose of clarification are not indicated overtly, as Dumbarton Oaks Medieval Library policy does not permit the use of angled or square brackets. The frequent use of πράγματα (things/matters), πάντα (everything), and similar indefinite or unspecified terms adds a sense of vagueness, so I have reworded such phrases to make them more specific and explicit. Similarly, instead of translating a pronoun I have often indicated what I believe it to refer to. In accordance with the guidelines of the series, I have restricted the notes to a minimum, offering the reader brief explanatory comments. The transliteration of proper Greek names, ancient and Byzantine, follows the *Oxford Classical Dictionary* and *Oxford Dictionary of Byzantium,* respectively. References to classical texts are taken from the standard Oxford Classical Texts or Teubner editions, unless otherwise stated.

In rendering the *On Morals* into English, I have profited from consulting Ioannis Polemis's modern Greek translation of the work,[27] although my debt to him extends much farther: his enviable familiarity with Metochites, both as editor and translator, informed discussions we had on particular points of the text. I would also like to thank him for kindly consenting to the reproduction of his 2002 criti-

cal edition accompanying my translation. In 2019, a more recent edition of the text appeared in the Teubner series, but this reached me too late for me to take full advantage of it (see Notes to the Text). I am grateful to Polemis for allowing me to consult the proofs of the edition. My deepest gratitude goes to my assigned reader from the Dumbarton Oaks Medieval Library's editorial board, Niels Gaul, who went through earlier drafts and subsequent versions with meticulous care, suggesting many improvements, particularly on tricky passages, and providing his scholarly expertise throughout. Professor Alexander Alexakis was another valuable collaborator, helping me decipher opaque passages and saving me from infelicitous renderings. An anonymous reader also offered sound comments on other portions of the translation, improving points of interpretation and style. Enormous thanks go to both of them. I am also deeply indebted to Dionysios Stathakopoulos for being an acute reader of the Introduction. Earlier sections of the translation were presented at the workshop "Defining and Theorising Emotions," part of the International Research Network "Emotions through Time: From Antiquity to Byzantium," which took place at the University of Edinburgh in October 2016. I would like to thank the audience for providing constructive suggestions. Finally, I am grateful to the series editor, Alice-Mary Talbot, for her guidance through the various stages of the publication of the volume, and to John Mulhall, Tyler fellow at Dumbarton Oaks, for diligently reviewing and formatting the Greek text and English translation together with Alice-Mary Talbot. This book is the beneficiary of the unyielding support of my husband, Petros, who first encouraged me to work on Metochites and has been a

constant advisor in the course of this endeavor. The book is dedicated to my brothers, Christos and Kyriakos.

NOTES

1 Verpeaux, "Le *cursus honorum.*" See also Kontogiannopoulou, *Η εσωτερική πολιτική του Ανδρόνικου Β'*, 95–101.

2 N. Ševčenko, "The Portrait of Theodore Metochites at Chora."

3 See the study by Magdalino, "Theodore Metochites, the Chora, and Constantinople."

4 Apart from the entry on Metochites in *ODB*, under "Metochites, Theodore" (vol. 2, pp. 1357–58), and in *PLP*, no. 17982, I also consulted the relevant entry by Martin Hinterberger in the forthcoming *LbA* (and I thank him for sharing it with me). On Metochites's life and work, see in general Beck, *Theodoros Metochites: Die Krise;* I. Ševčenko, *La vie intellectuelle;* I. Ševčenko, "Theodore Metochites, the Chora," especially 25–37; I. Ševčenko, "Vita: Theodore Metochites"; and de Vries-van der Velden, *Théodore Métochite.*

5 For a detailed treatment of the political history of this period, see Nicol, *The Last Centuries of Byzantium,* 39–167.

6 Smyrlis, "Financial Crisis."

7 On the intellectual background to this period, see, for example, I. Ševčenko, *Society and Intellectual Life;* I. Ševčenko, "Palaiologan Learning"; and Tinnefeld, "Neue Formen der Antikerezeption."

8 Gaul, "Performative Reading."

9 Escurial B. IV 24 (*olim* Z. IV 20), fols. 177–263; see De Andrés, *Catálogo de los códices griegos,* 58, 210. The overwhelming majority of the letters are now lost.

10 References to the published works by Metochites mentioned above can be found in the Bibliography under "Editions of Works by Metochites."

11 Bazzani, "Theodore Metochites"; Hunger, "Theodoros Metochites als Verläufer."

12 On Metochites's language, see Hinterberger, "Studien zu Theodoros Metochites." On his style, see Hult, "Theodore Metochites as a Literary Critic"; I. Ševčenko, *La vie intellectuelle,* especially 51–67.

13 Polemis, Ἠθικός, 2002 edition, 9*–10* n. 4, citing I. Ševčenko, "The Logos on Gregory," 223. Also in Polemis, *Theodori Metochitae carmina*. De Vries-van der Velden, *Théodore Métochite*, 260, shifted the date to 1297/1299, and before her, Hunger, "Theodoros Metochites," 15, suggested circa 1328.

14 Voudouri, "Representations of Power," 110–11.

15 Cunningham, Featherstone, and Georgiopoulou, "Theodore Metochites's Poem," 100.

16 Polemis, Βυζάντιος, 22.

17 I. Ševčenko, "Théodore Métochite, *Logos* 10," 142.

18 I follow Polemis, Ἠθικός, 2002 edition, 11*–16*.

19 Stobaios, *Anthology*, 2.7.2; see also 2.39.20–41.25.

20 Xenophontos, "The Byzantine Plutarch."

21 Polemis, "Ἡ ἡδονὴ τῆς θεωρίας."

22 Angelov, "The Moral Pieces."

23 On the history of the transmission of Metochites's texts from the time of their composition up to their arrival in the Greek manuscript collections of the Renaissance, see Förstel, "Metochites and His Books."

24 Sathas, Βιογραφίαι τῶν ἐν τοῖς γράμμασι διαλαμψάντων Ἑλλήνων, 144–45.

25 Meletiadis, Ἡ ἐκπαίδευση στὴν Κωνσταντινούπολη, 43–56. See also Note on the Text, last paragraph.

26 I discuss these issues in a forthcoming study entitled "Exploring Emotions in Late Byzantium: Theodore Metochites on Affectivity."

27 Polemis, Ἠθικός, 2002 edition.

ON MORALS OR
CONCERNING EDUCATION

Ἠθικὸς ἢ
περὶ παιδείας

I

Πολλάκις ἔγωγ᾽ εἱλόμην μέτρι᾽ ἄττα περὶ τῶν λόγων, ὡς δὴ τυγχάνω γινώσκων καὶ καθὼς ἂν οἷός τ᾽ εἴην, ἐρεῖν σοι, καὶ ὅπως ἂν ἀντὶ τούτων ἅπασαν ἥντιν᾽ ἔξεστι σπουδὴν αἱροῖο, παρακαλέσαι ὡς πόνον ἀγαθόν, οὐδὲ τὴν ἐπιμέλειαν αὐτοῦ καὶ κτῆσιν οὐκ ὄντα μᾶλλον ἢ ῥαστώνην ἀληθῆ τε καὶ φίλην.

2   Ἐπεὶ δ᾽ ἑκάστοτε προσεῖχον τὸν νοῦν, ταὐτὸν ἄρα ὥσπερ οἱ καθ᾽ ὕπνους ὄναρ ὁτῳοῦν ἐγχειρεῖν δοκοῦντες, ἐσκοπούμην μὲν καὶ μέχρι τῶν λογισμῶν μόνων ἦν ἐνεργός, ἀνάγκη δ᾽ ἦν ἔπειτα μηδὲν πλέον ἐπὶ τοῖς ἔργοις αὐτοῖς ἀπαντᾶν—μηδ᾽ ἂν ὅτι μάλιστα βιαζοίμην—ἔπεσθαι, ἀλλὰ πάντ᾽ ἔδρων μᾶλλον ἢ λέγειν προθέμενος ἤνυτον λέγειν, τῆς ἄλλοτ᾽ ἄλλης ἐμπιπτούσης ἀφορμῆς ἀπαγούσης βίᾳ, φροντίδων εἰς τὸν βίον ἀναπιμπλάμενον, οὐκ οἶδ᾽ ὧντινων, οὐδ᾽ ὅπως ἐρῶ, παντάπασιν ἀγεννῶν καὶ ἀνελευθέρων, καὶ πραγματιδίων φλαύρων καὶ οὐδὲν καθάπαξ ἱερῶν, οὐδ᾽ ἀξίων σπουδῆς, οὐδ᾽ ὧν οὐδείς ποθ᾽ ἑκών γε εἶναι προειδόμενος ἀνὴρ ἐλλόγιμος ὅλως ἅψαιτ᾽ ἄν, κάκιστ᾽ ὀλουμένων, μᾶλλον δὲ κακῶς ὀλλύντων καὶ κατατεμμαχιζόντων εἰς μυρίαν ὅσην ἀηδίαν τὸν ἐραστὴν τοῦ καλοῦ νοῦν.

ON MORALS OR
CONCERNING EDUCATION

Chapter 1

Many times I reached the decision of telling you a few things about education, as I happen to perceive them and to the extent that I am able to do so. I also wished to encourage you to undertake every possible effort for the sake of this education, because it is a worthy endeavor and its pursuance and acquisition is nothing but a true and pleasant leisure activity.

However, whenever this consideration crossed my mind, I used to ponder it, but my thoughts alone were active, as I—no matter how much I pressed myself—was prevented by necessity from further pursuing and acting upon them, exactly like those who dream while asleep that they are occupied with a task. Therefore, I did everything but manage to say what I intended to say, since each time some other excuse would come up and forcefully divert me, as I am enmeshed in countless and indescribable concerns of life. These concerns are completely base and inappropriate for free men, trivial affairs of no great significance at all, unworthy of any attention. No man of high repute will ever deal willingly with such matters, once acquainted with them beforehand. Damn them! Yet it is they that damn and completely smash into a thousand pieces of disgust the mind that longs for virtue.

2

Ἐδόκει δέ μοι καὶ τοῦτο μάλιστ' ἐργῶδες· εἰ γὰρ πει-
ρῴμην, ἀμελετήτως ἔχειν, ἅτ' ἤδη τῆς ἐν λόγοις ἧσπερ
εἰώθειν ξυντυχίας ἀπότροφος πολλοῦ γεγονώς· μελέτη δέ
τοι ἔργον ὀφέλλει, φησὶν ἡ ποίησις, ὃ δέ, μήτε τιν' ἄσκησιν
μήτε τὴν γιγνομένην ἐπικουρίαν ἀεὶ προσλαμβάνον, τὴν
ἕξιν, οἶμαι, καθ' ἑκάστην ἐξ ἀνάγκης ἀπορρεῖ, τοῖς ἀτη-
μελήτοις ἔοικε τῶν φυτῶν καὶ μὴ τῆς νομίμου τυγχάνου-
σιν ἀγωγῆς καὶ ὥσπερ οὐδ' ἐκεῖνα πρὸς τὴν φύσιν ἢ τὴν
φοράν, οὔτ' εὔδρομον οὔτε σῶφρον ἂν εἴη πρὸς ἅπασαν
ἐπιχείρησιν.

2 Ἐγὼ μὲν οὖν οὕτω δὴ μάλιστ' εἶχον πόρρω ἢ πρὸς τὴν
νῦν κατασκευὴν περὶ τὸν λόγον ταύτην καὶ ξυνουσίαν,
ἔμελλες δ' ἄρα, παντάπασιν αὐτὸς ἀφροντίστως ἔχων σαυτοῦ, ἐμὲ λοιπὸν πρὸς ἑαυτὸν ἐπιστρέψαι παρ' ὥραν ἤδη,
καὶ μηδὲν ἐπὶ σαυτοῦ μήτ' ἄμεινον βεβουλημένος μήτ' ἐξ-
ισχύσας, κατ' ἐμοῦ γέγονας ἰσχυρὸς πάντων μεταστῆσαι
πραγμάτων πλεῖν ἢ ἔγωγ' αὐτὸς τέως ᾤμην τε καὶ παρ-
εσκευάσμην, καὶ σαυτοῦ μὲν οὔπω σὺ καὶ νῦν γέγονας, ἐμὲ
δ', οὐκ οἶδα πότερον ἂν φαίην, εἴτ' ἐμαυτοῦ πεποίηκας
εἴτε, τἀληθέστερον, μᾶλλον σοῦ.

3 Ὧν γὰρ μήπω πρότερον δι' ἐμαυτὸν εἶχον μεταστῆναι
μήθ' ὅλως ἕξῆν, διὰ σὲ γίγνεται καὶ δοκῶ μοι πάντων περι-
έσεσθαι τῶν ἄλλων φροντισμάτων μεριμνῶν ἐπὶ σοί. Ὡς
γὰρ τῶν ἡμετέρων, οἶμαι, παντάπασιν ἀπεγνωκὼς καὶ ὧν

Chapter 2

However, the following also seemed to me extremely difficult: if I had attempted to deal with the topic of education, I would have been unprepared, since I have abstained for a long time now from the blissful engagement with education to which I had been accustomed. The poem says *practice advances every activity,* but I think that a skill not constantly honed by training and regular attention necessarily weakens day by day, resembling untended plants that are not treated properly. Just as those plants cannot follow the rules of growth or productivity, similarly this skill can neither function well nor undertake any venture prudently.

So, this is how I came to be so very far off from this present involvement in and composition of this essay on education. But it would be you who, having thoroughly neglected yourself, would finally make me turn myself around, though late in the day by now, and, although you neither made any better plans for yourself, nor managed to accomplish any, you prevailed over me in detaching me from all other matters to a greater extent than I, myself, had previously imagined or expected. And now, even though you have not mastered yourself as yet, I do not know what to say about myself: whether you brought me to my senses or whether it would be more true to say that you made me your servant.

It is for your sake that it became possible for me to overcome all these troubles, which I could never before escape for my sake, nor did I have any such possibility; and I believe that by taking care of you I will be able to transcend all my other worries. For, I think, when I am in complete despair

ἐλπίδων εἶχον ἐπ' ἐμαυτοῦ περὶ λόγους καὶ δευτέρων ἀμεινόνων, φασίν, ὧν ἑξῆς πλέως ἦν ἐπὶ σοί, ζημιούμενος, κάμνω καὶ δεινὰ πάσχειν δοκῶ μοι μηκέτ' ἀνεκτῶς, ὥσπερ ἄρα πρότερον ἔμοιγε ξυγγινώσκειν ἠξίουν. Καὶ τοῦτο μὲν ὃ μέγιστον ἠνάγκασεν εἰς τὸν παρόντα νῦν, οἶμαι, λόγον.

4 Ἀλλὰ μὴν ἔτ' ᾠήθην μάλιστα ὡς ἐκείνως μὲν ἴσως ἐπιχειρῶν εὐφημεῖν τοὺς λόγους, μελετῶν αὐτὸς ἐν αὑτοῖς καὶ συνασκούμενος, τἀμαυτοῦ θαυμάζειν ἀξιοῦν ἐδόκουν ἄν, καὶ οἷς ἄρα δὴ ξύνειμι, καὶ σὲ καὶ πάντας καθάπαξ σπουδάζειν, καθάπερ ἀμέλει τοῦτο δρῶσιν οἱ πλείους, τὰ οἰκεῖα αὐτῶν πρὸς ἑκάστους ἀνθρώπων συνιστῶντες καὶ καταπείθοντες ὁμολογεῖν καὶ σφίσιν ὡς βελτίστοις προσέχειν· καὶ τοίνυν οἱ μὲν πατρίδας αὐτῶν καὶ τόπους τινὰς καὶ ξυνοικίας, οἱ δὲ πολιτεύματα, οἱ δὲ βίων αἱρέσεις, οἱ δὲ ἕκαστα, ἅττα ἂν ἕλωνται καὶ μεθ' ὧν ὑπ' ἀνάγκης ἂν ἡστινοσοῦν συνῶσι, κόπτουσι πᾶσαν ἀκοὴν σεμνηγοροῦντες καὶ πραττόμενοι περὶ αὐτῶν ἀγαθὰς τῶν ἀκουόντων ἐλπίδας.

3

Νυνὶ δὲ ἔγωγε μάλιστα μὲν ἠβουλόμην οὐχ οὕτως ἔχειν ὡς ἄρα πέπονθα καὶ ἀπετράπην τῶν λόγων, πειρώμενος δ' ἴσως εὐφημεῖν, ὧν τέως αὐτὸς κατηλόγηκα καὶ

about myself and the hopes which I had of education for myself, and moreover when I pay the price of losing one after another the even better hopes with which, as they say, I was filled for you, I am distressed and seem to suffer dreadfully; but I cannot stand it anymore in the same way as I would have consented to this for myself in the past. I think this is the main reason that led me to compose this essay.

Furthermore, I thought that if I had tried to praise education in that way while studying and practicing it myself, I would have seemed to be expecting both you and everyone else to admire my own interests and fully pursue the areas I am engaged in, which is, of course, what the majority of men do: they recommend their personal interests to each individual and try to persuade him to agree with them and pay attention to their endeavors, as if they were the best. Therefore, some deafen everyone around them by speaking solemnly and cultivating fine expectations in their audiences about their country or various other places and communities, some speak about constitutions, others about lifestyles, and others about whatever they choose or on whatever they are necessarily engaged in.

Chapter 3

I now very much wish that I were not in the plight in which I currently find myself and had not turned away from education. However, in trying to speak highly of what I myself have recently neglected and abandoned against my will,

μακράν εἰμι, ἄκων ἀνάγκῃ πράγματος, ξυγχωρεῖν μᾶλλον, οὐκ ἐμαυτῷ καὶ οἷς προσήκει μοι χαρίζεσθαι δόξαιμ' ἄν. Οὕτω γε μὴν καὶ ἐμαυτὸν μᾶλλον ἐλέγχειν ἔσται ὡς ἔξω προνοίας ἀτυχοῦντα τῶν δοκούντων βελτίστων, ἐμαυτὸν δ' ἀξιῶν ἐλέγχειν, ὑπὲρ ὧν ἔδοξα πρὸς σὲ σπουδάζειν, πῶς οὐκ ἄν σοι πιστὸς εἴην ἐπιχειρῶν πείθειν; Καίτοι τοσοῦτόν γε νῦν ἐρῶ, μηδὲν ὑποκρυψάμενος ὥσπερ ἐν ἀρχῇ μεταχειρίζων καὶ προσποιούμενος τὸν λόγον, ὡς οὐδὲν ἢ προσήκει πλέον ἐπαινεῖν ἢ λέγειν εὖ παρεσκεύασμαι.

2   Εἰσὶ γὰρ δή τινες οἳ τοσαύτην ἀξιοῦσιν ἀποφλισκάνειν τῇ παιδείᾳ χάριν, ὥστ' οὐδὲν ἐῶσιν ἄρρητον, ὅ,τι ἂν εἰς τοὺς λόγους ὅλως ξυννοήσωνται φέρον ἡντιναοῦν σεμνότητα, ἀλλὰ πάντα πράγμαθ' ὑπὲρ αὐτῶν καταψεύδονται καὶ φασὶ καὶ ἀποσεμνύνουσιν, ὅσα ἂν οἷοί τε γένοιντο, καὶ εἰ σφίσιν ἄρα δὴ μὴ μέτεστιν αὐτῶν τἀληθοῦς, ἐμοὶ δοκεῖν, ἵν' ἰσχύῃ τὸ σπούδασμ' ἑαυτοῖς, ἑκόντες ἀμελοῦντες, ἢ τῷ σφόδρα βούλεσθαι πρότερον μὲν αὐτοί <αὑτούς>, εἶθ' οὕτως τοὺς ἄλλους ἀπατῶντες.

3   Καὶ τοίνυν οὐκ ἀνεπιτίμητον μὲν οὐδ' ἀνεμέσητον ἀμφοτέροις τούτοις ὁ τοῦ καλοῦ πλάνος καὶ τὸ τοῦ προσήκοντος ἀτυχεῖν, οὐκ ἀσύγγνωστον δὲ αὖθις τῶν μὲν ἡ φιλοκαλία, μέχρι καὶ τοσοῦτο πάσχειν, τῶν δὲ ἡ φιλαυτία μέχρι καὶ ψεύδεσθαι. Ἅπαντες γὰρ ἑαυτοὺς φιλοῦσιν, εἰς ὅσον ἂν ἥκῃ καὶ δύναιντο πλεῖστον, καὶ τοσοῦτον ἴσως ἀνεύθυνον, ὡς νομίζεται, ὥστε καὶ πάντα διὰ τοῦτο μόνον ῥᾳδίως τολμᾶν, καὶ βούλοιντ' ἂν τὰ πάντα σφίσι πρὸς τὸ

simply driven by compulsion, I might give the impression that I do not just defer to myself, nor do I favor whatever concerns me. In fact, I will have the opportunity to cross-examine myself even more, because due to lack of foresight I am failing to obtain what I consider best. And, as I also deem it appropriate to question myself, why would I not be trustworthy when I try to persuade you about the issues on which I have decided to instruct you? But now I will just say one thing without hiding anything, as if arranging my speech from the beginning for my own ends, because I am not prepared to praise or speak more highly of education than is fitting.

For there are some people who want to repay such a huge 2 debt of gratitude to education that they leave nothing unsaid that they tend to think could give learning some kind of solemnity. But for the sake of learning they tell all sorts of lies and praise it as much as they can, even if there is no truth to it. I think they do this in order to glorify their occupation, being willfully neglectful, or because of their great desire to praise education, deceiving first themselves and then everyone else in the same way.

In both these cases their straying from what is good and 3 their failure to do what is right cannot remain uncensored or without provoking indignation; still we can pardon the love of what is noble, which leads the first group of people into such error, and the self-love of the second group of people, which leads them to tell lies. For all people love themselves to the maximum degree they can manage, and this appears guiltless, as it seems, to the extent that one easily undertakes everything due to self-love alone. People who adore themselves would like all their things to be prepared

βέλτιστον ἐσκευάσθαι καὶ τὸ δεύτερον ἔτι μάλισθ᾽ οὕτως ἐσκευάσθαι δοκεῖν.

4 Ἀλλὰ μὴν καὶ τοῖς γ᾽ ἑτέροις, τοῖς ἀνάγκῃ δούλοις ἔρωτος, ἅπαντες ἕτοιμοι συγγνώμης εἰσίν, ὡς μηκέτι πρὸς ἄλλ᾽ ὁτιοῦν οὐδέν, καὶ τοῦτο μόνον ἄφυκτον καὶ παντάπασι βίαιον τὸ πάθος οἴονται, κἂν ὅτι πλεῖστον ἔλαθον ἑαυτοὺς ἀποιήτως ἔχοντες καὶ ἀπροόπτως, εἴ τις αἰσθάνοιτο καὶ ξυνορῴη ὡς οὐδένα λογισμὸν προσόντα, δι᾽ ὃν προσήκει σφίσι τῆς νόσου κρείττοσιν εἶναι.

5 Καὶ μὴν ἀμφότεροί μοι δοκοῦσιν ἁμαρτάνειν ἐνίοτε πρὸς ἐφεδρεύουσαν ἀκοήν, οὐχ οὗ σκοποῦσι καὶ βούλονται μόνον, πλέον τι τοῦ προχείρου τοῖς παιδικοῖς καὶ μετρίου πραττόμενοι, ἀλλὰ καὶ τῶν δικαίων ἔπειτα αὐτῶν καὶ ὧν μάλιστα ἐπ᾽ ἀσφαλείας ἐξῆν, οἶμαι, περαίνειν, καὶ τῇ λίχνῳ πρὸς ἅπαν κέρδος καὶ πᾶσαν ὑπερβολὴν ἐπιχειρήσει καὶ τόλμῃ τὸ κεφάλαιον ζημιοῦν, ὥσπερ ἄρα καὶ τῶν ναυτῶν οἱ ἀπληστότεροι ταῖς ἀεὶ παρενθήκαις τὸ σκάφος αὐτὸ καταδύουσιν.

6 Ἦν γὰρ ἄρα πρὸς ὁτιοῦν ὅλως ἐφ᾽ ἅπαξ ἀντιστῶσιν οἱ ἀκροώμενοι καὶ κρίνοντες καὶ ξυναίσθωνται νοσοῦν τοῦ ἀληθοῦς, αὐτίκα αὐτόθεν ἀνασεσόβηνται καὶ δραπετεύουσι τὴν ἀδικίαν καὶ πρὸς οὐκέτ᾽ οὐδέν εἰσιν εὐπειθεῖς, οὐδ᾽ ἀξιοῦσι συγχωρεῖν, ἀλλ᾽ εἰς ἕκαστ᾽ οὐκ ἀνυπόπτως οἷοί τ᾽ εἶναί φασι τῶν λόγων καὶ πειρωμένοις ἐπιβούλως οὕτως ἤδη ξυνέπεσθαι.

for the best, or at least to give the impression that this is how they have been prepared.

For the others, namely those who are by necessity slaves 4 to their desire, everybody is willing to show much more understanding than in any other case, and believes that this passion is the only extremely violent one and cannot be avoided. Everybody would excuse these people, even though they do not realize that they are largely unprepared and unwary of the future, if someone could see and understand that they have no idea how to properly overcome their disease.

However, if we listen to them carefully, both groups of 5 people seem to fail in some instances, not just in what they aim for and want, that is, to achieve something more than ordinary and mediocre in their favorite pursuits, but also fail in what is their just due and in what they could safely achieve, in my opinion; and, due to their greed for unbridled profit and every sort of excessive endeavor, they heedlessly destroy their capital, just like the most insatiable sailors, who keep adding new cargoes until they eventually sink their ship.

For, if critical listeners focus on any specific point of what 6 is being said and realize that it fails to conform to reality, they will immediately be shaken, will run away from injustice, and will believe in nothing anymore; nor will they be willing to forgive, but will say that it is impossible not to be suspicious of what is being said, and that they cannot follow people who try to trick them in this way.

4

Τοιγαροῦν οὗτοι δὴ καὶ μάλιστ᾽ ἐοίκασιν εἶναι, οἱ σπουδάζοντες ἀμέτρως οὕτως, οἱ τὴν πλείστην αἰτίαν ὑπὸ
τῶν πολλῶν κακηγορεῖσθαι παιδείαν παρασχόμενοι, μετ᾽
ἀδείας ὥσπερ ἐχόντων ἐντεῦθεν ἁπάσης ἀσελγαίνειν καὶ
βλασφημεῖν εἰς τοὺς λόγους καί, μετά τινος ἐμοὶ δοκεῖν
ἀναγκαίου δικαίου, τοῖς χειρίστοις συνεῖναι, βασκανίᾳ καὶ
ἀμαθίᾳ, ὥσπερ οἱ πατάγοις τισὶν ἀήθεσιν ἔκπληκτοι γενόμενοι καὶ πρὸς πάνθ᾽ ὁμοῦ φερόμενοι πράγματα.

2   Ἀλογοῦσι μὲν γὰρ δῆθεν ὡς οὐδὲν ὂν δεινόν, βασκαίνουσι δ᾽ ὡς ὑπερτέροις ἢ δύναιντο καὶ κρείττοσιν ἢ πρὸς
τὴν ἑαυτῶν φύσιν τυχεῖν, καὶ φασὶ μὲν μηδὲν εἶναι μέγα
μήθ᾽ οἷον μήτ᾽ ἐρᾶν μήτε κτήσασθαι, φθονοῦντες δὲ μάλα
ξὺν προθυμίᾳ δρῶσιν ἐναντί᾽ ἢ φασί, πείθοντες ἐντεῦθεν,
οἶμαι, ὡς ἄρα πρὸς τὰ μέγιστα βασκαίνειν ἐσκευασμένοις
ἐοίκασι καὶ ἀσυμφώνως οὕτως ἑαυτῶν ἔχουσι· καὶ τούτῳ
πρώτῳ δηλονότι τὰ σφέτερα αὐτῶν ὡς νοσεῖ καὶ ἀμαθῶς
ἔχει δεικνῦντες, ἀφ᾽ ἑστίας δοκοῦσί μοι περιπίπτειν, φημὶ
δ᾽ ὧν τις καὶ λόγος ἐστὶ βραχύς.

Chapter 4

Therefore those who are extremely passionate in what they do, seem to be particularly the ones who offer the best justification for most people condemning education; thus these latter have complete impunity to behave outrageously and level defamatory words against learning, and to participate in the worst of evils, that is, malignity and ignorance, with what seems to me a certain fitting necessity. They behave like those who have been terrified by some unexpected crash and are similarly scared of everything thereafter.

For on the one hand, they disregard learning, considering their attitude in no way dreadful, but at the same time they envy it, because it is far beyond what they can achieve and far surpasses what they can pursue with the help of their natural capacities. They therefore claim that learning is not a great thing, and not something suitable for people to love or acquire. Yet, by being intensely jealous, they act contrary to their words, since they persuade us, I think, that they seem to envy those who are prepared for the most important achievements, and thus contradict themselves. With this behavior they first and foremost indicate that they are suffering and that they are totally ignorant, and they seem to me to attack themselves. I refer to that group of people whom it is enough to mention only briefly.

5

Τῶν γὰρ δὴ πλειόνων τουτωνὶ τί ἄν τις καὶ μεμνῇτο, οἳ θρεμμάτων δίκην ἐπ᾽ αἰσθήσει μόνῃ τὸν ἅπαντα βίοτον ἐξανύτουσι, τῶν πλείστων αὑτῶν καὶ καλλίστων μερῶν τῆς ψυχῆς οὐδὲν ἐπαΐοντες, κατηλογηκότες παντάπασιν ἑαυτῶν καὶ τῆς φύσεως; Καὶ τοίνυν πρὸς τὴν τοσαύτην εὐμοιρίαν καὶ τὸν κλῆρον καὶ τὰ παρ᾽ αὐτῆς δῶρα οὔτ᾽ ἔγνωσαν ὅλως χάριν οὔθ᾽ ὅ,τι χρήσαιντο, ἀλλ᾽ ἄρα πάνυ τοι πλουτοῦντες οὕτω δή—οὐκ οἶδ᾽ ὁπότερον ἐρῶ, εἴθ᾽ ἑκόντες εἴτ᾽ ἄκοντες—ὅμως δ᾽ οὖν τὰ σφέτερα αὐτῶν καὶ τὴν οὐσίαν ἐμοὶ δοκεῖν ἠγνοήκασι, καὶ τὰ οἴκοι πατρῷα τόσα καὶ τόσα κατορύξαντες καὶ προέμενοι, πενίαν ἑαυ-τοῖς χειροποίητον κατεστήσαντο, οὐδ᾽, ἐξὸν ἐπὶ πλεῖστον ἀμέλει τρυφᾶν καὶ δὴ σεμνῶς, οὐ προὐνόησαν οὔθ᾽ εἵ-λοντο, ἀλλ᾽ ἐπ᾽ ἐλαχίστων καὶ φαῦλοι φαύλων τὸ ζῆν ὀλιγώσαντες, ἀσελγαίνουσιν.

2 Οἱ νοῦν φοροῦντες ἐν ἑαυτοῖς ἐλάθοντο, οὐδ᾽ ἐπι-στρέφονται καθάπαξ, οὐδ᾽ ἴσασι τοσοῦτον, ὅπῃ δὴ γῆς κατορώρυκται, καὶ τὴν τῆς ψυχῆς ἄσκιον αἰθρίαν καὶ τὸ τῶν λογισμῶν καὶ τῆς διανοίας διαφανὲς ἀμαυρώσαντες καὶ καταζοφώσαντες, ἐπετείχισαν πρὸς ἅπασαν ἐπιστήμης αὐγὴν καὶ θεωρίας, ἀσυλλογίστως ἑαυτῶν καὶ τῶν ὄντων, ἀσυλλογίστως τῶν ὁρωμένων ἔχοντες, ἀτεχνῶς ὥσπερ τὰ ἀνδρείκελα τῶν τυπωμάτων, μορφαῖς μόνον ἄνθρωποι, ἢν

Chapter 5

For who would ever make any mention of this multitude of people, who, just like sheep, spend their whole lives driven by their senses alone, ignoring the many levels and finest aspects of their soul, completely neglecting themselves and their nature? These men do not feel any gratitude for their immensely good fortune and their lot, nor for the many gifts they have been given by nature, and they do not even know how to use these things properly. Therefore, although they thrive so much—either willingly or unwillingly, I cannot really tell which of the two—they are still not fully aware, I think, of their possessions and their immense value. They have buried their huge ancestral fortune deep in the earth and abandoned it there, sentencing themselves to self-inflicted poverty. Although they could have lived luxuriously and even honorably for a long time, they did not make the necessary provision, nor did they choose this course of life; on the contrary, by shrinking their life to a very few, humble things, those "humble" men act outrageously.

Although these people have rationality within them, they 2 do not realize this; they totally abstain from introspection, and they do not know where they have buried their possessions. They have obscured the unshaded tranquility of their soul, the transparency of their judiciousness and intellect, and sunk into darkness. Then they have erected a wall against any gleam of knowledge and contemplation, so that they cannot comprehend anything about themselves and the things that actually exist, and cannot comprehend what they see either, just like unskillfully molded human statues.

ὁρῶσιν, οὐ ξυνιέντες ἔπειτα πρὸς οὐδὲν καθάπαξ, ἣν ἀκούωσι, περαίνοντες οὐκέθ' ὁτιοῦν, οὐ νῷ προσχρώμενοι—
πόθεν;—ὅν γε κατεχώσαντο παντάπασι συμπεπιλημένον
τοῖς τῆς σαρκὸς ἐπαχθίσμασι καὶ ὥσπερ ἀνεπιστρόφοις,
οἶμαι, καὶ ἀφύκτοις εἰρκταῖς κατακεκλεισμένον ταῖς τοῦ
σώματος λατομίαις, ὥστ' οὐδὲ διοίγειν ὅλως ἐξεῖναι τὰς
σαρκικὰς πτυχάς, οὐδ' ἀνακαλύπτειν, οὐδὲ προφέρειν ἑαυτούς, οὐδὲ δεικνύειν ἄττα οἴκοι κατακέκρυπται ἀγάλματα,
ὥσπερ οἱ ἐν ταῖς ὁδοῖς εἶχον Ἑρμαῖ πάλαι, ἀλλ' ἀτρέπτως
ὥσπερ ἐν τάφοις εἶρχθαι σφίσι νεκρὰ τὰ κάλλιστα καὶ ζῶσιν ἐμοὶ δοκεῖν ὡς ἂν ἀπηγχονισμένοι τῷ κρείττονι ἑαυτῶν
καὶ μόναις αἰσθήσεσι σαλεύοντες ἀνάρχοις, ἀλογίστοις,
ὑφ' ὁτουοῦν ἐντυγχάνοντος φορουμέναις καὶ καθάπερ ἐν
πελάγει τῷ βίῳ τὸν ἅπανθ' ἑαυτῶν αἰῶνα δυστυχοῦντες
καὶ δίχα κυβερνήτου προθέμενοι ναυαγεῖν.

3   Καίτοι, καθάπερ, οἶμαι, οἱ ταῖς φορταγωγοῖς ἔμποροι
χρώμενοι παρέλκονται κελήτι' ἄττα, ἐφ' ᾧ προσσχεῖν, εἴ
πῃ παρείκοι, τῇ γῇ καὶ ὑδρεύσασθαι καὶ πρὸς ἄλλην ἅπασαν ἡντιναοῦν ἑκάστοτε χρείαν ἀμέλει ῥᾷον εὐπορῆσαι
καὶ σκευαγωγήσασθαι, πρὸς τὴν αὐτὴν ἐμοὶ δοκεῖν χρείαν
ἐσκευάσθαι τῇ φύσει τὴν αἴσθησιν, ὡς τὸν μὲν ὅλον
σκοπὸν καὶ τὴν ἐμπορίαν τῆς φύσεως αὐτὸν ὄντα τὸν νοῦν
καὶ τὰ λογικὰ πράγματα, αἰσθήσει δὲ τοσοῦτο προσχρῆσθαι
δέον, ὅσα καὶ τοῦ παντὸς ἐλαχίστῳ μέρει, καὶ ἅμα μὲν

Indeed, they are human simply in appearance, and if they see something, they by no means understand it; likewise, if they hear something, they are completely unable to respond, incapable of using their intellect—how could they?—for they have hidden it entirely and repressed it, I believe, deep inside their overloaded flesh, and it is as if it were trapped in the quarries of the body, those prisons from which no escape or return is possible. In consequence, they cannot even open and completely unfasten the doors of their flesh, nor unveil themselves, display themselves, or expose those statues that are hidden inside them, as was the case in antiquity with the Herms in the streets. On the contrary, their most beautiful blessings are dead and imprisoned as if in graves from which there is no escape. I think they live as if the best part of their existence had been strangled. They move only because ungovernable and irrational senses control their bodies, senses that are transported by all sorts of stimuli. And, as if their life were a sea of troubles, they are unhappy for their whole life span, and without a helmsman are destined to be shipwrecked.

However, in my opinion, just as the merchants who sail 3 on cargo ships pull some small boats behind them in order to be able to reach land when there is an opportunity, to draw water for themselves, and be in a position to easily address any other need by bringing the necessary supplies on board and offloading goods, I assume that nature has spawned sensation for the very same reason; since the ultimate aim and business of nature centers on the mind and rational issues, whereas the employment of sensation must be restricted only to the affairs pertaining to the weakest part of the whole, and also when we need to interrupt vigor-

πρός τινα δὴ καὶ παῦλαν τῆς εὐτόνου μέν, ἐπιπόνου δὲ
μάλιστα τῶν λογισμῶν ἐργασίας, ὡς ἂν μὴ διαπαντὸς ἐξὸν
οὐριοδρομεῖν, ἅμα δὲ καί τινα ἐντεῦθεν πορίσαι διανοίας
ὕλην καὶ συλλογισμῶν προβλήματα καὶ πρὸς τὴν ἔσω
σπουδαζομένην πραγματείαν καὶ πολιτείαν διαδικασίαν
καὶ παρασκευὴν οὐκ ἀνέορτον καὶ ὥσπερ ἀνθεινά τινα καὶ
εὐανάδοτα πέμματα, οἷς τοῦτο μὲν ἐξέσται ῥαστώνῃ
χρῆσθαι, τοῦτο δὲ προσέσται πρὸς ὁτιοῦν χρόνοις ἔπειθ᾽
ὕστερον ἀνύτειν καὶ φέρειν ἡντιναοῦν πάντως ὄνησιν.

6

Ἀλλ᾽ ἡ μὲν ἐμοὶ δοκεῖν αἰσθήσεως αὕτη φύσις καὶ
χρῆσις, οὕτως ἄρα ἐπελθὸν μνησθῆναι. Ἐπεὶ δὲ τὴν τῆς
παιδείας ὁ λόγος ἐξετάζων φύσιν ἐδόκει δὴ τἀληθοῦς
μάλιστα φροντίζων καὶ μὴ πάντα ἐκ πάντων ἐπαινεῖν προθέμενος καὶ βίων αἱρέσεις ὥσπερ δή τινας λεωφόρους
ἀντιθέτους ἀνατεμεῖν—ἥντινα μὲν ἁπασῶν ἐκ παντὸς
τρόπου σπουδαστέον, ἔστι μὲν οὐδεὶς ὃς ἀμαθής, οἶμαι—
οὐ μὴν ἀλλὰ καὶ αὐτὸς ἐρῶ κατὰ βραχὺ νῦν γε εἶναι, πρὸς
ἀρχὴν ἐπανάγων ἀμέλει τὸν λόγον καὶ γνώμην τιθείς, ἥν
μοι ἔξεστιν, ὅτι δὴ μόνον τἀγαθόν ἐστιν, ἡ τοῦ Ὄντος
ἀλήθεια καὶ περὶ Θεοῦ φύσεως καὶ Προνοίας ἀπλανῶς
δόξαι καὶ ὥσπερ, οἶμαι, ἐνταῦθα ἐφορμεῖν ἀσφαλῶς καὶ
ἡδρασμένον καὶ ἠρτημένον ὡς ἀφ᾽ ἱερᾶς ἐντεῦθεν ὄντως

ous and toilsome mental activity, because it is impossible to travel constantly with a fair wind. Of course, another benefit we derive from employing our senses is that they help us to provide ourselves with material for thought and tasks for our reasoning, as well as to create motivations for our internal spiritual occupations and public arrangement of our lives, which will not be unpleasant, but will taste like sweet and easily digested pastries. These motivations we can now employ with ease, but we could also exploit them in different ways in the future to our own advantage and profit.

Chapter 6

To me this seems to be the nature and function of sensation, just as it occurred to me to expose it. But since my discourse exploring the nature of education seems to be aimed mostly at truth and is not intended to praise everything in every possible way or distinguish between diverse lifestyles that resemble roads going in opposite directions—although I believe there is no one who does not know what sort of all these courses of life they must by all means follow—I will still now mention this briefly, going back to the start of my speech and pronouncing my opinion as best as I can: the ultimate blessing is the truth of Being, and firm belief regarding God's nature and Providence. In my mind, one should rely steadily on such beliefs, one should be settled and fixed in one place, as if one lies moored at a truly sacred anchor, and then move toward the contemplation of the rest; more-

ἀγκύρας ὡρμῆσθαι μὲν πρὸς ἅπασαν τοῦ λοιποῦ θεωρίαν,
οὐ μόνον δὲ ἀλλὰ καὶ τολμᾶν καὶ φέρειν ἄττα ποθ᾽ ἑκάστοτε ξυμπίπτοι καὶ ὁ ῥέων προστρίβοιτ᾽ ἂν χρόνος, ἐν
ἀκύμονι ψυχῆς γαλήνῃ, εὖ μὲν παρασχόν, οὐκ ἐξιστάμε-
νον καθ᾽ ὁτιοῦν, οὐδ᾽ αἱρόμενον ἢ ᾽χρῆν πλεῖστον φρόνημα, μὴ τετυφῶσθαι, ἂν δὲ τοὐναντίον αὖθις, μηδ᾽ οὕτω
καθάπαξ ἡττώμενον, ἀλλὰ κατὰ τὸν Δωρικὸν κυβερνήτην
ἐκεῖνον πρὸς τὸν τοῦ βίου χειμῶνα καὶ τὸ κλυδώνιον καὶ
αὐτὸν φάσκοντα "ὀρθὰν τὰν ναῦν καὶ οὕτω καταδῦσαι" καὶ
μετὰ τῶν καλῶν λογισμῶν ἀτρέπτως τὸ σωματικὸν ναυάγιον ἑστήξειν φέροντα.

2   Ὁ μὲν δὴ λόγος οὕτω χρῆναί φησιν οἴεσθαι, πρὸ πάντων
εὐσεβῆσαι τὰς περὶ τοῦ Θεοῦ δόξας ἀληθεῖς, τὸ δ᾽ ἄρ᾽ εἶναι
ἐν ἀπορρήτῳ πίστει μόνον καὶ ἀναμφηρίστῳ περὶ τῆς τρι-
αδικῆς θεαρχίας καὶ τῆς τοῦ ὄντως ἀγαθοῦ, ἐν τρισὶν ἰδιό-
τησιν εἴτουν ὑποστάσεσιν, ἐνοειδοῦς φύσεως, ἢ δὴ πάνθ᾽
ὁπόσα ἐστὶ διὰ μόνον ἀγαθοῦ πλοῦτον, οὐκ ἐξ ἀνάγκης,
οὐδὲ δι᾽ ὕλην τινὰ προενοῦσάν τε καὶ συνοῦσαν, χρόνῳ
πρότερον κινήσασα, δεῦρο νῦν ἔχει. Οἰκονομεῖ μέν γε
λόγῳ καὶ πρυτανεύει τὴν ἅπασαν φύσιν, τάξιν ἣν ἐνέθετο
καλλίστην ἐκ πρώτου τηροῦσα, χρόνοις ὕστερον λῦσαι
βουλομένη. Καὶ γὰρ ἀμφότερα ἐνόμισεν, οὔτε τὸ γεγονὸς
φύσιν εἶναι μὴ λυθῆναι, γεγονὸς δή, οὔτε μὴ προνοεῖν τούτου τὸν Πατέρα καὶ Κατασκευασάμενον, μέχρις ἂν ἵστασθαι καὶ ἴσχειν βούληται.

3   Ἀλλὰ μὴν τοῦ ἀγαθοῦ πέρι καὶ Προνοίας οὕτω δὴ
νομίζοντες, ἔτ᾽ ἔχομεν ἀμέλει δόγμα μέγιστον ὄντως καὶ
περὶ μεγίστου πράγματος. Θαυμασίαν γὰρ δή τινα καὶ

over, one should also venture to endure in calm tranquility of the soul whatever happens on any occasion and whatever the passage of time brings. When things go well, one should not be at all excited or behave more arrogantly than is proper or be puffed up, and then again, if the opposite happens, one should not be at all discomfited, but, like that Doric captain of old, one should pronounce amid the waves and storms of life, "*I shall send the ship down upright,*" and, by thinking in the proper way, one should unflinchingly set the shipwreck of the body upright.

This oration indeed suggests that this is how we ought to think, and above all that we ought to revere the true beliefs regarding God. This is possible only through ineffable and unequivocal faith in the trinitarian divinity and the unified nature of the One who is truly good that entails three attributes, namely it has three substantial hypostases. This divinity previously set in motion everything that exists and even now sustains it all, precisely because it abounds in absolute goodness, and not by necessity, nor through some preexisting and coexisting matter. This divinity manages and controls through reason all of nature, maintaining the sublime order that it had imposed from the very beginning, even if it wishes to dissolve all these things later on. For it holds two related beliefs: that once something has been created, it will naturally not remain intact from the moment that it has been created, and that the Father and Creator will take care of it as long as he wishes his creation to exist and be kept alive. 2

If this is our opinion about the good God and divine Providence, we still have nevertheless another truly important doctrine relating to a very serious issue. For through 3

ὑπερφυῆ καὶ ξένην κοινωνίαν ἡ θεότης ἡμῖν ἐν μιᾷ τῶν αὐτῆς ὑποστάσεων κοινωνεῖ, ἄληπτον παντί, ἄρρητον καὶ κρείττω παντάπασιν ἢ ξυνιδεῖν. Ὁ γὰρ τοῦ ἀθανάτου Θεοῦ συναΐδιος αἰώνιος Λόγος ζῶν, ἡ μεγάλη καὶ παντοκρατορικὴ τοῦ Πατρὸς ἀνεκφοίτητος καὶ ἐνυπόστατος δύναμις καὶ σοφία καὶ ἀπαράλλακτος σφραγὶς αὐτοῦ, κινουμένη ἐφ᾽ ᾗ πρότερον αὐτὸς ὑπεστήσατο κτίσει, βουλῇ φιλανθρωπίας ἀπορρήτῳ ὀψὲ τῶν χρόνων ἐπιδημεῖ καὶ κάτεισιν ἀθορύβῳ δῆτα καὶ ἀσείστῳ καθάπαξ ἐντεύξει ταπεινωθεὶς ἡμῖν οἰκονομίᾳ μάλιστα καὶ προνοίᾳ τοῦ βελτίστου, ᾗπερ ἔδοξε συνοίσειν, καὶ γίνεται καθ᾽ ἡμᾶς διὰ Παρθενικῆς Μητρὸς πάντ᾽ ἄνθρωπος πλὴν τῶν παθῶν, ἃ φαῦλα καὶ διαβέβληται, προσλαβών τε σάρκα, μείνας ὅμως ὅπερ ἦν, ἐξ ἀμφοτέρων καὶ οὕτως εἷς ἐστιν ἀσυγχύτων καὶ ἀμφότερά ἐστιν ἀδιαίρετα ἐν ὑποστάσει μιᾷ.

4　　Τοῦτο δῆτ᾽ ἐστὶ τὸ ἡμέτερον τῆς εὐσεβείας μέγιστον δόγμα, τοῦθ᾽ ὃ παντάπασι καὶ νοῦ πᾶσαν καὶ λόγου νικᾷ φύσιν, τοῦτο ἡ τελείωσις τοῦ καλῶς θεοσεβεῖν καὶ οὗ χωρὶς οὐχ οἷόν τέ ἐστι Θεοῦ τυχεῖν, ἣν ἄρα τις μυηθεὶς ὅλως μὴ προσεῖτο.

one of its hypostases the divinity shares with us a wondrous, supernatural, and extraordinary communion, which is inconceivable in all respects, ineffable, and far beyond what people can perceive. For the living, coeternal, and everlasting Logos of the immortal God, the great, all-sovereign, inseparable, substantive power and wisdom of the Father, his indistinguishable seal, moved toward the creation which he himself had previously generated, and recently came to the world according to some secret plan of his love of mankind; this Logos came down to meet us without any commotion or tumult whatsoever, he humbled himself in his communion with us with absolute divine arrangement and provision for the best, in the way he decided would be the most profitable to us. He was born of a Virgin Mother, became a human being in all respects just like us, except that he was free from passions, which are debased and blameworthy. Although he assumed flesh, he nevertheless remained just as before, that is, God; he is one entity consisting of two natures, which are not confused but both inseparably united into one single hypostasis.

This is the most important doctrine of our faith, and this 4 is what surpasses the whole nature of rationality and logic in all respects. This is the culmination of correct religious belief without which, namely if an initiate does not wholly accept this, it would be impossible to reach God.

7

Ταῦτά γε μήν, ἅπερ εἴρηται, ὅστις ἄνθρωπος οὕτως εἶναι ἵλεῳ διανοίᾳ καὶ ἀσείστως παντάπασι πείθοιτο, ἐπ' ἀσφαλοῦς τε ὄντως ἑστήξει καὶ ἅμα δέοιτ' ἂν ἔτι καθάπαξ νομίζειν καὶ ὅσ' ἑκάστοτε καὶ ἐφ' ἑκάστοις κατὰ μέρος συνθήματα τετάχαται καὶ κατ' ἔθη τε καὶ ἤθη καὶ τὴν λοιπὴν ἱερὰν διακόσμησιν πολιτεύματα τοῖς παλαιοῖς ἐκείνοις ἡγεμόσι τε καὶ πατράσιν, οἷς καὶ τὸ πιστὸν ὁ χρόνος ἐκεῖθεν πολὺς δίδωσι, καὶ ὁμαλῶς εὖ μάλ' ἕπεσθαι ξὺν ἀπραγμοσύνῃ καὶ ἀπολύτως, ὡς ἡδέως ξυνεῖναι μήθ' ὁτιοῦν κινοῦντα μήθ' ὅλως πειρώμενον καταλογίζεσθαι καὶ κρίνειν.

2 Τῷ ὄντι γὰρ καὶ ἄριστον εἶναι καὶ ἀσφαλέστατον ἁπλοϊκῶς τε καθόλου καὶ ἐλευθέρως ἐν ὀλιγότητι γνώμης εὐσεβεῖν καὶ μηδὲν πλέον τοῦ προχείρου διατρίβειν πειρᾶσθαι, μηδὲ περαιτέρω ἢ κατὰ τοὺς πολλούς τε καὶ ἀγροικοτέρους φιλοσοφεῖν, ὡς ἔγωγε, ὅστις, ἐξὸν οὕτως ἀκινδύνως θεοσεβεῖν, ἔπειθ' ἑκών γε εἶναι πράγματα αἱρεῖται καὶ τἀπόρρητα καὶ καινότερα περὶ τῶν θείων ἐπιχειρεῖ σοφίζεσθαι καὶ ἰχνηλατεῖν μὴ πρὸς ἡντιναοῦν ἀνάγκην, μὴ πρὸς ἡντιναοῦν ὄνησιν, τοῦτον ἂν εἶναι φαίην δυστυχῆ σφόδρα καὶ ἀνούστατον καὶ τοῖς μὲν ἐμπόροις οὐκ ἂν παραβάλλοιμι τοῖς—δι' ἀπληστίαν κέρδους—κατασωτευομένοις τῶν

Chapter 7

Anyone who has such a kindly disposition and unshakably believes what we have said will stand on truly firm ground. At the same time, however, this man will also need to believe everything that has been prescribed from time to time on various occasions by those ancient leaders and fathers of the Church regarding religious covenants, the customs and behavior of the congregation, and the administration of the remaining aspects of the holy government of the Church. The credibility of these regulations is assured by the length of time from then until now; one should therefore follow them in a consistent and proper way, with freedom from worldly cares and absolutely strictly, adopting them happily without changing anything and without making any attempt to examine or judge.

For it is true that it is best and most secure for a person to behave piously through general simplicity and easygoing conduct, without resorting to much thought; to avoid exploring issues beyond the ordinary level and to not make more use of philosophy than the many and uneducated do. I would argue that a person would be extremely miserable and most stupid if he can act piously in accordance with the safe option I have just mentioned, but nevertheless chooses to enter such debates of his own accord and attempt in the mode of a sophist to articulate ineffable and novel pronouncements on divine matters and to investigate them in detail, motivated neither by necessity nor for any kind of advantage. I will not compare this person to merchants, who—out of greed for profit—disregard the amount of

2

ἀγωγίμων καὶ ἀεὶ παρεντιθεῖσι καὶ τὰ σκάφη καταδύουσιν, ὅτι τούτοις ἔρως γε τέως καὶ προσδοκία κέρδους τὸν ὄλε- θρον φέρει, τὸν δ᾽ ἀνάγυρον ὄντως εἴποιμ᾽ ἂν αὐτὸν κινεῖν παροιμιακῶς καὶ ὡς Καρπάθιον ἀμέλει τὸν λαγωὸν καὶ ὡς αἶγα φέρειν τὴν μάχαιραν καὶ σκάλλειν πῦρ ταῖς χερσὶ καὶ πάσαις δυσφημίαις ἐνέχεσθαι.

3   "Ἄνθρωπε," φαίην ἂν ἔγωγε, "μαίνῃ καὶ τῷ μεγίστῳ τῶν κινδύνων, μηδὲν δέον, παραβαλλόμενος ἀγνοεῖς. Ἤ πῶς οὐκ ἄν τις θαυμάσειεν ἢ πῶς οὐκ ἄν τις τὰ μέγιστα καταγνοίη περὶ τοιαύτης ἐργασίας, ἐν ᾗ κατορθοῦντι μὲν οὐδὲν ἔπειθ᾽ ὁτιοῦν ἀπαντᾷ κέρδος, ἀποτυχόντι δ᾽ εὐθὺς ὁ μέγιστος ὄλεθρος; Ἢν γάρ, οἶμαι δή, περιγένῃ παντάπα- σιν ἄπταιστος καὶ ἀλώβητος—ὡς ἔστι γε τοῦτο δυσχερές τε καὶ ἄπιστον—οὐδέν σοι πλέον ἐντεῦθεν οὐδὲν μᾶλλον ἢ ὥσπερ οὐδ᾽ ὅστις τὴν ἀρχὴν οὔτ᾽ ἐπεχείρησεν ὅλως οὔτ᾽ ἤνυσεν, ἀλλ᾽ ἕλκει βίον εὐσεβῶν ἀπράγμονα. Εἰ δ᾽ ἀπο- τεύξῃ τι παρεκκλίνας κατὰ βραχύ, φεῦ τῆς τόλμης, φεῦ τῆς ἀνοίας, φεῦ τοῦ πτώματος· οὐκ οἶδ᾽ ὁπότερον φαίην, ἢ κατὰ κρημνῶν ὦσας ἢ σαυτὸν ἀπηγχόνησας, καὶ τοῖς σαυ- τοῦ μὲν οὐχ ἑάλως πτεροῖς, τοῖς Ἰκάρου δὲ πτεροῖς παρα- πλησίως χρησάμενος, ἀφ᾽ ὕψους ἐκείνου τοσούτου ἑκών γε εἶναι ἀλόγιστος, αὐθέκαστος καταβέβληκας σαυτόν."

cargo they have already piled aboard a ship and by constantly adding new cargo eventually sink their vessel, because in the case of the merchants the destruction is brought about by their recent longing for and expectation of gain. For this person, by contrast, I would employ the following proverbs, leveling against him all the censure entailed in them: *let sleeping dogs lie, as the Carpathian hare, the goat carries the knife,* and *stir up the fire with your hands.*

I could then say to him: "My friend, you are a madman, because you do not realize that you are putting yourself unnecessarily at the greatest risk. How could one not wonder at you? Or how could one not condemn you harshly for acting thus, whereby, even if you are successful, you will get absolutely no profit, but if you fail, you will immediately suffer the most severe harm? Thus, I believe that even if you do not commit any kind of mistake and you remain unharmed—which is, of course, both difficult and unlikely—, you will gain nothing more from this than the person who from the very start did not try to do something similar and did not achieve anything, but spends his life free from worldly cares and piously. If you fail and somehow deviate slightly, alas for your daring, alas for your stupidity, alas for your downfall! I do not know which option to choose: Did you force yourself off the cliff or did you hang yourself? You were not caught by your own wings, but it is as if you used Icarus's wings, throwing yourself down from that great height willingly, thoughtlessly, at your own instigation." 3

8

Πυθαγορείοις μὲν δὴ λόγος εἷς τῶν χρυσῶν μὴ ταῖς λεωφόροις βαδίζειν, ἀλλ' ἀτραπὸν ἀνύτειν ἀήθη τε καὶ ἀνόδευτον· βούλεται δ', οἶμαι, σφίσι τοῦπος μὴ τοῖς τετριμμένοις τῶν δογμάτων ἐπιχειρεῖν, μηδὲ καθάπαξ ἐγκεῖσθαι, ὡς ἂν διὰ τὴν συνήθειαν ὑπὸ τῶν πολλῶν ὀλιγωρουμένοις, καὶ ἅμα μηδὲ κατάγχειν ἀείποθ' ὥσπερ ἐπὶ ῥητοῖς τὸν νοῦν, μὴ δὲ ξυνδεῖν, οὐκ οἶδ' αἷστισιν εἰρκταῖς, τὴν ἐπιστήμην, τεταγμένα κατὰ τὴν παροιμίαν βαδίζειν καὶ δειλανδρεῖν μή τι πλέον ἄλλεσθαι ἢ δέδοται, ἀλλ' εὐδρομεῖν τὰ πάντα καὶ τολμᾶν καὶ γυμνάζεσθαι καὶ ὥσπερ εἰς κοινόν τινα ἔρανον, ἤν τι καὶ δύνηται πλέον, φέρειν καὶ τοὺς πολλοὺς στρέφειν εἰς ἑαυτόν, ἄγασθαι τὴν εὐπορίαν.

2 Τοῖς μὲν οὖν οὕτω δὴ πρὸς δόξαν ἁμιλλωμένοις οὐδὲν ἀτόλμητον καὶ μάλιστ' ἴσως, ἐπειδὴ καὶ τούτων ᾠήθησαν ἔνιοι μηδὲν εἶναι πρᾶγμα περὶ τῶν θείων, καθ' ὅσον οἷόν τέ ἐστι, σπουδάζειν, ὡς οὐδένα τῶν ἀπάντων φλαῦρον οὐδὲν ὁτιοῦν περὶ τούτων οὔτε δοκεῖν ὅλως οὔτε λέγειν, ἀλλ' ἄττα ποτ' ἂν μάλισθ' ἡγοῖτο κάλλιστα, τούτοις τε πείθεσθαι καὶ πείθειν ἐπιχειρεῖν ὀντινοῦν. Τῶν οὖν δοκούντων φασὶ σφίσι βελτίστων, τούτων περὶ τοῦ θείου καὶ δοκούντων αὐτοῖς καὶ λεγομένων, οὔτε ποτ' ἂν αὐτὸ δυσχερᾶναι οὔτ' ἄλλον οὐδέν' εἰκός γε εἶναι τῶν ἀπάντων.

Chapter 8

One of the exhortations from the Pythagorean *Golden Words* says not to walk on busy roads, but to make our way on the less familiar and the little-used paths instead. The Pythagoreans mean to say with this verse, I think, that we should not make any arguments about well-known doctrines or get involved at all, because many people have become so accustomed to them that they take little heed of them. Moreover, we should not always oppress our minds as if with famous sayings nor confine our knowledge in who knows what sorts of prisons, in an attempt *to move on in absolute order* according to the proverb, and be scared lest we veer slightly beyond customary practice. The proverb incites us rather to constantly move forward, to dare everything, to train ourselves, and, if possible, to contribute even more, as if to a communal feast, until we attract the attention of the public, who will admire our resourcefulness.

For those people who compete with one another for fame 2 in such a way there is nothing they would not dare, and perhaps all the more so because some of them believe that there is nothing special about pursuing divine matters as far as possible, so that no one at all could possibly think or say anything bad about such issues; but they will adopt the opinions they consider best and then attempt to persuade everyone else about these matters. Those things that seem best for themselves, they say, seem best to them also about the divine and it is these things that they eventually say, namely they say that it seems unlikely to them that either the divine or any human being could ever be dissatisfied.

3   Ἡμῖν δὲ οἷς μεγίστη ζημία, οἷς ἐπαχθέστατον ἔγκλημα, ἑνὸς ὄντος τἀληθοῦς περὶ Θεοῦ, ὥσπερ ἄρα καὶ περὶ παντὸς ἄλλου πράγματος ἁμαρτεῖν κατὰ βραχύ, πᾶν ἄλλ᾽ ὁτιοῦν τιθεμένοις, τί τὸ κινοῦν, τίς ἀνάγκη καθ᾽ οὕτω μεγίστου κινδύνου κῦβον ῥιπτεῖν καὶ ὠθεῖσθαι, καὶ μάλιστα νῦν ἀμέλει τούτων τῶν καιρῶν, ἡνίχ᾽ ὡς οὐδὲν ἄλλο τι τῶν ἁπάντων τοῖς πλείοσι πρόχειρον ἐπὶ γλώσσαις ἐπενεγκεῖν ἔγκλημα δόγματος ἀλλοτριότητα καὶ κακοδοξίαν, ῥᾷον ἢ σκῶμμά τι τῶν οὐδενὸς λόγου;

4   Καὶ μέντοι παραλαμβάνουσα, οἶμαι, τὴν κακηγορίαν ἡ φήμη αὐτίκα αὐτόθεν κούφοις, ὅ φασι, πτεροῖς αἴρεται καὶ δείκνυσιν ἄρα ὅσον πλεονεκτεῖ ἡ τῶν φαύλων προκοπὴ καὶ κακολογία τὴν τῶν ἀγαθῶν εὐφημίαν καὶ οἱ πολλοὶ τῶν ἀνθρώπων καὶ φαῦλοι καὶ ἀλογώτεροι μάλιστα ἐν τούτοις εἰσὶ κατὰ τῶν ἐλλογίμων ἰσχυρότεροι· οἵ, καθάπερ αἱ βδέλλαι φύσιν ἔχουσιν ἐπὶ τοῖς πονηροῖς αἵμασι τρέφεσθαι, παραπλησίως καὶ αὐτοὶ προσανάκεινται καὶ ἀνιχνεύουσιν, ἤν τί που φλαῦρον καθ᾽ ὁτουοῦν τῶν εὐγενῶν καὶ χαριέντων προσαναμάξωνται καὶ προσανιμήσωνται καὶ πορίσωνται σφίσιν αὐτοῖς οὐκ οἶδ᾽ ἥντιν᾽ ἐντεῦθεν ἀηδίας ὕλην ἐντρυφᾶν, κακοὶ καὶ σοφισταὶ καὶ ἀγύρται καὶ σκηνῆς καὶ δράματος πλέω ἀγροικίαν ἐργολαβοῦντες δήμου καὶ προσποιούμενοι τὰ μηδαμῇ παρὰ σφίσιν ὄντα καὶ πρὸς ἅπαντα εἰρωνευόμενοι. Καὶ πολλὴ παρ᾽ αὐτοῖς ἡ ἀκρίβεια καὶ ἡ κακοήθεια καὶ ἡ βασκανία καταγοητεύουσα καὶ ἀεὶ κακῶν ἐφιεμένη κατὰ τῶν πεπαιδεῦσθαι δοκούντων καὶ νοῦν ἐχόντων καὶ σφόδρα ἀνύτουσα καὶ κατεργαζομένη.

CHAPTER 8

For us, however, who consider it the greatest harm, a 3
most dreadful crime, since there is only one truth about
God, to commit even the slightest mistake, as if we were
treating any other topic, turning our attention to a totally
different thing, what motive, what force could impel us to
throw the dice at such great risk? Especially in our own days,
when no other accusation springs more readily from the
mouths of most people than that of deviating from doctrine, and heretical belief, an accusation that is made even
more easily than trivial jests?

I think that rumor immediately seizes upon the accusa- 4
tion and from there soars on high with its *light wings,* as they
say, demonstrating the extent to which the prosperity of bad
men and the slander they utter prevails over the praise of
good men. It is especially in such cases that the many wicked
and uneducated men become more powerful at the expense
of men of high repute. Like leeches which, as is their nature,
feed upon the blood of wicked people, these men set off in a
similar way to try and discover any dark stain upon the noble and graceful, and then feed on it and let go after they
have provided themselves from there with who knows what
resources for their disgusting pleasures. They are vile sophists, beggars of the stage and the dramatic plays, who make
much profit out of the rusticity of people, pretending to
possess what in fact they lack, feigning ignorance about everything. They are very precise, and so it is their malignity
and envy that bewitches everyone and is always aimed at
harming those who are famous for their education and wisdom, operating in a highly successful and efficient way.

9

Πλάτων μὲν οὖν, τὸ τοῦ ἀγαθοῦ κράτος ἀποδεικνύων, ὁρᾶν ἔλεγεν ὅτι τἀναντία φύσιν ἔχει μάχεσθαι καὶ δρᾶν εἰς ἄλληλα, μέχρι τοῦ φθείρειν ὀρεγόμενα μὴ ξυνεῖναι, τὸ δ' ἀγαθόν τε καὶ τοὐναντίον, τὸ μὲν ἀεὶ πλεῖον ἐν βίῳ τὸ φαῦλον, τὸ δ' αὐτοῦ πολλοστόν, μένει μέντοι διαπαντὸς καὶ οὔπω καὶ νῦν ἐξέλιπε πρὸς τὴν μάχην, ὡς ἄρ' ἦν εἰκός, πρὸς τὸ 'φάμιλλον τοσοῦτο τοῦ κακοῦ πλῆθος· καὶ τό γ' εἶναι μέγα ῥώμης οἶμαι τεκμήριον.

2   Ὁ μὲν δὴ λόγος ἔοικεν ἀσφαλὴς ἔτι καὶ νῦν εἶναι, καίτοι γε κομψότερον εἰρημένος, μάλιστα ἀληθείας ἦφθαι. Ἡμεῖς δὲ νῦν ὅμως τοσοῦτο κατὰ τῶν ἀστείων ἐνίοτε καὶ ἐνίων τὸ τῶν βδελλύρων τούτων ἀνδρῶν καὶ φθορέων καὶ λήρων κράτος ὁρῶμεν, ὥστε τὰ μέγιστα κατὰ τοὺς λυσσώδεις δάκνοντας κῦνας ἰσχύειν, ἢ μᾶλλον κατὰ τῶν ζῴων τὰ ἰοβόλα κρύφα καὶ δολίως ἐπιφυομένους παντάπασιν ἐξολλῦναι. Ἦν γάρ τί που παραφθέγξωνται καὶ προστρίψωνταί τι τοιοῦτον ὁτῳοῦν ἔγκλημα, παραχρῆμα κατήνυσται καὶ οὕτως ἐνέδυ κατὰ τοῦ ἀνδρὸς καὶ ἥψατο δευσοποιὸν τὸ αἰτίαμα, ὡς θᾶττον ἂν κατὰ τὴν παροιμίαν ἐξεῖναι *κεραμίῳ τὴν θάλασσαν ἀντλῆσαι* ἢ τοῦ παντὸς ἐκεῖνον λοιπὸν βίου τοὔνειδος ἀπολῦσαι καὶ ἀποτρίψασθαι.

3   Οἱ δέ, ἐφ' ἑαυτῶν οἱ πλείους, μᾶλλον δὲ καὶ τοῖς πολλοῖς παρρησίᾳ, τίς ἂν ἐρεῖ, ὅσα καταφλυαροῦσι τῶν ἱερῶν, ἄττα δὴ καὶ κατακούειν σπουδαίοις ἀνδράσι πολλὴ ἀηδία

Chapter 9

In attempting to show the power of the good, Plato used to say that he had observed that the things that have opposing natures fight and act against each other, and they yearn not to be combined, even to the point of destruction. In the case of what is good and bad, however, although evil is always much more prominent in life than goodness, still the latter always survives and, as one would expect, it has never until now failed in its battle against the rivaling multitude of evil. This is of course a significant testimony, I believe, to the power of goodness.

This opinion seems to be sound even nowadays, and, although it is articulated in a rather lofty manner, it undoubtedly contains some truth. However, we sometimes now observe that the power of certain repulsive, destructive, and silly men over cultivated ones is so great that they prevail over them, just like rabid dogs, which bite; or, rather, completely destroy them like lurking venomous animals do with their treacherous attacks. For, if they utter any word or level any accusation similar to those mentioned above, they immediately hit their target and their accusation so intensely stains the person it touches that, as the proverb has it, it is easier *to draw the water out of the sea with a jar* than to try for the rest of your life to get rid of and rub out this disgrace. 2

On the other hand, who could possibly describe the nonsense many people utter with unfettered tongue on the holy issues not only privately, but even more so in the company of many people, words which cause much disgust and nau- 3

καὶ ναυτιᾶν ἔπεισι; Καταπομπεύουσί τε τἀπόρρητα, κακοὶ κακῶς τε καὶ ἀμαθῶς ἐκτραγῳδοῦντες καὶ κιβδηλεύοντες, καὶ σεμνοπροσωποῦσι (πῶς ἂν εἴπῃ τις;), ὡς ἥδιστα σφίσιν αὐτοῖς ἀνοηταίνοντες, μηδενὸς ἑπομένου μήθ᾿ ὅλως ἀντιπράττοντος. Οὐδὲ γὰρ ἔχουσιν, οἶμαι, τοὺς βασκαίνοντας, ἀλλ᾿ οἱ μὲν οὐδ᾿ ἀξιοῦσι προσβλέπειν, οὐδ᾿ ἐπιστρέφεσθαι πρὸς τὸν λῆρον, οἱ δὲ οὐ ξυνιᾶσιν, ἀλλὰ πρὸς μόνην φήμην ἐπτόηνται, ἡ μηδὲν κατὰ τῶν τοιούτων ἰσχυρὸν ἔχουσα, κατὰ τῶν ἐλλογίμων μάλιστα δρᾶν ἰσχύει, ὥσπερ αἱ κατ᾿ ἀντιτύπων ἀφέσεις καὶ τὰ βέλεμνα.

4   Ταῦτ᾿ ἄρα ἐγώ φημι παντὸς μᾶλλον εὐλαβητέον τὴν περὶ τῶν θείων πολυπραγμοσύνην, οὐ μόνον πολιτικώτερον οὕτω πρὸς τὴν ἐφεδρεύουσαν βασκανίαν, ὡς εἴρηται, κεχρημένους, ἀλλ᾿ ὅτι καὶ τῷ παντὶ βέλτιον ὡς ἀληθῶς καὶ λυσιτελέστερον σιγῇ τιμᾶν τὰ ἀνέφικτα καὶ τὸν ἐκ τοῦ μὴ τυχεῖν ἐπιχειροῦντα κίνδυνον δεδιέναι καὶ φεύγειν. Οὐ γὰρ ὅ,τι μὲν τεύξῃ οὐκ οἶδας, τοῦτο δὲ οἶδας εὖ μάλα, ὡς ἀποτυχὼν καὶ ἁμαρτήσας κατὰ βραχύ, ἢ ῥῆμα ἢ νόημα, αὐτίκα αὐτόθεν ἐξώλης τε καὶ προώλης γεγένησαι καὶ τόν γε πόθον καὶ τό γε σέβας οὐκ ἐκ τοῦ λέγειν ἑτοίμως, ἄττα βούλει, πάνυ τοι πλεῖστα, ἀλλ᾿ ἐκ τοῦ μηδὲ λέγειν, ἃ δὴ καὶ πρόχειρα, δηλοῦν ἐστιν.

sea to any educated person who hears them? Those miserable men trot out the ineffable mysteries of our faith in an
abominable and ignorant manner and pompously proclaim
and adulterate them. They even try to appear serious (how
shall I put it?), as if they derive the utmost pleasure from
their folly, since nobody follows them or resists them in any
way. There is certainly no one who envies them, I think; in
fact some people do not deem it worthy either to look at
them or pay attention to their foolishness, whereas others
do not understand anything, and the gossip they hear is sufficient on its own to stun them. This gossip does not have
any power against such wicked men, but it can cause serious
harm to highly regarded men, like discharged arrows which
bounce off against adversaries.

For these reasons, I therefore suggest that above all we 4
must beware of officious curiosity about divine matters, not
just because it is more publicly courteous to spare ourselves
the danger of slander that lies in wait, as I have said, but because it is truly much better and more beneficial in every respect to honor with silence that which we cannot achieve,
and to fear and avoid the risk that might lead to failure. For
you do not know what you might gain, but you do know this
very well: that if you fail and make even a slight mistake either in a word or notion, you will immediately be utterly and
completely destroyed. You can show your love and respect
not by blurting out instantly whatever you want on most issues, but by completely refraining from speaking even on
topics that seem ordinary.

10

Ἐπαναλάβωμεν δὲ τὸν λόγον. Ἐφάμεθα τοίνυν πρῶτον εἶναι καὶ μέγιστον καὶ πρὸ πάντων καὶ ὅ,τι τις ἂν ἐρεῖ μάλιστα τῷ μέλλοντι καλῶς βιώσεσθαι τὰς περὶ Θεοῦ καὶ τῶν θείων δόξας ὀρθῶς τε καὶ ἀπλανῶς εὐσεβῆσαι, καὶ τοῦθ᾽ ὡς ἀνωτέρω καὶ διελόντες διὰ πάντων ἐφάμεθα. Τούτῳ γε μὴν μάλισθ᾽ ἕποιτ᾽ ἂν ἑξῆς ἅπαντα ἀγαθά, ὅσα τις ἂν ξυννοήσειε καὶ κατερεῖ, ὡς μετὰ τούτου πάντη τε καὶ πάντως κάλλιστ᾽ ἔχοντα καὶ χωρὶς οὔ, ὥσπερ οὐδ᾽ εἴ τινι τυφλώττοντι καὶ περὶ τἀναγκαῖα καὶ κράτιστα δεδυστυχηκότι κάλλη καὶ κόσμους τις περιβάλοιτο καὶ οὐκ οἶδ᾽ ἥντινα φλυαρίαν καὶ ἀχρηστίαν. Καὶ γὰρ δὴ κἀνταῦθα τὸ μηδὲν ὡς ἀληθῶς εἶναι τοῦ θεοσεβεῖν χωρίς, καὶ βίος εὐγενής τε καὶ σώφρων καὶ λόγος καὶ πᾶν ὁτιοῦν. Ἐπεὶ δὲ τοῦθ᾽ οὕτως ἔχοι καὶ κέοιτ᾽ ἂν παντάπασιν ἀσφαλές τε καὶ ἄτρεπτον, λοιπὸν δὴ περὶ τῶν ἄλλων ἁπάντων θεωρῆσαι, οἳ μάλιστα χώραν ἕκαστα ἔχει καὶ τετάξεται.

2 Ὅτι μὲν δὴ τὰ πάνθ᾽ ἡμῖν κατὰ τὸν βίοτον τόνδε ῥεῖ καὶ οὐδὲν πιστὸν παντάπασιν, οὐδὲ μόνιμον οὔθ᾽ ἵσταται, ἀλλ᾽ ὅλως ἀλόγιστοι δή τινες αὗται καὶ ἀτέκμαρτοι μεταβολαὶ στρέφουσι ταῦτα καὶ μεταφέρουσιν, οἷς ἐχόμεθα καὶ περὶ ἃ σχολάζομεν, ξυνεωράμεθα μὲν οἱ πλείους, καὶ ἀκριβῶς ὅμως κατιδόντες καὶ λέγοντες παρρησίᾳ, καὶ αὖθις οὕτως ὥσπερ ἀρρήκτοις τισὶν ὑπὸ τούτων δεσμοῖς ἐχόμεθα, μήθ᾽ ἡμᾶς αὐτοὺς μήτ᾽ ἀλλήλους αἰσχυνόμενοι. Τὰ μέν γε

Chapter 10

But let us resume the argument. We said that the first and most important thing of all and what one should say, especially to anyone who proposes to lead the good life in the future, is that they should hold correct and unerring opinions regarding God and divine matters. This too I indicated above, having discussed it in great detail. All other blessings depend on this attitude to a large extent, all the blessings that people can think of or articulate, because only when they come with this proper faith do they prosper everywhere and in all respects; otherwise it is impossible. Similarly, even if someone invests a blind man with beautiful ornaments and who knows what sorts of useless and silly things, he is still deprived of the necessary and pivotal means of life. In our case too, noble origin, prudence, education, and anything else that is not coupled with divine respect is truly nothing. Since things are like this and are both certain and unchangeable in all respects, we should now discuss all our remaining topics, in the precise place and order that has been assigned to each one of them.

Most of us realize that everything in this life is fluid, and that we can trust nothing at all; that nothing is permanent or stable, and some completely irrational and unpredictable powers cause everything to which we are attached and with which we are concerned to move and change. And although we are fully aware of these things and admit them without any hesitation, we are nevertheless caught up in them through, as it were, some unbreakable chains. Yet we do not feel embarrassed either for ourselves or for one another.

παίζοντα καὶ κατειρωνευόμενα λείπει πάντως κεχηνότας ἡμᾶς καὶ σφόδρα ἐπτοημένους, αὐτίκα αὐτόθεν, μὴ προειδομένους μήθ' ὁτιοῦν προνενοηκότας, ἀποδιδράσκοντα, ἢ λείπεται δὴ παρ' ἡμῶν, οἶμαι (πῶς ἂν εἴπῃς;), ἀπρὶξ ἀντεχομένων τε καὶ συμφυομένων καὶ μηδέποτε καθ' ὥραν τῶν λογισμῶν τε καὶ τῆς προσδοκίας ἀπαλλαττομένων.

3   Καὶ οὐκ οἶδ' ὅ,τι δεῖ πλείω περὶ τούτων λέγειν, ὅπου γε μηδέν ἐστιν ἀμέλει καινόν, ὃ μήπω πρότερον ἐνίοις εἴρηται μήτε νῦν τοῖς πλείστοις ὑπείληπται καὶ προεώραται. Πάντες γάρ ἐσμεν ἐν τούτοις φιλοσοφεῖν εὔποροι καὶ τῷ πάνυ δήλῳ τοῦ πράγματος καὶ προχείρῳ συγχωροῦντες, οὐδ' ὁ ἀμαθέστατος ἡμῶν ἐνταῦθα ἀτυχῆσαί ποτ' ἂν μὴ οὐ τῶν δεόντων τι καὶ αὐτὸς κατιδεῖν τε καὶ κατερεῖν, ὥσπερ αὖ οὐδ' ὁ πολυπραγμονέστατος καὶ περιεργότατος ἔχει τι πλέον ἀνύσαι καὶ προενεγκεῖν, κἂν ὅτι μάλιστα βούλοιτο, ὃ μὴ δὴ πρότερον ξυννενόηται.

II

Καὶ τὰ μέν γε οὕτως ἔχει. Ἀρετὴ δὲ μόνον δὴ κατ' ἀνθρώπους ἐν τῷ βίῳ τῶν ἁπάντων κτῆμ' ἐστὶν ἀσφαλές τε καὶ τέλειον καὶ κατ' οὐδὲν ἐνδεῖ τὸ μὴ οὐ πάντῃ τε καὶ

These things that make sport of us and make fun of us depart suddenly, leaving us openmouthed and stunned, because we had not foreseen their departure, neither had we made any necessary provision. Alternatively, I think that it is we who (how should I put it?) abandon them, no matter how closely connected and united with them we are, no matter how impossible it is for us to free ourselves from thoughts and hopes in relation to them even for a single moment.

I do not think there is any reason for me to say anything more on these issues, since what I say is nothing new, nothing that has not already been said by others in the past or that most people nowadays do not accept and anticipate. For we are all resourceful in discussing theoretical issues of this sort and we agree on the quite obvious issue that readily comes to mind. Even the most ignorant individual among us would not fail to know and say something relevant on the topic, whereas on the other hand even the most knowledgeable and most curious man could not discover or contribute anything extra, anything that has not been conceived of by someone else before him, no matter how much he longs to do so.

Chapter 11

So this is how matters stand. Virtue, however, is the only possession of all those human life includes that is stable and perfect, and under no circumstances does it fail to be the most sublime thing everywhere, in all respects and at all

πάντως καὶ ἀείποτ᾽ εἶναι καλλίστη, ἡδίστη μέν γε μάλα
συνεῖναι ὡς οὐδὲν ἄλλο τίποθ᾽ ἓν τῶν ἀπάντων, οὐδ᾽ ὁμοῦ
πάντα· περὶ ὃ δὴ πλεῖστον κέχηνεν ἡ φύσις καὶ ἅμα κλέος
οὐρανόμηκες πρόσεστιν, εἴ τῳ μέλοι.

2   Μᾶλλον δὲ καὶ ὅστις ἄρα περιγέγονε, μὴ μέλον αὐτῷ
διὰ τὸ τῆς ἀρετῆς παντάπασιν ἀνεπίστροφον ταύτῃ, τὸ δ᾽
αὐτόματον ἔποιτ᾽ ἂν ἀποτρεπομένῳ. Καλλίσταις δ᾽ ἀείποτε
καὶ περὶ πάντα τὸν βίον ἐλπίσι συνοῦσα, ἔτι μᾶλλον ἐπὶ
τέλει δείκνυσιν. Οὐ γὰρ ὥσπερ, οἶμαι, τἆλλ᾽ ἅπαντα τελευτῶντα ἀπέδρα ἀπαλλαττομένων ἢ καταλέλειπται καὶ οὐ
πάνυ δὴ βούλεται ξυνέπεσθαι, οὐχ οὕτω λοιπὸν καὶ αὕτη,
ἀλλ᾽ ἥδε πιστὴ γηροτρόφος καὶ εὐμενὴς εἰς τέλος παρα-
μείνασα καὶ μεταλλαττόντων οὐκ ἔλιπεν, οὐκ ἀπεχώρησε,
τηνικαῦτα δὲ μάλισθ᾽ ὥραν ἔχει καὶ οὐδέπω προὔδωκεν,
οὐδ᾽ ἀπέδρα τὸν κτησάμενον.

3   Ἀρετὴ γάρ, κἂν θάνῃ τίς, φησίν, οὐκ ἀπόλλυται, ζῇ δ᾽
οὐκέτ᾽ ὄντος σώματος, ἀπαίρει δὲ συνέκδημος ψυχῇ καὶ
συμπέφυκεν ἀθάνατον μόνον ἀγαθὸν τῷ σπουδάσαντι,
μᾶλλον δέ, ὡς ἡμεῖς ἔγνωμεν ἀληθέστατα καὶ νομίζομεν,
ἵλεως ἀγαθῶν κληροδότις, ὧν οὐκ ἄν τις ἐνενόησε πρότερον, οἷ᾽ ἐστίν, οὔθ᾽ ὅλως ἐλογίσατ᾽ ἄν, ὧν ἔτι κἀνταῦθα
τὰς ἐλπίδας τις ἔχων μόνας, οὐκ ἠξίου πολιτεύεσθαι τὰ
παρόντα, ἀλλὰ μάλιστ᾽ ἐν δευτέρῳ ἐποιεῖτο καὶ ἀπεωθεῖτο,
μόνην δ᾽ ἐκείνην εὐδαιμονίαν ἐμνηστεύσατο, ἧς οὐχ ὅλως

times, and it is a greater delight to share in than anything else in the world, even if one sets against it the sum of all other blessings. As regards the possession of virtue, nature gapes in great amazement and, at the same time, if a man cares about the acquisition of virtue, his *fame is exalted to heaven.*

But even if someone does not care about virtue, although 2 he has conquered it (for virtue is thoroughly impervious to itself), fame comes on its own even if he shuns it. Throughout the entire period of life, virtue constantly coexists with the best hopes, and toward the end of life it proves its worth even more. For, as I perceive it, virtue, unlike everything else, which deserts a person as soon as he is dead, or is left behind, refusing stubbornly to follow him, does not behave this way at all, but remains a kind and faithful servant in old age until death comes. And when men die, virtue neither deserts nor leaves them; on the contrary, that is its greatest moment, and virtue has thus far never betrayed or abandoned the person who possesses it.

For, as has been said, *even when someone dies, virtue does not* 3 *vanish, but continues to live on even when the body no longer exists.* It departs in order to accompany the soul during its journey, and it is the only good blessing that is by nature immortal for the person who pursues it. To put this in a better way, as we know very well and believe, it is virtue itself that benevolently bequeaths all blessings, the value of which no one realized before or took full account of. In this world, a person who hoped only to acquire these objects does not consider it worthwhile to participate in ephemeral affairs; instead, he considers them of secondary importance and rejects them, seeking only the prosperity that is unaffected by change,

ἅπτεται τροπή, κατιδὼν τἀνθρώπεια πράγματα μηδὲν
ὑγιὲς μηδ᾽ ἑστάναι πεφυκότα, ἀλλ᾽ ἄνω καὶ κάτω στρεφό-
μενα καὶ φερόμενα, μυρίαν καὶ ἀκαταλόγιστον παντάπασι
μεταβολήν.

4   Ταῦτ᾽ ἄρα ἐπὶ γῆς ἑστὼς ἄνθρωπος εἰς οὐρανὸν ἄνω
ποιεῖται συνθήκας καὶ πραγματεύεται ἀντὶ τῶν παρόντων
τὰ μήπω δῆλα, μᾶλλον δὲ ἀντὶ τῶν ἀδήλων τε καὶ ἀστάτων
καὶ ῥεόντων τὰ ὄντως εὐπαγῆ τε καὶ εὔδηλα, γενναῖον
προϊστάμενος λογισμὸν καὶ ποθῶν ἀπλανές, οὐκ ἀπατη-
λὸν καλόν, οὐδ᾽ εὐρίπιστον, οὐδ᾽ ὅπερ αὖραι πάντοθεν
ἀντιπνέουσαι στρέφουσι, πλείω τὴν ἀηδίαν καὶ λύπην ἀεί-
ποτ᾽ ἐμποιοῦν τοῖς ἐνισχομένοις, ἀλλ᾽ ἄλυπον μέν, ἀνώ-
λεθρον δέ, καὶ πεπηγὸς μέν, κόρον δ᾽ οὐκ ἔχον, ῥᾳστώνην
δὲ συνεῖναι καὶ οἵαν ἄρρητον. Τοῦτό ἐστι τὸ πρῶτον κατ᾽
ἀνθρώπους, τοῦτο τὸ μόνον ἄτρεπτον ἀγαθόν.

12

Σπάνιον δὲ οἶμαι τόδε τὸ χρῆμα—καὶ σφόδρα σπάνιον,
κἂν εἰ πολλοὶ παρρησίᾳ καθ᾽ ἑκάστην οἱ ἀπογραφόμενοι
πρὸς τὸν βίον τοῦτον καὶ μετατατόμενοι, οἷς ὁ μὲν νοῦς
ἴσως ὀρθῶς ἔγνω καὶ ὁ λογισμὸς ὥρμηται, τὸ σῶμα δὲ
ὅμως κλᾷ καὶ οὐκ ἔρρωται καὶ τὸ τῆς φύσεως ἀστατοῦν τε
καὶ εὔτροπον ὑπὸ πάντων, ἅττα δὴ παρεμπίπτει.

since he sees that human affairs by their very nature involve nothing sound or stable, and that everything is turned upside down as a result of an utterly infinite and incalculable movement.

As a consequence, the human being who stands on earth 4 makes an agreement with the God who resides in heaven above and he exchanges his present possessions for what he cannot yet see, or rather, by giving up what is invisible, unstable, and fluid, he receives in return what is truly solid and manifest. He acts thus because he uses his noble reasoning as a guide and longs for a fixed rather than a deceptive or unstable good, which is tossed about by strong winds blowing in various directions, so that it produces even greater disgust and grief among those held fast by it; instead, he longs for something painless and indestructible, something solid with which a person can never be sated, a pleasure unspeakable, as it were, for those who experience it. This is the most important blessing given to humankind, this is the only one that is unchangeable.

Chapter 12

I assume that this good is rare—indeed very rare, no matter how many births and deaths are openly recorded every day. Some of these people perhaps think correctly and their mind is excited, although their body is weakened and loses its strength, while at the same time human nature is both unstable and easily affected by whatever happens.

2   Εἶδον ἐγὼ πολλάκις ἐνίους, μᾶλλον δὲ πλείστους εἶδον, γεννικῶς μὲν ἁψαμένους τοῦ πράγματος καὶ μετὰ λογισμῶν ἀκμαίων τε καὶ θερμῶν πρὸς τὸν βίον τοῦτον αὐτομολήσαντας—καὶ σχεδὸν οὐδεὶς ὅστις οὔ, οὐκ ἔμελλον δὲ ἄρα καθάπαξ ἀντισχεῖν, οὐδ᾽ εἰς τέλος τὸ λῆμμα διατηρῆσαι, ἀλλ᾽ οἱ πλείους, ἢ αὐτίκα καὶ μετ᾽ οὐ πολὺ ἢ μεσοῦντες ἢ τέως γε μήν, ἐνέδοσαν, καὶ τοῖς μὲν καὶ παντάπασιν ἡ θερμότης ἔσβεσται, οἱ δ᾽ οὐκέτ᾽ ἦσαν ὡς πρότερον αὐτῆς, ἀλλ᾽ ὅμως ὑφεῖντο καὶ τῶν γενναίων ἐκείνων λογισμῶν ἀνεχώρησαν. Οὕτως ἔστιν ἀνώμαλον ἡ φύσις καὶ μυρίων ἀεὶ μεταβολῶν καὶ τροπῶν ὑπὸ τοῦ σώματος καὶ τῶν τοῦ σώματος πλέως καὶ κομιδῇ τοῦτο δυσχερὲς ἁπάντων περὶ ὁτουοῦν εἰς τέλος καρτερῆσαι πράγματος τὰ δόξαντα, τῶν λογισμῶν ταραττομένων ὑπὸ τῶν ἐμπιπτόντων καὶ τρεπομένων ὁσημέραι καὶ ὅσαι ὧραι σχεδόν.

3   Ἃ γὰρ δή τῳ χθὲς καὶ πρώην ἔδοξε, σήμερον εἰς τοὐναντίον ἅπαν τἀνδρὶ μετέδοξεν, ὑφ᾽ ἑαυτῷ μάρτυρι καὶ πολλοῖς ἴσως τοῖς θεωμένοις, καὶ αὖθίς γε τοὐναντίον, καὶ τοῦτο πολλάκις, καὶ πάσης ἀνωμαλίας τε καὶ ἐναντιότητος καὶ ἀοριστίας, ἅ τε πράττομεν πλήρη καὶ ἃ νοοῦμεν οὐχ ἥκιστα δὴ καὶ λέγομεν, καὶ σφόδρα ἐστὶν ἀλόγιστον τοῦτο καὶ οὐκ ἀσφαλὲς ἐρεῖν, ὡς περὶ ὁτουοῦν αὐτῷ τινι τὰ αὐτὰ καὶ δόξειε καὶ εἰρήσεται μέχρι τοῦ βίου παντὸς καὶ ὡς τόνδε τινὰ δὴ τὸν βίον εἰς τέλος, ὃν εἵλετο, καταπράξεται.

I often saw certain persons, or rather I saw many persons,   2
who vigorously attached themselves to this activity and
came of their own accord toward this particular lifestyle
with a simultaneously keen and impetuous mind—almost
everyone begins this way. But it was not meant for them to
resist fully or to maintain their courage to the end. Most
people yielded either immediately, or after a while, or half-
way through, or in any case at some point in between. The
eagerness of some was entirely quenched, whereas others
no longer possessed their initial enthusiasm, but nevertheless they surrendered and abandoned their previous brave
disposition. Human nature is so inconsistent, always full of
countless reversals and changes that derive from the body
and from anything related to it. The most difficult thing of
all is to go on maintaining our opinions about a particular
issue until the very end, given that our thoughts are thrown
into turmoil by the accidents of life and shift on a daily or
almost hourly basis.

For the opinions a person held yesterday and the day be-   3
fore, he changes them today to the precise opposite, and he
is himself witness to his change of mind along with many
other people who likely observe him as well. After this, another reversal of opinion occurs, and the same thing happens over and over again, and all our actions and thoughts,
no less than all our words, are accompanied by every sort of
instability, contradiction, and imprecision. To claim the following is extremely stupid and dangerous, namely that a
person can hold and articulate the same opinions regarding
a particular point for his entire life and that he will fulfill the
particular lifestyle he has chosen until the very end.

13

Ούκοῦν διὰ ταῦτ' ἔγωγε ἐφάμην σπάνιον εἶναι κομιδῇ, ὅστις τὰ κάλλιστα ἑλόμενος μέχρι παντὸς ἐκαρτέρησε καὶ οὐκ ἐτράπη οὐδ' ἔλιπε τὴν τάξιν, ἣν αὐτὸς ἑαυτὸν ἐπὶ καλλίστου κατέστησε σχήματος, καὶ σφόδρα εἰσὶν ἐκ πολλῶν οἱ κατορθοῦντες ὀλίγοι, οἷς ὁ λογισμὸς εἰς τέλος ἔρρωται, οἵ κεν ἀνέρες πέλωνται τλησικάρδιοι, ὠκέες δέ σφιν ἵπποι καὶ πᾶσαν, αἱ πράξεις δηλαδή, περὶ τὰ τῇδε καὶ οἷς ἡμεῖς ἐχόμεθα προσπάθειαν ἀποτρέχουσι, μηδενὶ τῶν ἀπαντώντων, ὅ,τι ποτ' ἂν ᾖ καινότερον, μὴ διατιθέμενοι, μηδὲ στρέφοντες—ὡς οἴακα καθάπερ οἱ ναυτιλλόμενοι—πρὸς τὰς ἀντιπνοίας τοῦ βίου τὸν λογισμόν, ἀλλὰ πλοῦν ἀνύτοντες καινότερον καὶ ἀεὶ τὸν αὐτὸν πρός τε γαλήνην καὶ πᾶσαν ἐπήρειαν, ἀείποτ' ἐχόμενοι τοῦ σκοποῦ, βραχὺ μὲν τὸ τῇδε τῆς ζωῆς μέτρον, καὶ εἰ μήκιστόν τῳ ξυμβαίνει, καθορῶντες, μεγίστους δὲ τοῦ μέλλοντος καὶ ἀθανάτου βίου καρποὺς καὶ πολιτείαν εὖ τε πράξασι τῇδε καὶ μὴ καὶ τὸ νῦν ἑκάστοτε προσβαλόν τε καὶ ἐνοχλῆσαν ὅσον οὐκ ἤδη παρερχόμενον σφᾶς, τὴν δὲ δι' αὐτὸ τροπὴν τῆς ἐξ ἀρχῆς αἱρέσεώς τε καὶ γνώμης μεγίστων ἴσως ἀφορμὴν ὀλέθρων καὶ ἀτυχῆσαι παντάπασι τοῦ μέλλοντος ἐκείνου καὶ καλλίστου βίου, τοῦτο δ' οὐκέτι μὴ εἶναι χάλκεα χρυσέων, ἀλλὰ τὰ μὴ ὄντα καθάπαξ τῶν ἀεὶ καὶ μὴ τελευτώντων ἀλλάξασθαι.

Chapter 13

For this reason I argued that very, very rarely does a person make the best choices and maintain them to the end without changing his mind or dismissing the order that he imposed upon himself toward the best manner. Indeed, only a few people out of many succeed in this, those whose reasoning is vigorous until the end. Only men with a brave spirit succeed in this, those who possess *swift-footed horses* (that is, their actions) that race past every preference relevant to this life and the matters by which we are held fast, paying no attention to anything that happens to them, regardless of how strange it might be. They do not turn their mind—like a rudder, as sailors do—in the direction of life's adversities, but follow a rather novel route, the same in a calm sea and bad weather alike, always headed toward their destination. They realize that the measure of this life is very short, although it turns out extremely long for some, whereas the fruits and quality of living of the immortal existence to come are of great consequence both for those who have done good deeds here on earth and those who have not. They also consider whatever occasionally irritates or troubles them now to be something that has already passed them by, and they think that if as a result of these troubles they alter their initial choices and decisions, this will cause grave disasters and deprive them entirely of that marvelously beautiful life to come. This is no longer equivalent to an exchange of gold for bronze, but an exchange of things that will exist forever and never die for those that do not exist at all.

2   Τοιγαροῦν οἱ πλείους δὴ τούτων καὶ φυγῇ φεύγουσιν
ἡμᾶς καὶ τὰ καθ᾽ ἡμᾶς ὅλῃ γνώμῃ καὶ ῥώμῃ καὶ ἀποτρέπονται, οὐ μισανθρωπίαν ἀσκοῦντες—πόθεν; οἱ τοῦ μόνου
φιλανθρώπου καὶ κοινοῦ τῶν ὅλων δεσπότου ἐρασταί τε
καὶ ὀπαδοί—, ἀλλὰ τὸ ἀτύρβαστον σφίσι καθάπαξ σοφῶς
βουλόμενοι καὶ οἰκονομοῦντες καὶ μή τι προσπίπτειν ἐντεῦθεν πολέμου καὶ ἀσχολίας ἔχον ἀνάγκην, ἀλλ᾽ ἐφ᾽ ἡσυχίας ἁπάσης καὶ γαλήνης τῶν ῥεόντων τῶνδε, ὡς οἷόν τέ
ἐστι, τὸν σκοπὸν ἀνύτειν, καὶ τὰς ἐν πόλεσι καὶ μετὰ τῶν
πολλῶν κοινωνίας καὶ συνουσίας ὡς κῆρας ἀγαθῶν λογισμῶν ἀποδιδράσκουσι καὶ πᾶσαν τὴν ἀπὸ τῆς ὕλης ἀποχωροῦσιν ἐπιβουλήν, συνεργὸν τοῦ πόθου καὶ τῆς γνώμης
τὴν ἐρημίαν τῶν πάντων πραγμάτων ἀνθαιρούμενοι καὶ
τὴν ἐξ ἀρχῆς ἔνστασιν κρατύνοντες· οἷς αὖραι κατ᾽ ὄρεσφι
πνείουσιν ὀλβιόδωροι, αἱ παρὰ τῆς θεαρχίας αὐτῆς ἵλεω
συλλαμβανομένης ἐπίπνοιαι, τοὺς πόνους ἀναψύχουσαι
καὶ τὰς ἀπὸ τῶν πειρασμῶν φλογώσεις, ἐπιτολαί τέ τινες
ἄρρητον οἵαν ἐμποιοῦσαι γλυκυθυμίαν, ἃς καὶ ἴσασιν αὐτοὶ
μόνοι, ἀρραβωνιζόμεναι τὴν ὅσον οὐκ ἤδη μίμνουσαν
σφᾶς εὐπραγίαν καὶ ἴσχουσαι πρὸς ἑνοειδῆ καὶ μόνιμον
κίνησιν, ἄτρεπτον ὑπὸ πάντων, τοὺς λογισμούς.

3   Ἀμέλει δὴ σχεδὸν ἡμῶν παντάπασιν ἀνεπίστροφοι
γίγνονται, παράλληλα τιθέμενοι καὶ καθορῶντες ἐκ μετε-
ώρου, ἅ τε νῦν ἡμεῖς σπουδάζομεν καὶ πλανώμεθα, καθάπερ ὀνειρώττοντες οὐδενὶ θαρροῦντες πιστῷ, καὶ σφᾶς
ὅπῃ δὴ προήκουσιν, εὖ μάλα πεπεισμένοι, καὶ ἄττα

As a consequence, most of them actually flee from us and 2
reject our choices with full consciousness and strength, not
because they hate mankind—how could this be possible?
They are lovers and followers of our one, common benevolent God, the master of us all—but on the contrary, they
wisely seek absolute tranquility for themselves and also
manage to repel anything that might forcibly lead them
away from there to disruption and distraction. They wish to
fulfill their aim with as much calm and peace from perpetual
change as possible. They flee association and coexistence
with the many in the cities, as if these were destructive
plagues on good reasoning, and they run from every plot
that matter contrives, preferring instead isolation from all
things as a companion for their desires and expectations,
thus strengthening their initial way of life. Just as the winds
blow *on the mountains* bestowing bliss, so too the breezes
sent by the merciful divinity relieve their labors and the
flames of their temptations, and the rising of certain stars
produces an ineffable pleasure, a rising that only these people really know, which by means of a betrothal guarantees
their coming prosperity and keeps their thoughts in a unified and permanent movement unaltered by any influence.

And indeed, they are almost inattentive to us in all mat- 3
ters and they compare and examine in a haughty manner
what we do earnestly and at what points we wander, as if in a
dream, trusting nothing, while they are fully convinced of
how far they have progressed, and of the things they hope to

καρποῦνται ταῖς ἐλπίσι, καὶ μὴν ἔτι καὶ νῦν ἐνταῦθα, ὧν
οὐ πρίαιντ᾽ ἂν μήποθ᾽ ἅπασαν, ἣν ἄν τις δόξειε παρ᾽ ἡμῖν
εὐδαιμονίαν.

4   Οὗτοι μὲν οὖν οὕτω κατωλιγωρηκότες τῶν ὁρωμένων,
ἀειφυγίαν εἵλοντο τοῦ παντὸς βίου, μόνου τοῦ καλοῦ γεγονότες ὀπαδοὶ θερμοί τε καὶ ἄτρεπτοι καὶ λογισμῷ κρείττονι καθάπαξ ἀπαλλαγέντες ἔκ τ᾽ ἀνδροκτασίης ἔκ θ᾽
αἵματος ἔκ τε κυδοιμοῦ, ὑψηλοὶ καὶ ἀκροβάμονες καὶ ἀρι-
στεῖς κατὰ τῆς φύσεως, πρὸς ἣν οὐκ ἔκλιναν ὅλως οὔτ᾽
ἐνέδοσαν οὔτ᾽ ἐνετράπησαν, μᾶλλον δ᾽ εἰπεῖν καλλιστεῖα
καὶ ἀγάλματα ταύτης καὶ ὥσπερ πρωτοτόκια ἐντελεστέρας
τε καὶ ἀκμαζούσης καὶ πλήρους πλάσεως. Ὀλίγοι μὲν οὖν
ἐκ πολλῶν πάνυ, καὶ εἰ τοῦ παντὸς ἰσοστάσιοι, καὶ τοῦθ᾽,
ἥπερ εἴρηται, διὰ τὴν τῆς φύσεως νόσον καὶ τῆς ὕλης, ἃ
προβάλλεται πράγματα, καὶ τοῦ λογισμοῦ τροπὰς ἑκάστοτε καὶ ἐφ᾽ ἑκάστοις.

14

Ἔστι καὶ τῇδε κατ᾽ ἀνθρώπους ὅμως ἐν βίῳ μετουσία
τις ἀγαθοῦ καὶ κοινωνία, πολιτική τις ὡς ἔπος εἰπεῖν
ἀρετή, ἣ δὴ καθάπερ τῷ νομίσματι πρὸς ἀλλήλους χρώμεθα καὶ συγγιγνόμεθα καὶ ὅλως σύνεσμεν, ὡς οὐκ ἔστι
ταύτης χωρὶς πολιτείαν ἢ ὅλως ἀνθρώπεια πράγμαθ᾽
ἵστασθαι. Τὸ μὲν οὖν πρῶτον καὶ ἄκρατον ἀγαθὸν εἴρηται,

enjoy or currently enjoy, which they would not exchange even for everything that we consider happiness.

They accordingly despised what we can see, and they chose lifelong exile from social activities, since they became fervent and unwavering supporters of what is good alone, and because of their profoundly wise reasoning they freed themselves once and forever from slaughter, blood, and battles. Full of pride, they rise very high and triumph over nature to which they did not yield at all or succumb or flee in shame. I would say instead that these people are the fairest prizes of nature and its admired statues, who resemble the firstborn of a more complete, flourishing, and solid creation. These individuals are very few among the many, and if they are equal in value to the rest of the world, this is due, as has been said, to the weakness of nature and of matter, as a consequence of the many hurdles it puts forward, and to the deviation of our mind toward different paths on various occasions.

Chapter 14

There nonetheless still exists even in this human life some possibility of communion and partnership with what is good, almost a kind of political virtue, so to speak, which we use as if it were a currency in our daily interactions, and through which we cooperate and generally live together, because without this political virtue no society or human life at all can exist. We have already mentioned the primary and

καὶ σφόδρα σπάνιον εἴρηται καὶ δυσκαταγώνιστον, ὥστε καὶ τοῦτ᾿ αὐτὸ πολλάκις ἔνιοι καταλογισάμενοι καὶ δεδιότες, ὑποκεχωρήκασιν ὡς ἐργῶδες ἀνῦσαι καὶ παγχάλεπον. Τοῦ δὲ ἔξεστι πάντας ἱκνεῖσθαι καὶ ὡς ἐν ἀνθρώποις καὶ βίῳ ξυνόντας τυγχάνειν, ἀφορῶντας ἀείποθ᾿ ὡς πρὸς ἀρχέτυπα ἀνδρείκελα καί, καθ᾿ ὅσον, οἶμαι, ἔξεστιν, ἀφομοιουμένους τοὺς ἄνδρας ἐκείνους, ἃ μὲν οὖν ἔδοξεν ἐκείνοις φευκτά, παντὶ σθένει καὶ αὐτοὺς οἰομένους χρῆναι φεύγειν, ἃ δὲ τοῖσδε μή, κἀνταῦθα πειθομένους τε καὶ συνεπομένους.

2   Πλοῦτον μὲν οὖν καὶ τρυφὴν καὶ τὴν κατὰ κόσμον εὐεξίαν οἱ πλείους τῶν ἀνθρώπων τῶν κατὰ τὸν βίον ἁπάντων ἥγηνται κάλλιστα καὶ σφίσιν εὐκταιότατα παρεῖναι καὶ σχεδὸν περὶ ταῦτ᾿ ἐστὶν ἡ πάντων πᾶσα σπουδή. Τὰ μέν γε οὐκ ἄρα μόνον οὐδ᾿ ἡντινοῦν κοινωνίαν ἔχει πρὸς ἀρετήν, ἀλλὰ καὶ σφόδρα δὴ πρὸς αὐτὴν ἀντιπράττει καὶ τῆς ἐναντίας προδήλως ἐστὶν ἕξεως. Ἡ μέν γε τῶν ὄντων ἐρᾷ, τὰ δὲ τῶν τε χθὲς καὶ πρὸ τρίτης γενομένων καὶ τῶν ὅσον οὐκ ἤδη κατολουμένων, ἡ μὲν τῶν ἑστώτων τε καὶ μονίμων, τὰ δὲ τῶν ῥεόντων καί, μηδ᾿ ἂν ὅτι μάλιστα βιάζηταί τις, παραμεῖναι πρὸς ὀλίγον δυναμένων, ἡ μὲν τῶν ἀφθάρτων καὶ ἀνωλέθρων τε καὶ ἀτρέπτων, τὰ δὲ τῶν πάντῃ τε καὶ πάντως καὶ ἀείποτε τρεπομένων τε καὶ μεταβαλλόντων καὶ πλανώντων καὶ οὐδὲν πρὸς τοὺς κεκτημένους ἐχόντων πιστόν.

3   Οὕτως ἀπό τε τῶν ἐναντίων παντάπασιν ἀρχῶν ὥρμηνται καὶ πρὸς αὐτὰ τἀναντιώτατα φέρονται. Τοῦτο μέν γε ῥᾴδιον καὶ ὁτῳοῦν κατιδεῖν, μηδένα πώποτε τῶν ἀρετῆς

absolute blessing; we have said that this is extremely rare and difficult to achieve, so that some people many times tremble when they merely consider it, and have renounced it as laborious and extremely difficult to attain. This other blessing, however, can be attained and achieved by all who live among human beings, so long as they pay constant attention to and imitate those men as best as they can, I believe, as if they were exemplary images. Upon reflection, they must use all their strength to avoid matters these men consider contemptible, and they should, by contrast, comply with and accept matters they approve of.

Most people believe that wealth, luxury, and worldly prosperity are what is most beautiful in life and what is best to obtain, and everyone's attention focuses almost exclusively on these matters. Not only do these things not relate to virtue in any way, however, but they actually act strongly against it and obviously belong to an opposite habit. Virtue loves that which exists, whereas wealth, luxury, and worldly prosperity are linked only to that which was created yesterday or the day before and will very soon perish. Virtue belongs to the realm of stability and permanence, whereas the other matters just mentioned are ephemeral and cannot endure for long, no matter how much one tries. Virtue belongs to the realm of the incorruptible, indestructible, and unchangeable, whereas wealth, luxury, and prosperity belong to the realm of that which constantly in all cases and all ways changes, transforms, errs, and offers nothing trustworthy to those who possess it.

Virtue and happiness accordingly originate from radically opposed principles and have completely different ends. Anyone can easily understand that no one ever of those who

τελείας ἐπιμελουμένων τῶν τοιούτων ὅλως ἐπιστρεφόμε-
νον ὁρᾶν, ἀλλ' ὡς αὐτὰ δὴ τὰ σφίσιν ὀλεθριώτατα ταῦτα
παντὶ τρόπῳ χρῆναι φεύγειν οἴονται καὶ ἀποτρέπονται,
δεδιότες καὶ ὑφορώμενοι μέγιστον αὐτόθεν ἀπαντᾶν κίνδυνον, οἵ γε ὡς ἀληθῶς σπουδαῖοι καὶ σφόδρα ἠνυκότες
πρὸς τὴν ἐξ ἀρχῆς τοῦ βιοῦν αἵρεσιν.

15

Λόγῳ μέντοι πάνυ δὴ πρὸς τὴν ἀρετὴν κοινὰ πλεῖστα
καὶ μεγίστη συγγένεια πρός τε τὴν τῶν ὄντων καὶ τοῦ
βίου παντὸς σύνεσιν καὶ ἱστορίαν καὶ πρὸς αὐτὴν ἔτι τὴν
εὕρεσιν τοῦ ἀγαθοῦ καὶ θεωρίαν. Καὶ μὴν ἔτ' ἄλλα πλεῖστα
νῦν παρεῖται, ἅττα καθ' ὥραν ἴσως αὖθις ἔσται λέγειν καὶ
ὡς ἐξέσται.

2 Εἰμὶ μὲν οὖν ἔγωγε, καὶ πρότερον εἴρηται, οὐ τῶν
σφόδρα πασχόντων τῷ πράγματι καὶ προστετηκότων,
οὐδὲ τῶν πάνθ', ὅσ' ἂν οἷοί τε γίγνοιντο, ἐπιθειαζόντων
τε τοὺς λόγους καὶ ἐξισταμένων ὡς ἄρα μόνον ἐν
ἀνθρώποις καλὸν καὶ μόνον ἐστὶν αἱρετὸν καὶ μόνον ἡδὺ
καὶ μόνον ἱερὸν καὶ ἀθάνατον καὶ ὡς οὐκ ἔστιν οὐκ ἄλλως
ἢ μετὰ τούτου βιωτὸν ἀνθρώπῳ νοῦν ὅλως ἔχοντι, καὶ οὐκ
ἔγωγ' ἐπαινῶ τὰ περιττὰ ταῦτ', οὐδὲ πείθομαι, ἀλλὰ καὶ
σφόδρα δὴ θαυμάζω τῶν τε πάλαι ἐκείνων πρότερον καὶ

seek *perfect virtue* sees himself as completely paying attention to matters such as wealth and luxury, but that truly excellent men and those who generally succeed in the lifestyle they have chosen from the first believe that they should avoid them by every means possible, because they are extremely destructive for them; and they avoid them because they are afraid and suspect that they will immediately encounter the greatest danger.

Chapter 15

In fact, virtue has much in common with reason, and there is a quite substantial relationship in regard to their comprehension and knowledge of what exists and of life as a whole and, in addition, with regard to the actual discovery and contemplation of what is good. I will now pass over the many other similarities they share, which I will perhaps be able to discuss on the proper occasion and in the proper manner.

As I said before, I myself am not one of those who are 2 profoundly passionate about or engrossed by this issue, nor am I one of those who applaud learning with as much praise as they can muster, and who argue excitedly that education is mankind's only blessing, the only possible choice, the only source of pleasure, the only sacred and immortal thing, and that a rational person cannot possibly live except together with it. I do not approve of such exaggerated claims, nor do I believe them. In fact, I marvel greatly at our ancestors as

ὅσοι νῦν τὰ τοιαῦτα φιλονεικοῦσι καὶ βιάζουσι καὶ μαρ-
τύρονται ἄκαιρον καὶ ἀνήνυτον ἔνστασιν. Ἐρῶ δὲ ὅμως
περὶ αὐτοῦ δὴ τούτου παρρησίᾳ, ἄττα μοι δοκῶ καὶ ἃ ξυν-
νενόηκα καὶ ὡς ἄν τις, οἶμαι, ἐρεῖ μετρίως, καὶ μάλιστα
πρὸς ἤδη σὲ παρακαλεῖν εἰς αὐτοὺς ὡρμημένος.

3   Παιδεία τοίνυν, ἓν τοῦτο καὶ πρῶτον, καὶ τὰ τῆς σοφίας
ἀγαθὰ παραμένει τῶν κατὰ τὸν βίον ἁπάντων πιστῶς εἰς
ἄπασαν τῷ κτησαμένῳ τὴν ζωὴν καὶ οὐκ ἔστιν οὐκ ἀφαι-
ρεῖσθαι μήτε τὸν ἀπὸ ταύτης πλοῦτον ἐχθρόν, ὅτι μὴ
πέφυκε, μήτε τὴν ἀπὸ ταύτης δόξαν, ὅτι μὴ κρείττω γενόμενον. Τῷ ὄντι γὰρ πρὸς ταύτην ὥσπερ εἰς ἄσυλόν τι τέμε-
νος ηὐτομοληκότα τινὰ καὶ καταστάντα, ἔξεστιν ἐπ᾽ ἀσφαλοῦς ἑστήξειν καὶ μηκέτι καθάπαξ ἔπειτα μὴ δεδιέναι μήτε
χρόνων ἐπιβουλὴν καὶ ἀνωμαλίαν μήτε τυράννου βασκανίαν τε καὶ πλεονεξίαν μήτ᾽ ἄλλην ἅπασαν ἐχθρῶν ἐπήρειαν, ἀλλὰ πάντ᾽ ἂν μᾶλλον ἄνω καὶ κάτω γίγνοιτο καὶ
μεταχωροίη καὶ τρέποιτο ἢ νοῦς ὁτῳοῦν ἀφαιρεθείη σώφρων καὶ λογισμὸς ἔντεχνος καὶ ἣν ἐπιστήμη καὶ παιδεία
τοῖς θιασώταις καὶ σπουδασταῖς φέρουσα ἐνῴκισεν εὐδαιμονίαν καὶ τρυφήν.

16

Καὶ ταῦτα δὴ μάλιστα λόγῳ πρὸς ἀρετὴν κοινά, τό τε
μόνιμον κτωμένοις παντάπασι καὶ πιστὸν καὶ τὸ μηδόλως
ἐχθροῖς δουλεύειν μήθ᾽ ἡττᾶσθαι, κἂν ὅτι μάλιστα βλά-

well as at our contemporaries who quarrel over such issues, argue vehemently, and muster endless ill-timed objections. I will nonetheless set forth my opinion and my reflections on this topic frankly and as one might put it, I believe, measuredly, since I have already set out to urge you specifically toward education.

First and foremost, education and the blessings of wisdom remain faithfully with the man who possesses them for his entire life more than any other human possession does. No adversary can deprive the possessor of the wealth that comes with wisdom, because it is unnatural for this to happen, nor is it possible to deprive him of the glory that comes from wisdom, because the enemy does not surpass the possessor in this same area. Indeed, if someone seeks refuge in education and stays by its side, this person will feel safe, just as in a temple no one can violate, and will have no fear thereafter of either the deceitful plots or the vicissitudes of time, or of a tyrant's envy and arrogance, or of any other hostile abuse. Everything could turn quite on its head or disappear or change completely, but no one can deprive a person of a sober mind and skilled reasoning, the happiness and delight that knowledge and education bring out and instill in their followers and students.

3

Chapter 16

These, then, are the common features virtue and reason share, namely their stability and reliability for all those who possess them, as well as the fact that they cannot be en-

πτειν ζητῶσι, μήτε προδήλοις ἁρπαγαῖς ἰσχύουσι μήτ᾽ ἐλ-
λοχήσεσι καὶ ἐνέδραις καθάπερ ἀμέλει τἄλλ᾽, ἃ πρότερον
εἴρηται, παντάπασιν ἄπιστα καὶ οὐκ ἔμμονα, καὶ πρὸς
πᾶσαν ἐπιβουλὴν καὶ κακόνοιαν ἔφεδρον ἐμπίπτει καὶ μετ-
οχετεύεται καὶ πᾶσι πρόκειται τοῖς μεῖζον ἐχθροῖς ἰσχύουσι δρᾶν ὁτιοῦν κακὸν καὶ τρέπειν ἢ βούλονται καὶ καθ-
ιστάναι μείζονος ἀνίας αἴτια τοῖς κτησαμένοις, ἐπ᾽ ὀλίγον
ἔστιν ὅτε καταγοητεύσαντα καὶ παραχρῆμα ἀποιχόμενα
καὶ ἀναχωρήσαντα, ἢ καὶ θάτερον, πλεῖστον συνῳκηκότα
χρόνον καὶ συνήθειαν δόντα τροπῆς ἀνυπονόητον καὶ μηκέτι τοῖς λογισμοῖς ὑποπτευομένην, ἔπειτα κακῶς ἀπαλ-
λαττόμενα καὶ πρὸς βίαν ἀποτεμνόμενα τῶν μήτε προσδο-
κησάντων καὶ σφόδρα ἀντεχομένων τε καὶ πασχόντων.

2 Τοῖς πλείστοις δὲ καὶ τῶν ἐσχάτων ταῦτα συμφορῶν
ἀφορμαὶ γίγνονται, πλοῦτός τε καὶ δόξης κράτος ἀκμάζον,
ἢ φθονηθεῖσιν ἢ ὑποπτευθεῖσι, καὶ καθάπερ ἄρα τὰ ἐν
πελάγεσι σκάφη, ὑπὸ πνευμάτων ἀκμαίων οὐριοδρομή-
σαντα, ὑπ᾽ αὐτῶν δὴ τούτων ἐνίοτε τελευτῶντα περι-
ετράπη καὶ κατηνέχθη, τὸν αὐτὸν ἐμοὶ δοκεῖν τρόπον καὶ
οὗτοι βαρυπενθεῖς τε καὶ παλαμναίας ἠλλάξαντο τύχας,
ὑφ᾽ ὧν ἔδοξαν εὐδαιμονῆσαι. Παιδείας δὲ θησαυροὺς
καὶ κλέος οὐδεὶς μὴ ποτ᾽ ἴσχυσεν, οὔτ᾽ ἐνεδρεύσας—καὶ
εἰ μάλιστα φθόνῳ τήκοιτο—οὔτ᾽ ἐπιδήλως ἐπιθέμενος,

slaved in any way or defeated by their enemies, regardless of how much the latter wish to cause harm. For their enemies can seize them neither openly nor by means of trickery and ambush, as is doubtless the case with the other matters mentioned previously, which are entirely untrustworthy and impermanent, fall victim to every scheme and impending malice, and are diverted and lie exposed to every stronger enemy who has the power to do them harm and overturn them as he likes, in this way making them the cause of much greater sorrow for those who possess them, since they sometimes charm such persons for only a brief period and then suddenly depart and desert them. There is also the alternative case, that these things accompany a person for a long time and that he becomes so accustomed to them that he no longer envisages or suspects by means of reasoning the possibility of change, and then they will be taken away from him in an unpleasant fashion and cut off by force; for he will not expect this and will be so greatly devoted to them that he will suffer.

These things, namely wealth and the power of glory when it is in full bloom, cause the most severe miseries to the majority of people, who attract either envy or suspicion. Just as ships that are propelled by favorable winds in the open sea are occasionally ultimately capsized and sunk by the very same winds, in the same way, I think, these people are driven to deep misery and abominable fate by what they once considered to be their happiness. No one has ever managed to take the treasures and prestige of education away from their owner, however, neither by plotting—although he might be worn away by jealousy—nor in face-to-face conflict. To the

ἀφελέσθαι τοῦ κτησαμένου, μένει δ᾽ οἷον συμφυὲς κάλλος καὶ ἀναπάλειπτον, οὔτ᾽ ὄμμασι βασκάνοις οὔτε χερσὶ τεμνόμενον, καὶ ταύτην, οἶμαί, τις λέγων μόνην παρασκευὴν ἀκαταγώνιστον πρὸς πᾶσαν δυσμένειαν καὶ ἀνεπιχείρητον, οὐκ ἂν ἴσως ἁμάρτῃ λέγων. Ὅλως μὲν γὰρ οὐκ ἔστι κατ᾽ αὐτῆς ἐξισχῦσαι καὶ ὑποποιήσασθαι, καθάπερ οἱ πλέον ἰσχύοντες μαχόμενοι πάντα καταστρέφονται καὶ δουλοῦνται.

3   Ἢν δ᾽ ἄρα τις ἕλοιτο πολεμεῖν καὶ προπηλακίζειν, καὶ μάλα ἀμυνεῖται καὶ σφόδρα καιρίως καὶ ὡς οὐκ ἔστιν ἰᾶσθαι, καὶ πόρρω μάλιστ᾽ ἀείποτε τῶν χρόνων, ὥς τις ἔφη, "σοφὰ δ᾽ ἄκλαυστα καὶ πολύδηκτα βέλη." Καὶ τοῦτο μάλιστα δάκνει καὶ λυπεῖ τοὺς ἐν δυναστείαις κακοήθεις, αἰσθανομένους καὶ δεδιότας τὸ τῆς σοφίας ἀνεπιχείρητον μέν, ἰσχυρὸν δὲ καθ᾽ ὁτουοῦν, εἰ βούλοιτο, κακῶς δρᾶν καὶ ἀμύνεσθαι.

17

Ἐλύπει Πλάτωνα Διονύσιος, εἶτα μετεμέλετό τε καὶ ἤχθετο καὶ ἐπυνθάνετο, "Ἦ που Πλάτων ἐν Ἀθήναις καὶ Ἀκαδημίᾳ γενόμενος, πολὺν ποιήσει λόγον περὶ ἡμῶν τε καὶ καθ᾽ ἡμῶν." Καὶ ὁ μὲν ξυνενόει τε καὶ ἔμφροντις ἦν, βραχέα λυπῶν τὸν ἀμυνεῖσθαι πλεῖστον δυνάμενον, ὁ δέ, ἡδὺς ἦν καὶ μεγαλόφρων ἐκ φιλοσοφίας, ἐδείκνυε μὴ

contrary, they continue to abide with their possessor like an innate and ineradicable beauty, which cannot be harmed by envious eyes or hands. It would probably not be a mistake, I think, if one were to say that education is the only invincible and unassailable equipment against any adversity. For no one can defeat it in any way or conquer it, as happens in all other cases, in which the strongest fighters destroy and capture everything.

Even if someone chooses to fight education and assault it, education will defend itself vehemently and mortally against the attacker, so that he cannot be healed no matter how much time passes; as someone said, *"the arrows that a wise man shoots do not make one cry, but they do bite deeply."* This is exactly what eats at and causes sorrow to wicked men who exercise public power, because they realize fearfully that no one can combat wisdom, whereas wisdom, by contrast, is powerful enough to harm and repel anyone, if it wishes to do so.

Chapter 17

Dionysius caused Plato grief, and afterward he regretted it and was vexed, and he said: "Surely, when Plato has gone back to Athens and the Academy, he will have a great deal to say about me and against me." Such were Dionysius's anxious thoughts, because he had caused some minor grief to a person who could retaliate in numerous ways. Plato, on the other hand, was both pleasant and high-minded due to his

μέλον αὐτῷ καὶ "Μήποτε γένοιτο" ἔφασκε "τοῖς ἐν Ἀκαδημίᾳ τοσαύτη σχολή, ὡς περὶ σοῦ λόγους ποιεῖσθαι καὶ
φροντίσματα." Τῷ ὄντι γὰρ ὅ γε δὴ σπουδαῖος δύναται
μέν, οὐχ αἱρεῖται δέ, φιλοσοφίᾳ καὶ λογισμοῖς ἑαυτοῦ
δεσπόζων, μήθ᾽ ὑπὸ παντὸς πάσχειν δυσχεροῦς ξυμπίπτον-
τος, μήτε πρὸς πάντα κινεῖσθαι, ἀποχρῶσάν τε δίκην
ἡγεῖται τῷ δυσμενεῖ δεδιότι τὸ δέος αὐτὸ καὶ τὴν περὶ τῆς
ἀμύνης φροντίδα νύττουσαν. Οὐ γὰρ ἔστιν ὅπως ἀπαλ-
λαγὴ γένοιτ᾽ ἄν, ἀλλ᾽ ἀείποθ᾽ ὑπόνοιαι τὸν ἄνδρα καὶ βα-
σκανίαι δειναὶ ταράττουσιν, ἔμμονον ἀλγηδόνα φέρουσαι,
μὴ δυνάμενον τῶν πολεμίων ὅπλων κρατῆσαι καὶ ἀφελέσθαι.

2 Ὁ δὲ ἀπεριφροντίστως ἀνύτει τὸν βίον καὶ ἀμερίμνως,
καὶ μήν, ἢν ἄρα τι καὶ ἀνιαρὸν ἀπαντῷη, οἷα δὴ καθόλου
τἀνθρώπεια καὶ πειρώμεθα πάντες καὶ οὐδεὶς ὅστις οὔ, ὁ
δὲ ἄχθεται μέν (πῶς γὰρ οὐ μέλλει, θνητὸς ὢν καὶ μετὰ
σώματος εὐπαθοῦς συνοικῶν καὶ πολυδεοῦς τε καὶ πολυ-
τρύτου;), αὐτίκα δ᾽ ὅμως, ὥσπερ ἀπὸ δυοῖν ποδοῖν ἀμέλει
φασί, καθάπερ εἰς ἀλεξητήριόν τι τοὺς λόγους αὐτοὺς
ὥρμηται καὶ τὴν ἀπ᾽ αὐτῶν παραμυθίαν ἐπὶ τῷ δεινῷ καὶ
συμμαχίαν καὶ ῥᾷον ἢ κατὰ τοὺς πολλοὺς διαφέρει τὸν
ἐμπεσόντα κλύδωνα τοῦ βίου.

3 Ὀφθαλμοῖς μὲν γὰρ κάμνουσιν ἥδιστον καὶ πλείστην
ὡς ἀληθῶς φέρει παραμυθίαν τόποις ἐνδιαιτᾶσθαι χλοε-
ροῖς καὶ διηνθισμένοις, ἀνδρὶ δὲ ἀστείῳ καὶ περὶ τοὺς
λόγους ἐσπουδακότι μάλιστα, ὑπὸ δὲ τῆς βιωτικῆς ἀνωμαλίας ταραττομένῳ τε καὶ φλεγμαίνοντι μεγίστην ἐμποιεῖ
τοῖς λογισμοῖς λειότητα καὶ γαλήνην ἡ τῆς σοφίας, οἶμαι,

philosophical education, and showed that this issue did not bother him; he said: "May the people at the Academy never have so much spare time, as to discuss and be concerned with your issues." Indeed, the educated man, although he can, never chooses to suffer from any sort of unpleasant event or to be stirred up against everything, since he controls himself by virtue of his philosophical spirit; he thinks that for a frightened adversary that kind of fear, together with his painstaking care to protect himself, are sufficient punishments. It is impossible to avoid these sufferings, but terrible suspicions and envy trouble this man constantly, producing chronic pain, since he cannot prevail over the enemy's arms or take them away from him.

The educated man, by contrast, spends his life free of 2 anxieties and troubles. Indeed, even if he encounters some grief, because we all experience the full range of human problems and there is no one who does not, he is certainly grieved (how could he possibly not be, given that he is mortal and inhabits a body that is easily injured, needy, and much abused?). Nevertheless, *using both feet energetically*, as they say, he quickly rushes off, as if in the direction of a protective remedy, toward education itself and the consolation that comes from it and the assistance it offers in combating the disaster. He thus alleviates the troubles of life that have befallen him more easily than most people do.

Spending time in a green and flowery place furnishes 3 weary eyes with a very pleasant and genuinely great relief; especially for a cultivated and highly educated man, I think, who is agitated and disturbed by the vicissitudes of life, communion with wisdom and its blooming meadows brings enormous relaxation and calm to his mind, once he turns

συνοίκησις καὶ οἱ κατ᾽ αὐτὴν ἀνθηροὶ λειμῶνες, πρὸς
αὐτοὺς τραπομένῳ τε καὶ συννενευκότι, καὶ ἵλεων δὴ καὶ
ἀκύμονα καθίστησι τὴν ψυχὴν ἡ πρὸς αὐτὴν καταφυγὴ
καὶ παρ᾽ αὐτῆς ὑποδοχὴ καὶ καρποφορία τε καὶ ξενία
φέρειν οὐκ ἀγεννῶς τὰ λυποῦντα.

4   Τὸ μὲν γὰρ ὅλως κακῶς πρᾶξαι κοινὸν καὶ ὥσπερ τὸ
νοσεῖν ἀνθρώπειον καὶ τῆς φύσεως, ὁ δ᾽ ἄρα νοσήσας ἐκεῖνος καὶ τάχιστα τὸ δεινὸν ὑπερέσχε καὶ ῥάων γέγονε καὶ
μάλιστα ἤνεγκεν ἐν τῷ πάθει κοῦφος, ὅτῳ ἔδωκεν ὁ Θεὸς
εὐκαιρίαν τε τόπου καὶ τὴν ἄλλην περὶ αὐτὸν κατάστασιν,
τῇ φύσει πάντη συμμαχοῦντα πρὸς τὸν ἐγερθέντα τῆς
νόσου ταύτης πόλεμον γεννικῶς ἀντιπράττειν, ᾧ δὲ μή,
τοὐναντίον ἅπαν, δεινῶς ἔχει καὶ κατενήνεκται, οἷα δὴ
καθ᾽ ἑκάστην ὁρῶμεν καὶ γίγνεται. Καὶ ταὐτὸν ἄρα τοῦθ᾽
ὡς ἀληθῶς, οἶμαι, ἔχει πρὸς τύχην πολεμοῦσαν, ὅτῳ λόγος
ἐστὶν ἐπαναπαύσασθαι καὶ τὴν γιγνομένην ἐπικουρίαν
πλείστην ὄντως ἐκεῖθεν λαβεῖν, καὶ ὅτῳ μή, ἀθλίως σφόδρα
γεγυμνωμένῳ πάσης πάντοθεν συμμαχίας.

5   Καὶ ἔγωγε εἴκασα πολλάκις τὸν τοιοῦτον κατασκοπούμενος, ἀνδρὶ τόπους ἐρήμους τε καὶ ἀσκίους ὁδοιποροῦντι,
ὅς, ἐπιπεσόντος ἀθρόον χειμῶνος καὶ ἅμα νιφετοῖς καὶ
ῥαγδαίοις κοπτόμενος πάντοθεν πνεύμασιν, οὐκ ἔσχεν
οὔθ᾽ ἑαυτῷ χρήσασθαι οὔτε ποι καταφυγεῖν καὶ πρὸς ὀλίγον τὴν ἐπίκλυσιν παραμυθήσασθαι καὶ δυσχέρειαν τοῦ
καιροῦ, ἀλλὰ κακῶς ὅλλυται, τλήμων, ἄθλιος, ξένος, ἀνέ-
στιος, ἀλήτης ὥς, οὐκ ἔχων ἡντινοῦν ἀσφάλειαν, οὐκ ἔχων
λιμένα πρὸς τὸ ναυάγιον, ἀλλ᾽ ἅμα τε προσέπεσε τὰ λυποῦντα καὶ τῶν λογισμῶν αὐτῶν κάθηται παντάπασιν

CHAPTER 17

and inclines in its direction. And his seeking refuge in wisdom renders his soul gentle and calm, while the acceptance it provides and its fertility and hospitality make his soul bear the sad events nobly.

For suffering unfortunate events is a common experience 4 for everyone, and precisely like sickness, this is human and natural. If God has offered to someone who has become sick an appropriate place to live and other settled conditions for him to fight back bravely in the war that has erupted against this sickness in alliance with nature as a whole, the man gets over the suffering very quickly and recuperates and endures his misfortune quite easily. But for the person to whom God has not granted any of these things, everything is the reverse; he suffers enormously and is defeated by the sickness, just as we see happening every day. I truly believe that the same is the case when our fate is fighting against us; the man who is able to seek refuge in education for the sake of recreation certainly derives great assistance from it, whereas the person who is not educated has utterly and miserably stripped himself of external support.

I also often compared this latter man, as I pondered his 5 case, to a person who walks on remote paths without protective shade, and when a sudden storm occurs, is buffeted by snow and strong winds from all directions. In such a case he can do nothing, nor can he retreat anywhere to protect himself for a while from the floods and bad weather conditions, and instead this wretched person perishes utterly, in complete misery, far from his country, without a roof over his head, like a vagabond, lacking any place of security or a harbor to sail to in case of shipwreck. Whenever something bad happens to this man, he sits completely separated from

65

ἀφειμένος, μᾶλλον δὲ ἀφῃρημένος, μηκέτ᾽ ἰσχύσας ὅπῃ ἄρα τοῦ λοιποῦ προσδραμεῖν καὶ ἀποχωρῆσαι καὶ τὴν διάνοιαν κατασεισθεῖσαν ἐφορμῆσαι καὶ ἀνακαλέσασθαι διενεγκεῖν τὸν ἐπιβρίσαντα πόλεμον, ἀλλ᾽ ἀγόμενος καὶ φερόμενος καὶ τί γὰρ οὐ τῶν ἀθλίων πάσχων ὑπὸ τῆς πικρᾶς καὶ δυσκόλου τύχης.

6   Ὁ δὲ σπουδαῖος ἐκεῖνος ἄνθρωπος, καθάπερ οἱ πολεμίων ἔφοδον ἤδη κρατοῦσαν οἰκονομοῦντες, ἐπ᾽ ἄστεος ἐγγειτόνων ἀναχωροῦσιν, εἴκοντες μέν, ἀσφαλιζόμενοι δ᾽ ὅμως ὡς οἷόν τέ ἐστι τὴν ζωήν, παραπλησίως πρὸς τὴν ἔξωθεν τῶν βιωτικῶν ἀντιπράττουσαν ἀκμὴν οἱονεὶ κρησφύγετον εὑρίσκει τοὺς λόγους, εἰς οὓς καταφεύγων ῥώννυταί τε καὶ οὐκ ἐᾷ σκίδνασθαι, καθιστάνων ὡς οἷόν τέ ἐστιν ἐκ τῶν παρόντων μὴ παντάπασιν αἰχμάλωτον κινδυνεῦσαι τὸν λογισμὸν καὶ ποριζόμενος ἐκεῖθεν ἀνίας ἰσχυρὰ φάρμακα, ὥσπερ εἴς τινας αὐθόρμητος ἀγαθοὺς συμβούλους τοὺς λόγους αὐτοὺς καταφεύγων καὶ παραμυθίας ἀποκειμένους θησαυροὺς ἐν καιρῷ χρείας ὅτου τις ἂν δέοιτο.

18

Καὶ γὰρ ὄντως ἐν τοῖς τοιούτοις εἰώθαμεν ἄνθρωποι μάλιστα δὴ φίλων δεῖσθαι συμμαχούντων καὶ νομίζουσιν οἵ γε γνησίως φιλοῦντες ἐνταῦθ᾽ ὥσπερ τινὰ τοῦτον

or, rather, deprived of rational thinking. He lacks the strength to run and retreat for the future to a place where he can moor his shaken mind and then recall it so as to confront the impending war; to the contrary, he is ravaged and there is no misery he does not suffer as a consequence of his bitter and difficult fate.

The aforementioned educated man, however, behaves 6 just like people who, in order to deal with the now-victorious attack of their enemies, withdraw to a neighboring town, and although they retreat are still able to preserve their lives. In a similar fashion, a man of such a sort employs education as a refuge against the external attack of life's calamities that opposes him. By resorting to education, he becomes stronger and does not allow himself to be disorganized, bracing himself as much as he can against the risk of having his mind completely captivated by his current problems and, as a result of his education, providing himself with powerful drugs against distress, seeking at his own instigation refuge with education as with good counselors and like a precious legacy of consolation that is kept in reserve in time of necessity for whatever he might need.

Chapter 18

It is indeed in such cases that we human beings normally need the support of our friends in particular. It is in this case that genuine friends consider it a sort of necessary contribution and required obligation to sit by the side of a friend

ἀναγκαῖον ἔρανον καὶ ὀφειλόμενον ἀπαιτεῖσθαι φίλῳ
κάμνοντι συγκαθιζῆσαι καὶ συμπαραμεῖναι καὶ πάθος
φλεγμαῖνον λόγοις παρακλητικοῖς καὶ βιωτικὴν ἱλαρῦναι
καὶ καταστορέσαι δυσχέρειαν. Καίτοι γε τίνας ἄν τις μᾶλλον καὶ φίλους καὶ συμβούλους ἀμείνους εὑρήσει ἢ τοὺς
ἐκ τῶν βίβλων διαλεγομένους ἡμῖν παλαιοὺς ἐκείνους ἄνδρας, οἳ καὶ πείρᾳ πρότεροι τὰ καθ᾽ ἡμᾶς ἔγνωσαν καὶ
προεῖδον καὶ σοφίᾳ τὰ κατὰ τὸν βίον ἐσταθμήσαντο
πάντα; Τίνες δ᾽ ἂν καὶ παραμείναιεν ἀχώριστοι τούτων
πλέον, τίνες ἄρα καὶ κρεῖττον, ὁποῖον ἂν εἴη, λόγοις ἀλη-
θινοῖς καὶ γενναίοις τὸ λυποῦν σωφρονίσαιεν; Εἰσὶ γὰρ
ὄντως, εἰσὶ πάλαι λόγοι περὶ πάντων ἐσκευασμένοι τοῖς
ἀνδράσιν ἡμῶν ἕνεκεν εἰς ἕτοιμον χρῆσιν, κἂν θάνατος
φιλτάτων ᾖ τὸ λυποῦν, κἂν πενία, κἂν νόσος, κἂν ὕβρις
ἐχθροῦ, κἂν ἄλλη τύχης ἡτισοῦν ἐπήρεια. Ἐνταῦθα δὴ
ζητήσας ἐξ ὑπογυίου πορίσῃ φάρμακον, ἐνταῦθα λόγοις
τε ἄλλοις ἐκ φιλοσοφίας ἰσχὺν ἔχουσι καὶ παραδείγμασι
πρὸς παραμυθίαν χρήσῃ τῇ κοινωνίᾳ τῆς συμφορᾶς.

2   Πλάτων μὲν οὖν χρῆναί φησιν ἰέναι τοὺς νέους παρὰ
τοὺς γέροντας καὶ χαίρειν συνόντας καὶ πυνθάνεσθαι δὴ
τῶν ἀνδρῶν τὰ κατὰ τὸν βίον· αὐτοὺς γὰρ ἂν ἔχειν μάλιστα καὶ εἰδέναι, ἅτε προωδευκότας, ᾗ βαδιστέον ἐστὶ καὶ
ᾗ μή, καὶ προειπεῖν τὴν βελτίω τε καὶ λυσιτελεστάτην. Τὸ
μὲν οὖν ἁπλῶς οὕτως ἰέναι τινὰ παρὰ τοὺς γέροντας οὐκ
ἂν ἴσως εἴη τι προὔργου, ἐπεὶ μηδὲ πᾶσιν οἷόν τέ ἐστι νοῦν
ἔχουσιν ἐντυγχάνειν, μηδὲ προμεμαθηκόσι μηδ᾽ ὧν ὄναιτ᾽
ἄν τις μηδ᾽ ὁτιοῦν. Ἄλλωστ᾽ οὐδὲ πᾶσιν, οὐδὲ τοῖς ἀρίστοις
ἐξέσται συνεῖναι, ἀλλ᾽ ὀλίγοις μὲν ἴσως τῶν ἐφ᾽ ἑαυτοῦ,

who is suffering and support him both by lessening the sorrow that burns him with consoling words and by keeping the misfortune of his life in check. Yet could anyone find better friends and advisors than those ancient men who converse with us through their books? From experience our predecessors understood our problems, they anticipated everything and wisely calculated all the issues that arise in our lives. Who could possibly remain closer by our side than these men? Who could better moderate our distress, of whatever kind it is, with sincere and genuine words? Indeed, words of advice exist for all sorts of situations, devised long ago by those men for our sake for ready use, whether the source of our grief is the death of a beloved one, poverty, sickness, a nasty insult by an enemy, or some other misfortune. If you look here, you will find the remedy immediately, here, amid your adversity, you can console yourself with other teachings that derive their strength from philosophy, as well as with exemplary cases.

Plato says that young men should approach the elderly ₂ and take pleasure in conversing with them and ask them about various matters in life; for the elderly are in a position to be well aware of which path we should choose and which to avoid, since they have already tested them, and could thus tell us the better and most beneficial route in advance. Approaching old men, however, without any serious reason is perhaps somewhat useless, because not all of them will turn out to be in possession of their senses, nor can they all know ahead of time what sort of thing will benefit each individual. At any rate, young men cannot approach all old men, nor even only the best of them, but most likely merely a few of

ὀλίγοις δὲ τούτων ἔτι πολλῷ ξυνεωρακόσι, περὶ ὧν
βούλοιτ᾽ ἄν, καὶ λέγειν ἀσφαλῶς ἔχουσιν.

3   Ἀλλ᾽ ἔμοιγε δοκῶ κάλλιστα ἂν οὕτως ἔχειν τὸν λόγον
καὶ μάλιστα ἐξεῖναι καὶ πλείοσιν ξυντυγχάνειν καὶ ἅμα
ἀρίστοις καὶ καλῶς προωδευκόσι τε καὶ προεγνωκόσι καὶ
δυναμένοις περὶ πάντων εἰπεῖν, εἴ τις τοῖς πρὸ ἡμῶν ἐκείνοις σοφοῖς καὶ θεσπεσίοις ἀνδράσι δι᾽ ὧν καταλελοίπασιν
ἡμῖν ἐν ταῖς βίβλοις συγγίγνοιτο λόγων, εὖ μάλα προσέχων
τὸν νοῦν καὶ δεξιῶς ἐπακροώμενος καὶ καταμανθάνων,
ἄττα βούλοιτ᾽ ἂν ἕκαστα.

4   Ποῦ γὰρ ἄν τις ἄλλοις συγγένοιτο κρείττοσι, καὶ γῆν
ἀναμετρήσας πᾶσαν καὶ θάλασσαν, ἢ τίσιν ἄλλοις καὶ
ῥᾷον ἢ τούτοις, οἳ πᾶσι πρόκεινται βουλομένοις ἀπραγμά-
τευτος ἀπόλαυσις, εὔωνον ἀγαθόν, εὐπόριστος θησαυρός,
κοινὴ καθάπερ ἀέρος μετουσία καὶ οὐρανοῦ καὶ τῶν ὑπ᾽
αἴσθησιν πάντων κατασκόπησις; Ἢ περὶ τίνος ἄρα καὶ
ζητήσας οὐχ εὑρήσεις αὐτίκα αὐτόθεν πάλαι τοῖς ἀνδράσιν
ἐσκευασμένα δόγματα καὶ λόγους ἠσφαλισμένους καὶ τὸ
πιστὸν ἔχοντας, ἐπεὶ καὶ περὶ πάντων ἀκριβέστατα προεῖπον καὶ προὔθεντο νόμους καὶ κλήρους αὐτάρκεις ἀπολαύειν ἀπόνως τοῖς ἑξῆς ἡμῖν, καὶ οὐδὲν οὔτ᾽ ἀνεπίγνω-
στον οὔτ᾽ ἄρρητον παρεῖται, ἀλλ᾽ ἅπασιν εἴαται, πᾶσιν
ἀνεπληρώθη, πάντως εἰς τὴν κοινὴν φορὰν ἕκαστος εἰσ-
ηνέγκαθ᾽ ὁτιοῦν καὶ βέλτιόν ἐστι τῷ ὄντι κατὰ τὸν πα-
λαιὸν εἰρημένον λόγον συγχρωτίζεσθαι τούτοις καὶ νεκροῖς ἢ τοῖς ζῶσι νεκροῖς καὶ μηδ᾽ ὅτι ζῶσιν ἐπαΐουσι, καὶ

their contemporaries, and yet only a few of these really understand the issues that concern a young man or can discuss them with any certainty.

I still believe, however, that Plato's statement is quite well expressed, especially because young men can converse with many noble men who have already traveled successfully over life's path, so that they are well informed in advance and able to talk about everything, if one approaches the splendid wise men of antiquity through the legacy they have bequeathed us in their books, paying full attention, listening to them attentively, and thus learning whatever one wishes in every case. 3

Where could one find other teachers better than these, even if he searches the whole earth and sea? Or can we approach other men more easily than those who lie in front of anyone who needs them, like a free offer, an affordable commodity, an easily procured treasure like the common enjoyment of the air, the observation of the heavens and of all the other things that can be perceived by means of our senses? Is there any topic for which, if you inquire, you could not readily find opinions formulated in the past by the ancients, along with secure and trustworthy theories? For they have already discussed every topic quite precisely and have established laws for us who came after them and a sufficient legacy for us to enjoy with no effort. They have left nothing distinctly unknown or unspoken, but they released their wisdom to everyone and supplied it to us all. Each of them has certainly contributed something to the common treasury. As the ancient saying goes, it is certainly better to be in contact with them, even if they are dead, than with the living dead who do not even know they are alive. It is also 4

πρὸς τὴν ἐπείγουσαν χρείαν ἢ καθὼς ἄν τις καὶ ἕλοιτο,
μετὰ ῥαστώνης ἁπάσης ἐπιδημεῖν ἑκάστοτε ἑκάστῳ καὶ
προσιέναι.

5   Ἐοικέναι γὰρ ὄντως ἔμοιγε δοκεῖ τὸ πρᾶγμα ὥσπερ ἐν
ἑκάστου καθ᾽ αἵρεσιν ἅπασαν ἀπαντᾶν καὶ οἷον ἐπιξε-
νοῦσθαι κομιδῇ φιλοφρόνως ὑποδεχομένου καὶ πᾶσαν ἐπί-
δειξιν, οἶμαι, καὶ φιλοτησίαν σπουδάζοντος καὶ ξυνεῖναι
καθάπερ ἐν φιλικῇ πανδαισίᾳ τρυφᾶν ἔχοντα ταύρων ἠδ᾽
ἀρνειῶν ἑκατόμβας μῆλά τ᾽ ἀδινὰ καὶ εἰλίποδας ἕλικας
βοῦς, ἃ δὴ καὶ παντοῖα καὶ κάλλιστα διδάγματα περὶ ὁτουοῦν προβάλλονται τρυφᾶν ῥᾷστα καὶ ἀπολαύειν οἱ ἄνδρες
ἄφθονα, νικῶντες τῇ περιουσίᾳ τὴν χρείαν.

19

Διογένης μὲν οὖν ὁ κύων ἡμέρας μέσης, δᾷδα ἡμμένην
ἔχων, ἐζήτει περιιὼν ἄνθρωπον, ἤν που λάχῃ, ὡς ποθεινὸν
καὶ πάνυ τοι δυσπόριστον ὂν τὸ χρῆμα καὶ ἅμα ἐμοὶ δοκεῖν
ἐπισκώπτων ἀνεκτῶς τοὺς παρόντας τῇ καινότητι ταύτῃ
καὶ σωφρονίζων ἑαυτῶν ἐπιστρέφεσθαι. Τοῖς δ᾽, οἶμαι,
λόγου συντρόφοις ἀνδράσιν ἔξεστιν ἄρα ἀπόνως τε καὶ
ἀθρόον τοῖς ἀπ᾽ αἰῶνος ἀρίστοις καὶ εὐδοκίμοις ἀνθρώποις
καὶ νοῦν συνειληχόσιν ὅτι πλεῖστον ξυνεῖναι καὶ διαλεγο-
μένων ἐπακροᾶσθαι τὰ βέλτιστα, περὶ ὧν δέοιτ᾽ ἄν τις, καὶ
μηδὲν ὁτιοῦν πολυπραγμονήσασι, μηδὲ περιεργασαμένοις,

better in the case of pressing necessity, or alternatively by one's own choice, to visit and approach everyone of the ancients on any occasion with due easiness of temper.

It seems to me that the matter is the same as when a person visits the house of each of them according to his own choice, and the man welcomes him and offers him hospitality quite kindly, being eager to demonstrate to the full his friendly sentiments. It is as if one partakes in a friendly banquet and can enjoy the sacrificial offerings of bulls, lambs, fat *sheep,* and *oxen with rolling gait,* which are the wonderful advice of every kind that the ancients offer us on any issue to easily feast on and enjoy in endless supply, satisfying our needs by means of that abundance.

Chapter 19

Diogenes the Cynic philosopher used to wander around in broad daylight, holding a burning torch and seeking to find an honest man, if that was somehow possible. But since this was desirable but simultaneously not easily achieved, I think that by means of this strange attitude Diogenes made fun of those he encountered in a tolerant manner, urging them toward repentance. But I believe that the friends of education can associate painlessly and with no delay with the great men generally, that is those who have been honored and allotted great sagacity from time immemorial, and can listen to them as they dispense the best advice, depending on the needs of each individual. Without much worldly

μηδ᾽ ἀναγκασθεῖσι κατὰ ζήτησιν ἴσως γῆς καὶ θαλάττης
ἄλλοτ᾽ ἄλλας περιόδους, ἔστιν αὐτόθεν οἴκοι ξυλλαχεῖν
μετὰ ῥαστώνης ἁπάσης, ὅτου τις ἂν εἴη χρεῖος, καὶ ἅμα
ὁ πόθος τἀνδρός—ὅστις ἄρα—ἅμα ἡ ζήτησις, ἅμα ἡ
ξυντυχία, χωρὶς πλάνης ἡστινοσοῦν, χωρὶς δαπάνης, χωρὶς
πραγμάτων ἁπάντων. Καίτοι γε, εἰ καὶ τοῦτ᾽ ἦν ἀνάγκη
ξυμβαίνειν, τίς ποτ᾽ οὐχ εἵλετ᾽ ἂν τῶν φιλοκάλων ἀνδρῶν
καὶ σωφρόνως βιοῦν ἑλομένων καὶ πάνθ᾽ ὡς οἷόν τέ ἐστιν
ὑπὲρ τῶν λυσιτελούντων πονεῖν ἀξιούντων;

2   Νυνὶ δ᾽ ἀμέλει καὶ πρόχειρος ἐνταῦθα ἡ χρῆσις καὶ ἅμα
κατ᾽ οὐδὲν ἐνδεής, ἀλλ᾽ εἰς ὅσον ἄν τις ἐρῴη—μέτρα δ᾽ οὔ
φασιν ἔρωτος—καὶ πάνυ καταπολαύειν πλείστη. Καὶ μήν,
εἰ τοῦτο κάλλιστόν ἐστιν ὡς ἀληθῶς καὶ λυσιτελέστατον,
ἀνδράσιν ἀστείοις ἀεὶ συνεῖναι καὶ συνετοῖς τε καὶ νοῦν
ἔχουσι, καὶ τοῦτο σπουδάζουσιν οἱ πλεῖστοι καὶ φιλοδο-
ξοῦσιν, ὡς ἀνάγκην οὖσαν ἐντεῦθεν τῆς καθ᾽ ἡμέραν τι
φέρειν κοινωνίας τῶν ἀγαθῶν ἀνδρῶν καὶ συνδιατίθεσθαι
καὶ δεῖγμα μέγιστον εὖ ἔχειν, ὅστις χρῷτο, καὶ τοιοῦτός
ἐστιν ἕκαστος οἷσπερ ἥδεται συνών, καὶ τοῦτο πρόσεστιν
ἐνταῦθα μάλιστα καὶ τοῖς βελτίστοις ἔνεστιν ἐξ ἀρχῆς
ἄνωθεν πᾶσι καὶ σώφροσι καὶ πεπαιδευμένοις ἀείποτε
συγγινόμενον ἄλλου δὴ πάντως ἄλλο τι τῶν καλλίστων
καὶ πάντων ἅπαντα πρὸς κατόρθωσιν βίου καὶ προκοπὴν
ἐπιστήμης καὶ διανοίας καὶ ἡρμοσμένην ἕξιν καὶ σώφρονα
πορίζεσθαι.

trouble or effort, without having to take different routes in searching through land and sea, they can stay right at home and collect whatever is needed with no difficulty whatsoever. Once a man desires something—whatever that might be—as soon as he asks for it, he can immediately find it without any wandering or expense, with no annoyance whatsoever. Nonetheless, even if this were to happen by necessity, what man who loves goodness, opts for a life of moderation, and has decided to strive as hard as possible for what is beneficial, would not choose it?

Now in this case, the use of this advice is both readily accessible and lacking nothing, and it has reached the extent to which someone would desire it—they say that love has no limits—so that he can enjoy it to the full. Indeed, if this is what is truly best and most profitable, namely to constantly associate with cultivated, wise, and sensible men, this is precisely what the majority of people pursue and aspire to, due to the need that exists therein to obtain something from daily contact with noble men to use to their mutual advantage. This is also the clearest sign that anyone who employs their advice is in a good condition. In addition, everyone is similar to those with whom he likes to associate, and this is especially pertinent here. From ancient times to now, everyone is constantly used to engaging with the noblest people, the wisest, and most educated, deriving from each one of them a different blessing, but in their entirety everything that is necessary for the reform of his life, his progress in knowledge and intellect, and his regulated and moderate disposition. 2

20

Διὰ τοῦτο καὶ Σωκράτης ἐκεῖνος τοὺς θησαυροὺς τῶν παλαιῶν καὶ σοφῶν ἀνδρῶν, οὓς ἐν ταῖς βίβλοις κατέλιπον, ἔλεγεν ἀνελίττειν ἀεὶ καὶ κοινῇ μετὰ τῶν φίλων διέρχεσθαι, ὡς ἐντεῦθεν σφόδρα ἐνὸν ἄριστον καὶ νοῦν καὶ βίον συλλέξασθαι καὶ κομιδῇ τὴν τῶν ἀνδρῶν οὖσαν ἐπέραστον καὶ λυσιτελεστάτην συνουσίαν. Ὁ δ᾽ αὐτὸς οὗτος, ἀεί τινι τῶν κατ᾽ αὐτὸν ἑαυτοῦ κρείττονι καὶ σοφωτέρῳ σπουδάζων ἐντυχεῖν καὶ καθ᾽ ὅσον οἷόν τέ ἐστι τἀνδρὸς ὄνασθαι, πάντων πειρώμενος, πάντας ἤλεγχε καὶ ἀπεωθεῖτο καταφρονῶν, ὡς μηδένων ὄντων, μηδέ τι μὴ χρήσιμον ἐχόντων, ἀλλ᾽ ἢ μόνον δόκησιν ἄλογον καὶ κομπώδη φλυαρίαν, τοῖς δ᾽ ἐκείνων τῶν ἀνδρῶν θησαυροῖς ἡδέως συνῆν καὶ τοῖς φίλοις κοινωνεῖν τῶν ἐκεῖθεν ἀγαθῶν ἠξίου. Πάντως δ᾽ εἰ μὴ λόγου καὶ σπουδῆς ἄξιον ᾤετο τὸ πρᾶγμα, κέρδη ψυχῆς ἐντεῦθεν καὶ λογισμοῦ προκοπὴν ἀποφερόμενος—ἃ δὴ μόνα Σωκράτης ἀντὶ πάντων ἐπόθει τε καὶ ἐτίμα—καὶ θησαυρούς τινας ἐκεῖθεν, ὡς αὐτός φησιν, ἀρυττόμενος, οὐκ ἄν ποτε ἄρα ἡδέως οὕτω συνῆν καὶ πρὸς τοὺς πυνθανομένους ἐν τίσιν ἐστίν, ἐπὶ τούτοις ἐλαμπρύνετο.

2   Οὕτω δὴ παντάπασιν, ἔοικε, περισπούδαστόν ἐστι καὶ ὀνησιμώτατον ἡ τῶν σοφῶν καὶ κοσμίων ἀνδρῶν συντυχία καὶ συνδιατριβὴ καὶ τοῦτο πάντες ἂν συμφαῖέν τε καὶ συνθεῖντο. Τὸ δ᾽ ἄρα πολὺ μᾶλλόν ἐστι καὶ πρόδηλον ἐν αὐταῖς ταῖς βίβλοις καὶ τοῖς λόγοις, οὓς οἱ παλαιοὶ

Chapter 20

For this reason, the celebrated Socrates used to say that he always perused the treasures the ancient wise men left in their books, and discussed them in the company of his friends, for he believed that from those treasures one could gather information about the best way to think and live, and that association with these men is both extremely pleasant and highly profitable. Socrates himself would always try to engage with any of his contemporaries who was better and wiser than himself, and to benefit from this man as much as possible. While he was testing everybody, he questioned them all and rebuffed them in contempt, because he considered them unimportant and incapable of offering anything useful but only irrational fancies and braggart nonsense. But he dealt indulgently with the treasures of those ancient men and deemed it worthwhile to disseminate the blessings he derived from there to his friends. At any rate, if Socrates did not believe that this activity was noteworthy and important, if he did not derive any profit from it for his soul and the progress of his mind—precisely those very things Socrates desired and honored above all else—and if he could not draw from there, as he puts it, some treasures, he would never have engaged so eagerly with them or have expressed his pride in dealing with them to people who asked him what his interests were.

It thus seems that association and communion with wise 2 and decent men is in every respect highly desirable and very useful, and everyone will agree with me and approve this. And this becomes even more obvious in the case of the

πρότερον ἄνδρες ἐκεῖνοι κλῆρον καταλελοίπασι τοῖς ἐλλογίμοις.

3 Ἄλλωστε μὴν ποῦ τηνικαῦτα Σωκράτης τοσούτους
εὕρατο θησαυρούς, ὁπόσους νῦν ἡμεῖς ἔχομεν, τῶν ἀπ'
ἐκείνου τοσούτων χρόνων μεγίστην τὴν προσθήκην ἐμ-
ποιησάντων τοῖς κληρονομοῦσί τε καὶ ταμιουχοῦσι, καὶ
σχεδὸν ἐκεῖθεν ἡμῖν τὰ πλείω καὶ καλλίω τῶν λόγων κει-
μήλια, οὔτε φιλοσοφίας οὐδέπω καὶ τότε καθάπαξ ἠκρι-
βωμένης καὶ τοσαῦτα προενεγκούσης, οὐδὲ πρὸς πάνθ'
ὡς ἔπος εἰπεῖν ὡρμημένης τε παρρησίᾳ καὶ ἀραμένης
φρόνημα καὶ πρὸς τὴν τῶν ὄντων ἅπασαν καὶ τῆς φύσεως
ἑτερότητα ἐπιχειρούσης, μηδ' εἰς μυρίους ὅσους ὀχετούς,
ὥσπερ ἐκ μιᾶς τινος τὴν ἀρχὴν πηγῆς κατατετμημένης
τὸν ἀνθρώπινον τοῦ βίου λειμῶνα πολυσχιδῶς καταρ-
δεύοντας, οὔτε ῥητορικῶν λόγων ἐν τοῖς δικαστηρίοις
ἀνθούντων καὶ ῥεόντων ἔμμετρα, μᾶλλον δ' ὁσημέραι
κοπτόντων τὰ βουλευτήρια, οὐδέπω τῆς τέχνης ἐν κατα-
στάσει γεγονυίας καὶ πεπηγμένης, οὐδ' ὅρους ἐντελεῖς
οὕστινας ἄρα καὶ μέτρα καὶ συνθήματα δεξαμένης καὶ τε-
ταγμένης, ἀλλ' ὥσπερ ἐν ἀορίστοις τισὶ τεμμαχίοις καὶ
ἀσυνδέτοις κάλλεσι προκειμένης, ἕκαστος ὁτιοῦν ὡς ἔτυχε
συλαγωγῶν τε καὶ ἀφαιρούμενος, ἐδόκει περιστέλλειν
ἑαυτὸν καὶ κατακοσμεῖν ὡς οἷός τ' ἦν.

4 Καταπεποικιλμένης δὲ διὰ πάντων καὶ ὥσπερ ἡρμοσμέ-
νης τε καὶ παντάπασιν ἐξυφανθείσης εἰς περίβλημα διανοίας κάλλιστον οὐδείς πω ἔτυχεν ἔτι. Καίτοι τί λέγω;
Ἀλλ' οὔπω δὴ καὶ τότε μάλιστα τῶν κατὰ τὸν βίον
πραγμάτων αὐτῶν ἐπιδεδωκότων, οὐδ' ὥσπερ τοῦ κόσμου

books and works those ancient men have bequeathed to scholars as an inheritance.

Where could Socrates possibly have found as many trea- 3 sures in his lifetime as those we have today? For the enormous number of years that have elapsed since the time of Socrates have assembled a great addition for the heirs and keepers of the treasuries, and it is from that time that the largest number of and most significant intellectual jewels we have today were created; back then, philosophy had not yet been explored in detail and had not brought forth so many doctrines, it could not turn toward all intellectual disciplines openly, so to speak, or elevate its spirit, it did not venture to discuss in its totality the complexity of what exists and of nature, it was not yet split, as from one initial fount, into myriad streams to irrigate in numerous different ways the meadow of human life. In the time of Socrates, the performances of orators did not blossom in the law courts, nor did they flow with metrical rhythm; instead, they caused great commotion in the council chambers on a daily basis, because the art of rhetoric was not yet mature or established; it had not yet acquired or determined its complete terminology, rhythm, and rules, but in a way offered irrelevant aspects and unrelated beauties, so that every individual supposed that he could clothe himself in whatever he could despoil and steal and that he could adorn himself however he could.

No one yet had access to an art of rhetoric that was fully 4 embellished and, as it were, harmonious and completely woven into a superb garment for the intellect. But what am I saying? Especially back then the course of human history had not yet progressed, and the utmost point of the world's

τῆς ἀκμῆς αὐτῆς ἐπελθούσης, καθάπερ ἔπειθ' ἑξῆς εἴπετο
πραγμάτων Ἑλληνικῶν καὶ Ῥωμαϊκῶν ὄγκος τοσοῦτος·
ὑφ' ὧν, ὥσπερ ἐστὶ φύσις, ἐξαπτομένη προδήλως ἡ σοφία
συμπαρέθει καὶ ὅλοις, φασίν, ἱστίοις καταπνεομένη ἤρετο,
καὶ κατ' ἀνάγκην ἅπασαν παραβαλλομένη, πρὸς ἅπασαν
ἰδέαν τε καὶ φορὰν ἑαυτῆς ἐπέδωκεν, ὡς πρὸς ὕλην ἑαυτὴν
ἀνιστῶσα καὶ ἀναφλεγομένη μεγίστην καὶ ἀεὶ πλείω καὶ
τοῖς καιροῖς αὐτοῖς ἐπιδιδοῦσί τε καὶ τοῖς πράγμασι συμ-
παρεκτεινομένη τε καὶ προκόπτουσα—ἀρχὴ δ' ἄρα παντός,
φασίν, ἥμισυ—καὶ ὥσπερ εἰς μέγιστον θέατρον καὶ ἐπι-
δείξεως ἀκμὴν μετ' ἐπιμελείας ἁπάσης καὶ ῥώμης ἀποδυο-
μένη.

5   Τοιγαροῦν ὥσπερ οἳ τὰ πόνοις πολλοῖς κατορθωθέντα
προγόνοις καὶ προσγενόμενα, κτήσεις τε καὶ χρήματα,
εἰώθασιν ὡς τὰ πολλὰ τρυφᾶν αὐτοὶ καὶ καταχρῆσθαι,
μηδὲν ἔτι προσπονοῦντες, μηδ' ἐπικτώμενοι, παραπλησίως
ἐμοὶ δοκεῖν καὶ ἡμῖν τὰ τῶν παλαιῶν ἐκείνων καὶ σοφῶν
ἀνδρῶν παραλαβοῦσιν ἀμερίμνως ἐστὶν ἔχειν, πᾶν ὁτιοῦν
ἄρα βουλομένοις τε καὶ ποθοῦσι ῥᾷστα πάνυ τοι καὶ ἐκ
τοῦ προχείρου πορίζεσθαι καὶ ἀπολαύειν ἐξόν, νῦν μὲν
φιλόσοφον ἔννοιαν προκεχειρισμένοις δόγματα πλεῖστα
ὅσα καὶ κατὰ πᾶσαν ἰδέαν καὶ λογικὰς ἐργασίας, καὶ ταῦθ'
ἥπερ ἄρα βούλει καὶ τὴν γνώμην ἐκίνησεν ἔρως, εἴτε μεθ'
ἧς ἔχει φύσιν ἀπλαστίας καὶ πρεσβυτικῆς εὐγενείας φιλο-
σοφία καὶ ποθεῖς τὸ ἀνεπιμέλητον μὲν παντάπασι διὰ σω-
φροσύνην, ἄκομψον δὲ διὰ μεγαλοψυχίαν καὶ τὴν ἐν
ἀξιώματι τοσούτῳ τῶν τοῦ νοῦ δογμάτων τοσαύτην ἀναγκαίαν ὄντως καὶ λυσιτελεστάτην [. . .]

advancement had not yet arrived, as followed later on with the immense dignity of the Hellenic and Roman world. Kindled by this progress, knowledge evidently evolved, as was natural, and marched ahead side by side with historical developments, it raised all its sails to the winds, as they put it, and being completely exposed by necessity, it progressed in every form and direction it could attain, like a huge pile of firewood that burns and sends its flames as high as possible. Thus knowledge always expanded together with the times and situations as they themselves advanced, and it progressed—for *beginning is half done,* they say—and it revealed its strength in open display with all diligence and force, as if in a huge theater.

Just as some men routinely enjoy and abuse everything 5 their ancestors achieved and obtained with much toil, be it property or money, and do not busy themselves any longer or desire to acquire anything, in a similar way, I think, it is possible for us to inherit the precepts of those ancient wise men without the slightest care, and then we can receive and enjoy very easily and readily whatever else we wish and desire. When we examine a particular philosophical notion, we can procure whatever doctrines pertain both to every form and to rational activities, and these in whatever manner as you like, and however desire has prompted your judgment, whether you seek the complete simplicity that comes through moderation, with which philosophy shares a nature of purity and elderly nobility, the lack of stylistic ornament that comes through magnanimity, and in this enormous value of intellectual doctrines the truly necessary and highly beneficial [. . .]

21

Νῦν δὲ συμπλανώμενος πανταχοῦ Ῥωμαίοις καὶ ἐπ᾽ αὐτὰ Λιβύης τε καὶ Εὐρώπης τὰ ἔσχατα καὶ πάνθ᾽ ὁμοῦ καὶ περὶ πάντων ἔχων ἰσχυρίσασθαι ὡς ἀμέλει νῦν ἐκεῖθεν ἐπιδεδημηκώς. Καὶ μὴν καθ᾽ ἑκάστην ὁρῶμεν ἐνίους διά τιν᾽ ἐμπορίας χρείαν ἢ πρεσβείας ἢ ἄλλην, οὐκ οἶδ᾽ ἥντινα, ἀνάγκην ἀποδεδημηκότας ἀλλοτρίοις γένεσιν, οἳ δοκοῦσιν ἐπανιόντες πάνυ τοι φιλοτιμεῖσθαι τὴν πλάνην καὶ ἥδονται (πῶς ἂν εἴπῃ τις;), εὖ μάλα καὶ σεμνολογοῦσιν ἐπιδεικνῦντες ἃ σφόδρα κατεῖδον, καὶ ὥσπερ τινὲς θαυμαστοὶ καὶ μεγάλων αὐτόθεν ἐπιτυχεῖς γεγονότες, μακαριζόμενοι τῆς ἱστορίας ταύτης ὑπὸ τῶν ἀκουόντων. Οὕτω δὴ πολλοῦ τινος ἄξιον ἅπαντες ἥγηνται πλεῖν ἢ πρόχειρόν τι γινώσκειν καὶ τοῖς πολλοῖς εὔληπτον.

2 Καίτοι τί ποτ᾽ ἂν εἴη τοιοῦτον, πόσον δ᾽ ἄν τις περιόδου τινὸς ἀποφέροιτο κέρδος, πόσον δ᾽ ἐργῶδες τοῦτ᾽ ἐστὶ καὶ οἵας ἄρ᾽ ἔχει τὰς πάντοθεν δυσκολίας κατασκοποῦντι; Νυνὶ δ᾽ ἔξεστι μετὰ ῥαστώνης ἁπάσης καὶ ἀδαπάνως καὶ πάσης ἀπηλλαγμένον δυσκολίας ἅπαντα ἐπιέναι οἴκοι μένοντα ἐν ταῖς βίβλοις, καὶ τόπων καινότητας καὶ πράξεων παμπληθῆ καὶ παμμεγέθη φοράν—παλαιά τε καὶ νέα—καὶ βίους οὕστινας ἄρα καὶ πολιτεύματα, ὀλίγῳ δὴ κομιδῇ τῷ χρόνῳ, ὀλίγῳ δὴ κομιδῇ καὶ τῷ πόνῳ, ὥσπερ ἐν πανδήμῳ πανηγύρει γενόμενον, πάνθ᾽, ὁπόσ᾽ ἂν βούλοιτο, πρίασθαι.

3 Ἀνεμνήσθην δὲ ἤδη καὶ αὐτῆς πέρι πανηγύρεως, ὡς οἱ

Chapter 21

On the other hand, by traveling everywhere with the Romans, to the farthest points of Europe and Libya, you can talk in detail about all those places as if you had just returned from them. Every day we encounter people who have traveled among foreign races for commercial purposes, or for an embassy, or for some other reason I cannot identify. When these individuals return, they seem very proud of their journey and very happy (how can one put this?), and they solemnly describe the sights they saw as a way of showing off; their listeners praise them for their narrative as if they were some remarkable people who had just accomplished something amazing. Everyone thus believes that it is quite important to know more than what is customary and easily accessible to the masses.

But what could this really be about? How much gain can 2 one get from such a journey? How much effort does it demand, and what sorts of difficulties does it pose for the individual conducting the investigation? In our case, a person can travel anywhere very easily, with no expense or difficulty whatsoever, by staying in his own house and immersing himself in books: novel places, numerous significant events, and various different lives and constitutions—old and new alike—rapidly, with minimal effort, in the same way that a man attends a fair for all townsfolk to buy anything he wants.

I have already discussed this very fair, saying that most 3

πολλοὶ τῶν ἀνθρώπων σπουδάζουσι ταῖς παμμεγίσταις καὶ παμπληθέσιν ἑκάστοτε ἐπιδημεῖν θέας ἕνεκα πλείστων τε καὶ παντοίων πραγμάτων. Ὧν εἴ τις ἐνταῦθα, ὡς ἔοικεν, εἰς τοὺς ἐν ταῖς βίβλοις θησαυροὺς τὸ φιλοκερδὲς τρέψοι καὶ τὴν τῆς γνώμης πολυπραγμοσύνην, πλεῖστον ὅσον ὀνίναιντ' ἂν καὶ μέγιστον ἵμερον ταῖς ψυχαῖς ἐμβαλεῖται σοφίας καὶ ἡδονήν, θηρωμέναις περὶ ὧν ἄρα ἐπόθουν. Εἰ δὲ μὴ τοῦτο, πάντως εὔδηλον, ὃ πάλαι πρότερον εἴρηται, ὡς οἷς μὲν ἔχουσιν ὀφθαλμοῖς, καὶ ἴσασι καὶ ἥδονται χρῆσθαι, οἷς δ' οὐκ ἔχουσιν, οἶμαι—νῷ καὶ ψυχῆς ὄμμασιν —οὔτ' ἔχουσι χρήσασθαι οὔτε μὴν οὐδὲν ἐπαΐουσιν ἀμέλει περὶ αὐτῶν.

22

Ἐθαύμασα δὲ ἔγωγε κἀνταῦθα τὴν Ἕλληνα τύχην ὅπως ἠνέγκατο πλέον, τυχοῦσα πλειόνων ἢ κατὰ τοὺς ἄλλους ἀφηγήσεων καὶ λόγων, ἐν οὐκ ἀφθονωτέροις ἴσως τοῖς πράγμασι, μᾶλλον δ' ὡς ἀληθῶς ἐθαύμασα ἔγωγε κἂν τούτοις τὴν Ἕλληνα καὶ σοφίαν καὶ γλῶτταν, ἐπεὶ τὰ σφέτερα ὁρῶμεν ὡς ηὔξησε μάλιστα καὶ προὔθετο τὰ οἰκεῖα αὐτῆς ἐφ' ἑαυτῆς δαπανῶσα καὶ ἀφ' ἑστίας, ὃ δή φασιν, ἀξιοῦσα χαρίζεσθαι τοῖς ἑξῆς ὑπομνήματα. Τῷ ὄντι γὰρ καὶ τοῦθ', ὡς ἔοικε, κέρδος ἐστὶ σοφίας, τὰ συγγενῆ τιμᾶν πλεῖστον τῶν ἄλλων, ἀξιολόγῳ μνήμῃ μάλιστα.

people try to visit the largest and most crowded ones every time, in order to see as many different commodities as possible. Now, in my opinion, if these people were to direct their love for gain and their curiosity toward the treasures found in books, they would make a massive profit and would instill in their souls an immense yearning for wisdom along with the pleasure derived from obtaining what they desire. Alternatively, that which was said long ago becomes obvious in every respect, namely that they know how to use the eyes they have and are happy to do so, but that when it comes to the eyes they lack—that is the mind and eyes of the soul—in my opinion, they cannot use them and do not understand anything about them.

Chapter 22

In this case as well, however, I admired the fortune of the Greeks, how it brought forth more historical narratives and stories than the others, without necessarily having accomplished greater exploits. Better put, in this case too I truly admired Greek wisdom and language, because we see that both made great progress and advanced their affairs using their own resources and qualifications, as they say, and deeming it worthy to bestow on future generations aides-mémoire of the events that occurred. Indeed, this seems to be the advantage of wisdom, to honor mostly its own accomplishments rather than the accomplishments of others by means of particularly remarkable commemoration: for

Ἕλληνές τε γὰρ δὴ πλεῖστα συνεγράψαντο τῶν ἄλλων, καὶ περὶ αὑτῶν δὴ μάλιστα πλεῖστα ἢ περὶ τῶν ἄλλων.

2 Καὶ τοίνυν ἅπαντα τὰ αὑτῶν ἴσμεν παμπλήρη, καὶ μείζω καὶ μείω καὶ περιφανῆ τε καὶ μή, ἀλλ' ἥττονος δόξης, καὶ οὐδὲν ὅ,τι μὴ σχεδὸν ὠλιγώρηται, μὴ τυχεῖν μνήμης, ἀλλ' ἴσμεν ὅσα τε δὴ μέγιστα ἐν τοῖς Μηδικοῖς Ἀγῶσιν ὡς ἀληθῶς τῶν ἐκ παντὸς τοῦ χρόνου γενομένων ἔργα, καὶ Μαραθῶνι καὶ Πλαταιαῖς καὶ τῆς ἐν Σαλαμῖνι ναυμαχίας τὰ τρόπαια, καὶ τὸν αὐτὸν τρόπον ὡς ἔπλευσε ναυσὶ Σόλων τρισὶν ἐς Σαλαμῖνα ὀλίγῳ πρότερον καὶ παρεστήσατο, ἴσμεν καὶ μὴν ἔθ' ὡς Περικλῆς ἐκεῖνος, οὗ πλεῖστον Ἕλλησιν ὄνομα, δέκατος στρατηγὸς τὸ μέγιστον τεσσαράκοντα ναυσὶν ἐπέπλει κατὰ τῆς Σάμου καὶ περιέπλει γε ἑκατὸν μεθύστερον ἔπειτα τὴν Πελοπόννησον, ὁ δ' αὐτὸς οὗτος στρατηγὸς αὖθις αὐτοκράτωρ πεντεκαίδεκα ναυσὶν Ἄντρον ἐδουλοῦτο καὶ Χαβρίας ἑκατὸν μὲν ναυσὶ τρίτος στρατηγὸς Αἴγυπτον ἀφίστη τοῦ βασιλέως, δυοκαίδεκα δὲ μόνος αὐτοκράτωρ Χίους ἐπολιόρκει καὶ Ἰφικράτης ἕβδομος παραπλησίως εἰς Αἴγυπτον καὶ αὐτοκράτωρ τρισὶ ναυσὶ Σηστὸν παρεστήσατο καὶ Σαμία μία ναῦς τὸν Πελοποννησιακὸν συνεκρότησε πόλεμον καὶ Λύσανδρος τὴν μεγίστην καὶ καλλίστην Ἑλλήνων πόλιν Ἀθήνας θαλάττης ἄρχουσαν καταστρεψάμενος καὶ τείχη καθελών, μετὰ βραχὺ κρεωδότης ἦν Ἀγησιλάου καὶ μετ' ὀλίγον αὖθις ἐν Ἁλιάρτῳ καθαπερεὶ πελταστής τις ἢ ὁπλίτης Λάκων εἷς ἔπιπτεν.

Greeks have written more works than other peoples, and they wrote mostly about themselves rather than about others.

We therefore know in detail every single deed they ac- 2 complished, be it great or not, famous or not, or of lesser repute. They have scarcely failed to mention any of their achievements, and we know of their many exploits in the Persian Wars, truly the greatest that ever occurred in all time, namely the battles at Marathon and Plataea and the naval victory at Salamis. We know equally well how Solon, just before these events, sailed with three ships against Salamis and conquered the city. In addition, we know that Pericles, the man whose name was the most renowned among the Greeks, sailed with nine other commanders against Samos with forty ships at most and afterward circumnavigated the Peloponnese with a hundred triremes. As a general with absolute power, Pericles also captured Andros with fifteen ships, while Chabrias, the third general, with a hundred ships urged the Egyptians to oppose the Persian king. The same general alone with twelve ships and full authority besieged the island of Chios, and in a similar way the seventh general Iphicrates sailed to Egypt and with complete authority conquered Sestos with three ships. We also know that a trireme from Samos became the pretext for the Peloponnesian War, and that Lysander captured the largest and most beautiful Greek city, Athens, which reigned supreme over the sea, and destroyed its walls, and shortly thereafter became quartermaster of Agesilaus's army, and soon after that was killed in Haliartos as a peltast or a Lacedaemonian heavily armed soldier.

3   Ὁ δ᾽ αὐτὸς Ἀγησίλαος, ἄριστος τῶν ἐν Σπάρτῃ καὶ ἰδι-
ωτῶν τε καὶ βασιλέων, ἀνταίρει τε καθ᾽ ἕω πρὸς ἅπασαν
τὴν Περσικὴν δυναστείαν, καὶ μέγιστα ἐκεῖνα τότε καὶ
κάλλιστα τῶν Ἑλληνικῶν, οὐ πολλοῦ δ᾽ ἔπειτα χρόνου
κατέπλεεν εἰς Αἴγυπτον πάνυ πρεσβύτης, μισθοῦ συμ-
μαχῶν στασιώταις καὶ περιτρεπόμενος ἐπὶ θάτερα τοῖς
μεῖζον ἰσχύουσιν ἢ διδοῦσί τι πλέον, ὥσπερ ὁτιοῦν ὅπλον
τοῦ νικῶντος ἀεὶ γιγνόμενον.

23

Καὶ ταῦτα δὴ πάντα καὶ μνήμης ἠξιοῦτο πλείστης καὶ
συγγραφόντων, ὧν ἐπὶ σοφίᾳ μέγιστον κέρδος, καὶ οὐδὲν
ὅ,τι μὴ παρείαται καὶ κατωλιγώρηται, καὶ τῶν ὀλίγου καὶ
μηδενὸς ἀξίων, ἀμνηστίᾳ. Καίτοι πόσαι ταῦτα καὶ χῶραι
καὶ πόλεις καὶ ἄνδρες—καὶ ἰδιῶται καὶ ἄρχοντες—κα-
τεπράξαντ᾽ ἂν ἀτυχεῖς συγγραφῆς; πόσοι δὲ τὰς αὐτὰς ἢ
καὶ μείζους ἔν τε παρασκευαῖς καὶ ἀγώνων κράτει ἐπε-
δείξαντο πράξεις; ἃ δή, μηδενὸς ἢ βραχέος ἀξιωθέντα
τυχὸν ἔνια λόγου, κατετάκησαν ὑπὸ τοῦ χρόνου κατὰ
βραχὺ καὶ λέλυνται παντάπασιν, οἶμαι, λήθης ἐντελοῦς
ὀλέθρῳ.

2   Καὶ τὰ μὲν ἄλλ᾽ ἐῶ. Πόσαι δὲ πόλεις ὅμως ἐν δημο-
κρατίᾳ καὶ πολιτεύμασι τὸν αὐτὸν ὅνπερ Ἕλληνες τρόπον,
ἔν τε Βιθυνίᾳ καὶ Φοινίκῃ καὶ Ἀφρικῇ παραπλησίαις

Agesilaus himself, who was the greatest among the citizens and kings in Sparta, campaigned to the east against the entire Persian empire, and this campaign became the greatest and noblest Greek feat of the time. Not much later, however, when he had reached an advanced age, he sailed to Egypt as a mercenary to fight along with some partisans, and would change sides depending on which of the two was stronger at any particular point, or which offered the highest pay, so that he resembled armor that always belonged to the victor. 3

Chapter 23

All these events were deemed worthy of detailed mention and were treated by authors whose wisdom yielded the greatest profit. Nothing was overlooked or marginalized in obscurity, no matter how insignificant and worthless it might have been. Yet how many countries, cities, people—ordinary citizens and rulers alike—may have accomplished the same deeds but lacked an author to record their actions? How many people achieved the same feats and even greater ones, both in their preparations and in how powerfully they fought? But all these have faded away little by little due to the passage of time and have utterly disappeared due to destruction by overwhelming oblivion, in my opinion precisely because some of them were deemed worthy either of only brief mention or of no mention at all.

I pass over the rest. But really, how many cities in 2 Bithynia, Phoenicia, and Africa, which were democracies

ἀρχαῖς χρώμεναι, παραπλησίοις στρατηγοῖς καὶ στρα-
τεύμασι, παραπλησίοις δὲ καὶ οὐδὲν ἥττοσι καὶ αὐτοῖς
πράγμασι, παραπλησίας οὐκ ἔτυχον μνήμης, μὴ γλῶτταν
ἔχουσαι νικῶσαν ἐπὶ παντός, ὡς ἔοικε, τοῦ χρόνου καὶ
κέντροις ἔρωτος φιλοκάλου πρὸς ἑαυτὴν τοὺς πολλοὺς
ἕλκουσαν; Καίτοι τί λέγω; Ἢ οὐ καὶ νῦν ἔτι μάλιστα ὁρῶμεν ὡς οὐκ ὀλίγαι τῶν ἐν Ἰταλίᾳ πόλεις ἐν τοῖς αὐτοῖς εἰσι
καὶ μεθ’ ὁμοίων, οἶμαι, τῶν πραγμάτων καὶ γῆς ἅπτονται
καὶ θαλάττης καὶ τὰ πρὸς ἀλλήλους βουλεύουσί τε καὶ
μεταχειρίζουσι;

3   Κατ’ οὐδὲν μέν γε ὡς ἀληθῶς αὐταῖς ἐλλείπει ἢ ἐκείναις
τότε πρότερον ἐνομίζετο, οὐ βουλευτήριά τε καὶ δικα-
στήρια, οὐ πολέμους καὶ μάχας καὶ ναυμαχίας, οὐ παρα-
σκευάς, ἃς ὁρῶμεν ἑκάστοτε, οὐκ ἀρχαιρεσίας, οὐ στρα-
τηγῶν τόλμας καὶ ἴσως γνώμας, οὐκ ἄλλο τι οὔ. Ἀλλὰ
ταῦτα μὲν οὔτ’ ἐπισημαινόμεθ’ ὁρῶντες οὔτε καινόν τι
νομίζομεν οὔτ’ ἀξιοῦμεν προσέχειν τὸν νοῦν ὁτιοῦν συλ-
λογίζεσθαι, ἀλλ’ ἡσυχῇ τῶν λογισμῶν ἐσμεν, ὥσπερ ἂν εἰ
μηδὲν ἴσως γίγνοιτο. Πρὸς δ’ ἐκεῖνα πολλή τις αἰδὼς καὶ
χρώμεθα ἔν τε βίοις εἰκόσι καὶ λόγοις ἐπιχειροῦντες καὶ
πάσῃ τιμῶντες μνήμῃ, “ὁ δεῖνα τὰ καὶ τὰ πάλαι ποτ’ ἔφη
καὶ τὰ καὶ τὰ κατεπράξατο,” ἅπαντα ἡγούμενοι τοῖς γε
ἀστείοις κέρδος καὶ μηδὲν ὅ,τι βραχύ, μηδ’ ἀδοξίαν, ὅστις
χρῷτο. Σεβόμεθά τε δὴ μάλιστα καὶ σπουδάζομεν τὴν
ἀγγέλλουσαν γλῶτταν, ὡς οὐκ ἂν ἄλλως ἀξιώσασαν περὶ

and had constitutions identical to those of the Greek cities, using similar administration, governors and troops, and accomplishing similar deeds not at all inferior to those of the Greeks, failed to eventually achieve similar commemoration simply because they lacked a powerful, timeless sort of language, it seems, which attracts audiences with the lure of its elegance? But what am I saying? Do we not see even today that many cities in Italy are in the same situation as the cities of ancient Greece? Pursuing similar goals, they seize control of land and sea, I think, and they plan and undertake their relations with one another.

Truly, no customary usage among the ancient Greek cities is absent from the contemporary cities of Italy: neither council chambers and law courts, nor wars, battles, and naval conflicts, nor military preparations that we see on all occasions; neither elections of magistrates, nor generals who are equally brave and presumably have the same spirit; nor is there anything else they lack. Although we see all these things, we do not perceive them, we neither consider them novel nor do we pay them any attention or infer anything from them, but we keep calm, acting as if nothing has occurred. By contrast, we display great respect toward the achievements of the Greeks making use of their images and words in our lives during our endeavors, honoring them by making constant references, such as "Such and such a person said and did this and that in the past." We even consider all this a profit for cultivated men and believe that nothing is disgraceful, however insignificant, for the person who uses it. Above all, we respect and study the language that communicates these deeds, because otherwise such a language would not have deemed it worthwhile to discuss such

αὐτῶν καὶ λέγειν, εἰ μή τι νόμιμον ἦν ἀνάγκη παντὸς
μᾶλλον, ὡς ἔοικεν, ἀξιολόγῳ μνήμῃ τιμᾶσθαι τὰ δόξαντα
δηλαδὴ τῶν ἔργων κάλλιστα.

4   Καὶ γὰρ δὴ σφόδρα ἕλκουσί τε πρὸς ταὐτὰ καὶ
ἐπιστρέφουσι Θουκυδίδαι τε καὶ Ξενοφῶντες καὶ Θεόπομ-
ποι, Ἀττικαῖς εὐγλωττίαις χειρούμενοι καὶ τῇ παρασκευῇ
τῆς φωνῆς μέγιστον ἀνύτοντες πρὸς ὑποδοχὴν καὶ τὸ
παραλαβεῖν, ἃ σπουδάζουσιν οὕτω καὶ κατατείνουσιν ἑαυτοὺς πράγματα. Οὕτως ἄρα τῇ τῆς φωνῆς, οἶμαι, τύχῃ
πολλῷ γέγονε τὰ τῶν Ἑλλήνων ἐπικυδέστερα καὶ παρῆλθε
παντάπασι τἄλλ᾽ ἅπαντα παλαιά τε ὁμοῦ καὶ νέα καὶ ὅσα
καθ᾽ ἕω καὶ ὅσα τῆς λοιπῆς μοίρας, ἐν τοῖς αὐτοῖς ἴσως
ὄντα.

24

Καὶ πρὸς ἔτι ἐξαίρω μέντοι λόγοις τὰ Ῥωμαίων αὐτῶν,
ἃ τοσοῦτον ὑπερέσχεν ἅπανθ᾽ ὡς ἔπος εἰπεῖν ἀξιώματι καὶ
δόξῃ καὶ τῷ τῶν πράξεων αὐτῶν ἀπαραμίλλῳ καὶ κράτει
τῶν ὅλων καὶ ῥώμῃ καὶ ἀνδρῶν γνώμῃ καὶ τόλμῃ καὶ
πᾶσιν ὁμοῦ, ὥστε πᾶσαν εἰς ἑαυτὰ κεκίνηκε γλῶτταν ἀφη-
γεῖσθαί τε καὶ θαυμάζειν, πάντων ἀφεμένους τῶν ἄλλων,
ὥσπερ ἄρα ἐν ταῖς καινοτομίαις εἰώθαμεν ἄνθρωποι, καὶ

matters, unless it was inevitably more legitimate than anything else, apparently, to honor with worthwhile mentions the actions that are judged finest.

Of course writers such as Thucydides, Xenophon, and Theopompus powerfully attract their audiences and turn their minds toward these actions, overwhelming them with their Attic eloquence, and by means of the power of their expression they have a significant impact on the acceptance and reception of the topics that they studied in this manner and to which they devoted themselves so deeply. In my opinion, precisely because the Greeks were fortunate in their language, their actions were glorified even more and surpassed in all respects all previous deeds, both ancient and contemporary, both those that occurred in the east and those in the rest of the world, although these too were presumably just as valuable as those of the Greeks. 4

Chapter 24

Moreover, in our discourse we extol the deeds of the Romans themselves, all of which were almost so superior in terms of their quality and fame, and in the incomparable manner of their accomplishments, their control over everything, the strength, spirit, and bravery of their men, and in general in every single matter, that they prompted every tongue to narrate these deeds and marvel at them, neglecting everything else, just as we human beings are accustomed to do when faced with novelties; all these feats, I assume,

πάντα, οἶμαι, νοῦν ἦρε, καὶ εἰ πρότερον ὀλίγος ἦν, μὴ
καθεύδειν, ἀλλ᾽ ἐγρηγορέναι καὶ προσέχειν καὶ λογίζεσθαι
πρὸς τοσοῦτο τοῦ χρόνου καὶ τῆς οἰκουμένης θαῦμα.

2   Δημάδης μὲν οὖν ἔλεγε, πυθομένων Ἀθηναίων Ἀλέξαν-
δρον ἐν Σούσοις τελευτῆσαι καὶ ταραττομένων, μὴ πείθε-
σθαι· πάλαι γὰρ ἂν ὄζειν τὴν οἰκουμένην νεκροῦ, ὡς τὸ
ἐκείνου σῶμα τῆς οἰκουμένης σχεδὸν ὂν καὶ ταύτην ἀναγκαῖον συμπάσχειν ὁτιοῦν αὐτῷ πεπονθότι. Τὰ δὲ Ῥωμαίων
αὐτὰ γέγονε σχεδὸν ἡ οἰκουμένη καὶ οὐκ ἦν οὐδένας
ἀνθρώπων οὐκ ἀμερίμνως ἔχειν, οὐδ᾽ ἀλογίστως ὁτιοῦν ἐν
ἐκείνοις γιγνόμενον, ἀλλ᾽ ἅμα τέ τι παρὰ Ῥωμαίοις ἦν ἢ
ἐγίγνετο—ὅ, τι ποτ᾽ ἂν ἦν ἢ ἐγίγνετο—καὶ ἅμα τοὺς ἀπαν-
ταχοῦ τῆς γῆς ἀνθρώπους εἶχε ξυναίσθησις καὶ θάμβος
καὶ λόγος πλεῖστος ἐθριάμβευε διὰ πάντων, ὥσπερ ἑνὸς
ὁρῶμεν σώματος μέρους ὁτουοῦν δράσαντός τι ἢ παθόντος
αὐτίκα αὐτόθεν τῷ παντὶ ξυναισθάνεσθαι συμβαίνει.

3   Ὅπερ δὲ περὶ Ἀθηναίων ἔφη Θουκυδίδης, πεφυκέναι
τοιούτους, οἵους μήτ᾽ αὐτοὺς ἡσυχίαν ἄγειν δύνασθαι
μήτε τοὺς ἄλλους ἐᾶν, τοῦτο δὴ μάλιστα Ῥωμαίους εἶχεν,
ἀεί τ᾽ ἐν μεγίστοις ἐξεταζομένους πράγμασι καὶ αὐτούς τε
ὄντας ἐνεργεῖς κρειττόνων ἢ κατὰ τοὺς ἄλλους, μᾶλλον δ᾽
ἢ κατὰ τὰ πρότερον ἀεὶ σφέτερα αὐτῶν καὶ πάντας μὴ
καθεύδειν διὰ ταῦτα συγχωροῦντας, ἀλλ᾽ ἀνίστασθαι καὶ
ὡς ἔνι μάλιστα τῷ λογισμῷ τῶν πραγμάτων ἅπτεσθαι καὶ
ξυνορᾶν. Τοιγαροῦν ἅπανθ᾽ ὡς ἀληθῶς κατέσχον τῇ δόξῃ
καὶ πλέω γε τῆς αὐτῶν γέγονε τύχης καὶ τοῦ περὶ αὐτῶν
λόγου καὶ πλεῖστοι δή, πλεῖστα περὶ αὐτῶν συγγραψάμε-
νοι, φιλοκαλίας τε περὶ αὐτῶν δόξαν καταλελοίπασιν ἡμῖν

incited every mind, even if it was previously of a limited character, not to fall asleep but to be vigilant and alert and turn its attention to this great marvel of time and the world.

When the Athenians learned that Alexander had died at 2 Susa and were thrown into confusion, Demades told them not to believe this, because the whole world would have smelled his corpse long ago, since Alexander's body in a way belonged to the world, so that the world would necessarily share his suffering if anything happened to him. Roman affairs, on the other hand, came to comprise virtually the entire world, and no one could ignore or refrain from observing what was happening to the Romans. To the contrary, as soon as something occurred in Rome—whatever it might be—everyone throughout the whole world could immediately feel it, and amazement and much discussion overtook everyone, in the same way as, when one part of our body does or suffers something, we see that our whole body can immediately sense it.

What Thucydides said about the Athenians, namely that 3 they are by nature unable to remain quiet or leave other people to rest in peace, also affected the Romans in particular, who were always put to the test in the most significant affairs and themselves accomplished many more splendid deeds than other peoples, or rather their subsequent achievements were always superior to their previous ones. In this way, the Romans did not allow other people to relax, but they kept them on the alert and made them observe and examine their deeds as attentively as possible. They therefore truly reigned supreme over everything thanks to their glory, and everything was overwhelmed by their fortune and their fame. Many authors composed numerous works about them and bequeathed to us their fame as lovers of beauty

καὶ ἡδίστην ξυνεῖναι διατριβὴν πλεῖν ἢ κατὰ τὰς ἄλλας ἴσως συγγραφάς τε καὶ ἱστορίας.

25

Καθόλου μὲν οὖν παντὸς ἡδονὴ πράγματος, ᾗ φησι Πλάτων, περόνη τίς ἐστι πρὸς αὐτὸ καὶ συνδεῖ (πῶς ἂν εἴπῃ τις;), σφόδρα καὶ οὐ διάλυτον, οὐδ᾽ ἀπότμητόν ἐστι ῥᾷστα ὅτῳ ἂν ξυμβαίνοι τὸ τοιοῦτον πάθος πρὸς ὁτιοῦν. Ἡ δὲ περὶ τὴν ἱστορίαν ὅλως ῥοπὴ καὶ πραγμάτων μετρίως ἐποπτεῦσαι παλαιῶν ἀφηγήσεις οὕτως ἀκάματον ὡς ἀληθῶς ἔρον ἐνέσταξε τῇ ψυχῇ καὶ τοσοῦτο δηγματῶδες ἀεὶ νύττον θέλγητρον, ὡς οὐκ ἄλλο τίποτ᾽ οὐδέν, οὐδ᾽ ἔστι καθάπαξ ἀναμαθεῖν, ὅστις ἄρα μὴ πεπείραται παθών.

2 Οὐ γάρ ἐστιν ὅπως ἄν τις κόρος καὶ μέτρον ὁτιοῦν γένοιτο τῇ περὶ ταῦτα φιλοπραγμοσύνῃ, οὐδ᾽ ὅπως ἀγαπήσειεν ἂν ἀμέλει καὶ ἠρεμίᾳ τινὶ σχήσειν ἑαυτήν, ἀλλ᾽ ἀείποτέ τι προσλαμβάνων ὁ σπουδάζων, οἶμαι, πάντως ἀεί πως ἱμέροις ἀγρύπνοις τε καὶ ἀτρύτοις προστέτηκε καὶ ζητεῖ καὶ προσεξεργάζεται, τῷ τῶν ληφθέντων ἤδη κέντρῳ τἀφανὲς ἰχνηλατῶν αὖθις καὶ ἀνορύττων, ἅττα δὴ πάλαι πρότερον χρόνων καὶ πραγμάτων ἄλλαις ἐπιδρομαῖς συγκέχωσται.

3 Τοιγαροῦν, ὥσπερ οἱ φιλοπλουτοῦντες αὐτοὶ οὐδὲν ὅ, τι ἄρα μέτρον ἐνόμισαν, οὐδ᾽ ἔστησαν, οὐδ᾽ ἐπαύσαντο, οὐδ᾽

and a leisure activity that is highly pleasant to associate with, far more pleasant, perhaps, than other historical accounts and stories.

Chapter 25

As Plato says, in general the pleasure that comes from everything is a pin that fastens the individual firmly to it (how can one put this?), and when a person happens to experience this sort of passion for something, he can neither be loosened nor easily cut off from it. But the inclination toward history instills in the soul a truly invincible passion to study in due moderation the narrative of past events, along with such an incomparable charm that it constantly stings and pricks it, and no one can understand it at all, unless he has experienced it personally.

For human curiosity on such issues can never be sated or moderated in any way, nor would it be content to maintain itself in tranquility. To the contrary, the person who studies history and is always learning something, in my opinion, is somehow constantly engrossed by sleepless and untiring longing, and searches for and accomplishes things previously unknown to him. Because of the goad of his previous discoveries, he looks for the traces of hidden events and unearths those that took place long ago and have been buried by additional onslaughts of events that have occurred in the meantime.

Therefore, just as people who seek wealth do not understand what moderation is and never stop or desist from as-

ἐφ' ὅτῳ δήποτ' ἂν γενόμενοι, καὶ ἀποχρῆναι τοῦ λοιποῦ
φαῖεν καὶ κατασχεῖν ἄρα σφᾶς ἕλοιντο, ἀλλ' ἀεὶ γῆν καὶ
θάλατταν περινοοῦσι σπουδῇ πάσῃ συλλογιζόμενοι πάνθ'
ὁμοῦ χρήμαθ' ἃ ξυνίσασι γεωργοῦντα πλοῦτον, τὸν αὐτὸν
ἐμοὶ δοκεῖ κἀνταῦθα καὶ οὗτοι τρόπον, οὐκ ἔχουσιν ὅπως
ἂν ἔπειθ' ἑαυτῶν γένοιντο καὶ ἀποσταῖεν εἴ πῃ ἄρα καὶ
παύσαιντο τῆς περὶ τὴν ἱστορίαν τῶν παλαιῶν λιχνείας
ταύτης καὶ ξυλλογῆς, ὅρον ὁντινοῦν προστησάμενοι, ἀλλ'
ὡς ἀληθῶς ἀπέραντα κατεπείγονται καὶ κάμνουσι τοῖς
ἠνυσμένοις ἤδη λοιπὸν καὶ φθάσασι τὸν ἀεὶ μαθημάτων
νέον ἀνακινοῦντες πλοῦτον, μηδὲν ἀπαμβλυνόμενοι, μηδ'
ἐν τοῖς ἐλαχίστοις ἀποκνοῦντες κάματον κέρδους ἅπαντα,
ἀλλὰ μετεῖναι πάντων ὅλως ἐξόν, ἅπαντα αἱροῦνται σφίσι
παρεῖναι καὶ οὐδὲν ὅ,τι οὔ, ὥσπερ οἱ ἐν περιουσίαις καὶ
πλούτῳ τρυφᾶν ἑλόμενοι καὶ Συβαριτικὰς σπουδάζοντες
καρυκείας οὐ μόνον τἀναγκαῖα καὶ ὧν ἀπαραίτητος ἡ
χρῆσις, ἀλλ' ἅπαντα πρὸς τὸ ἁβρότερον ἐσκευασμένοι
προτιθέασι καὶ περινοοῦσι καὶ μαγγανεύουσιν, εἴ τί που
ἔξεστιν ἔτι νέον, καὶ ὁπόσα φέρουσι γῆ τε καὶ θάλασσα καὶ
οἷοί τ' ἂν ὦσι πραγματεύεσθαι, πρὸς οὐδὲν ὅλως ἀποκναί-
ουσιν οὔθ' ἵστανται, παραπλησίως ἀμέλει καὶ οὗτοι πρὸς
οὐδὲν ὁτιοῦν ὀλιγωροῦντες, ἀλλ' ἅπανθ' ὡς ἀληθῶς τρυ-
φῶντες ἡδονὴν εὐγενῆ τε καὶ παραμένουσαν.

4   Τῆς δ' ἄρα ἡδονῆς, οἶμαι, ταύτης οὐ μόνον ἐν ἱστορίᾳ
καὶ τῷ παλαιοῖς οὕτω συμπλέκεσθαι πράγμασι πειρῷτο ἄν
τις, ἀλλὰ καὶ πρὸς ἅπασαν αὕτη σοφίαν ἐπαγωγόν ἐστι
σφόδρα καὶ διὰ πάσης ὡς ἔπος εἰπεῖν συμφύεται, εὐφυής

piring to get more, and no matter how much they have amassed, they do not admit that they have enough for the future and choose to restrain themselves; to the contrary, they constantly contrive enormous projects with great zeal on both land and sea, and they think of every possible means they can to harvest wealth, I assume that the lovers of history follow the same route in this case. They too are unable to control themselves or abstain from their passion even for a moment, and they cannot relinquish their obsession with investigating past events and collecting information or set a limit on their passion. Indeed, they rush about endlessly and strive to mix in the new riches of constant studying with their previous accomplishments, without losing their force or shrinking from any profitable labor in even the most trivial matters. If they can possess everything, they prefer to keep it all by their side and be lacking nothing, like extremely wealthy men who choose to enjoy luxury and arrange sybaritic banquets. Nor do they employ only the necessary and indispensable ingredients, but instead they serve every food delicately prepared, and try to think of something novel and dress their dishes artificially to the extent this is possible; they also attempt to avail themselves of the products of the land and the sea and all other available commodities, without hesitating or excluding anything. Likewise, the lovers of historical research neglect nothing and truly enjoy everything as a permanent, noble pleasure.

I believe, however, that a person would not find this pleasure only in history and past events, but that it also greatly attracts one toward every sort of knowledge, and, to put the matter differently, it is naturally suited to every kind of wisdom, and is graceful and extremely beautiful, and 4

τε καὶ καλλίστη ἑαυτῆς προμνωμένη τοῖς ἀπαντᾶν
βουλομένοις χάριν οἵαν δή τινα καὶ ῥαστώνην οὐκ εὐκα-
ταφρόνητον, ὥσπερ ἀμέλει καὶ οἱ παμφόρα πεδία καὶ λει-
μῶνας εὐκάρπους φιλοπονοῦντες ἐοίκασιν αὐτοὶ πρώτως
αὐτόθεν οἷοί τ᾽ εἶναι μάλιστα ἥδεσθαι. Ὥστε οὐ μόνον
κατὰ τὸν Πυθαγόραν ἔξεστιν εἰπεῖν ὡς "ἑλοῦ βίον τὸν ἄριστον, τοῦτον δὲ ἡδὺν ἡ συνήθεια ποιήσει," ἀλλὰ καὶ τοῦθ᾽,
ὡς "οὐχ ἥκιστα ἑλοῦ βίον τὸν τῆς σοφίας ἄριστον ὡς
ἀληθῶς ὄντα" καὶ ὄν, οἶμαι, κἀκεῖνος μάλιστα ἠβούλετο,
"τοῦτον δὲ ἡδύτατον τῶν ἄλλων εὑρήσεις," ὡς οὐκ ἔστιν
ὅ,τι ποτ᾽ ἂν ἥδιον ἄλλο γένοιτο ἀνδρὶ νοῦν ὅλως ἔχοντι
τῆς ἐν λόγοις αὐτῆς ξυνουσίας τε καὶ διατριβῆς.

26

Καὶ μήν, εἰ τοσοῦτο δὴ τῆς ἡδονῆς ὁρῶμεν αὐτῆς κατὰ
πάντων ἀνθρώπων τὸ κράτος καὶ οὕτως εὖ μάλα περὶ
αὐτὴν καὶ μικροὶ καὶ μείζους κεχήνασι, κατ᾽ ἄλλος ἄλλο τι
πάντως ἢ ἄλλα καὶ πάντες ἅπανθ᾽, ὡς οἷόν τέ ἐστι, ταύτην
θηρώμενοι (οἱ μὲν δόξῃ καὶ τύφῳ κάτοχοι καὶ προστε-
τηκότες καὶ τὸν τρόπον τοῦτον ἥδεσθαι προελόμενοι καὶ
τετιμηκότες, οἱ δὲ φιλοπλουτίᾳ, οἱ δὲ κυνηγεσίοις, οἱ δὲ
γυμνασίοις, οὐκ οἶδ᾽ οἷστισι, καὶ πόνοις, οἱ δὲ καὶ τοὐναντίον, ἀπονίᾳ δηλαδὴ καὶ ῥαστώνῃ πάσῃ, οἱ δὲ τρυφαῖς καὶ
τοῖς αἰσχροτάτοις αὐτοῖς, ἀσελγείαις καὶ ᾄσμασί τε καὶ

promises beforehand to those who want to engage with wisdom delight and recreation of a sort that is difficult to despise; this is what happens with people who laboriously cultivate fertile plains and fruitful fields and who because of this seem to be able to be the first to get delight from them. According to Pythagoras, we can say not just *"Choose the best way of life, and habituation will make it pleasant!"* but also "Above all, you should choose the truly best way of life, the life of wisdom," which Pythagoras himself greatly desired, I believe, "and you will see that this is the most pleasant one, more than all the others." Nothing could become more pleasant for a wise man than this engagement with and commitment to education.

Chapter 26

Therefore, if we see that the power that pleasure exerts upon all mankind is so great, and that everyone, whether young or old, gapes at it in eager expectation, and everyone chases after it as much as possible, each for a different reason or reasons (some are possessed by fame and arrogance, and are engrossed by them and honor them, preferring to get their pleasure in this way; others are lovers of wealth, hunting, athletic exercises of one sort or another, or physical exertion. Yet others, by contrast, take pleasure in laziness and every kind of relaxation, whereas some prefer luxury and its most shameless manifestations, namely licentiousness, songs, pipes, and indecent dances. In gen-

αὐλοῖς καὶ κορδακίσμασιν, ἕκαστος δὲ πάντως καθ᾽ ὁτιοῦν
πρὸς ταύτην ἐπείγονται καὶ ἀνύτουσιν, Ἐπίκουρος δὲ καὶ
συχνοὶ τῶν ἐλλογίμων παλαιῶν ἀνδρῶν, στασιῶται τῆς
αἱρέσεως, ἡδονὴν τὸ πᾶν ἐν βίῳ τέλος καὶ τῆς ἀνθρωπίνης
ὁρμῆς καὶ γνώμης νομίσαντες, ἔδοξαν οὐ πάνυ τοι φορτικῶς οὐδ᾽ ἀηδῶς ἀποφήνασθαι, ἀλλὰ καὶ πολλοὶ προσή-
καντο τὸ δόγμα καὶ προσέθεντο, νοῦν ἔχειν ἀξιοῦντες), ἢ
που χάριέν ἐστιν ὡς ἀληθῶς καὶ παντάπασιν εὐφυές τε καὶ
οἰκεῖον καὶ λυσιτελέστατον ἡ παρὰ τῶν λόγων καὶ περὶ
τοὺς λόγους αὐτοὺς γιγνομένη τοῖς σπουδαίοις ἡδονὴ καὶ
τοῖς ἄπασαν, οἶμαι, τὴν τοῦ βίου γνώμην καὶ πορείαν ἐνταῦθα κόπτουσι καὶ τῶν ἄλλων προελομένοις.

2   Ἡδονή τε γὰρ δὴ μάλιστα πλείων ἢ κατὰ τἄλλ᾽ ἄπαντα,
ὅστις πεπείραται καὶ ὤναθ᾽ ὁτιοῦν καὶ μετρίως, ἄπαντες
ἂν συμφαῖεν, βεβήλοις δ᾽ οὐδὲν ὅλως μὴ δοτέον—ἀλλὰ
πύλας ἐπιθέσθων, τῶν κρειττόνων ἀπαθεῖς αὐτῶν καὶ
καθάπαξ ἀνήκοοι καὶ ἀναίσθητοι, βοσκημάτων τρόπον ἐπὶ
τῷ σώματι μόνῳ τὴν ἡδονὴν ὁρίζοντες.

3   Ἡδονή τε δή, ὅπερ ἔφην, ἐνταῦθα πάνυ τοι πλείστη καὶ
ἅμα καλλίστη καὶ καθαρὰ καὶ τοῦ θειοτέρου μέρους ἄκρατος, αὐτῆς μόνης τῆς ψυχῆς, οὐκ οἶδ᾽ ὡς εἴ τί γ᾽ ἄλλο,
φόρτου καὶ μολυσμάτων ἀγνεύουσα καὶ καθιστῶσα μὲν ἐν
ἀπαραμίλλῳ γλυκυθυμίᾳ τε καὶ ῥαστώνῃ ταύτην εὖ πως
ὑγροτέραν καὶ κεχυμένην καὶ ἵλεων, ὁπλίζουσα δὲ μάλιστα καὶ ἀνεγείρουσα καὶ τελεσιουργὸν τῶν ἑαυτῆς, ἣ
δὴ πρότερον εἴρηται, παρασκευάζουσα, διανοίας τε καὶ

eral, every person rushes and makes his way toward pleasure for entirely different reasons. Epicurus and many of the ancient philosophers who were followers of his school thought that pleasure was the ultimate goal of life and of human activity and the mind; not only were they not seen to have said anything vulgar or distasteful, but to the contrary many people embraced the doctrine and became members of this school, because they believed that the Epicurean attitude was reasonable), then I think that the pleasure that comes to educated men and to those who have devoted themselves exclusively to this attitude and activity in their lives and have preferred this to anything else, the pleasure that arises from engagement with and about education, is truly and in all respects graceful, appropriate, and fitting for human beings, as well as highly beneficial.

For this pleasure is superior in comparison to all other 2 pleasures, and everyone who has experienced it and profited from it even moderately will agree. But we should certainly not offer it to the unhallowed—let those who are unmoved by these better things, the utterly deaf and insensate, who restrict pleasure to the body alone, as animals do, close their ears!

As I just noted, in this case the pleasure is great, ex- 3 tremely beautiful, and pure, partaking exclusively of divinity, pertaining to the very soul more than anything else, and uncontaminated by excessive burdens and stains. It brings the soul into incomparable indulgence and relaxation, and in a quite beautiful way it makes the soul more pliant and overflowing with mildness, while at the same time it equips it greatly, stimulates it, and prepares it to undertake the tasks that pertain to it, namely the intellect and knowledge,

ἐπιστήμης, καὶ ἀμφότερα ὡς ἔνι δηλαδὴ κάλλιστα, νοῦν
ἐνεργῆ μέν, ἀλλ᾽ ἐπαφρόδιτον, καὶ ἡδονὴν μέν, ἀλλ᾽
ἔντονόν τε καὶ σώφρονα, οἷόν τι χρῶμα καὶ θέαμα καθορῶ-
μεν ἐπ᾽ ἀέρος ἐνίοτε σύγκρατόν τε καὶ κάλλιστον, εἰ ἄρα
μεσημβρίᾳ καὶ θέρει φλέγοντι αὐτόματον ὗσε καὶ ταῖς
ἡλιακαῖς ἀστραπαῖς νοτίδες ἄνωθεν συνυφαίνονται καὶ
συμπλέκονται, τὰς τοῦ πυρὸς λαμπάδας ἐπανθίζουσαί τε
καὶ κατατέμνουσαι καὶ κεραννῦσαι κατάστασίν τινα καὶ
κάλλος οἷον ἀδόκητόν τε καὶ ἥδιστον.

4   Καὶ δὴ λοιπὸν καὶ τῆς σοφίας αὐτῆς οὐ καθάπαξ τὸ
δραστικὸν οὐκ ἀνέορτον, ἡ δ᾽ ἀκμὴ παντάπασιν οὐκ αὐ-
στηρὸν τίποτ᾽ ἐστίν, οὐδ᾽ ἀτόλμητον, ἀλλ᾽ ἕκαστος καθ-
εωραμένος οἷός τε ἔσται θαυμάσαι τὸ κεκραμένον ἄρα καὶ
εὐξύμβλητον ὥρᾳ τοσαύτῃ καὶ χάριτι.

27

Καὶ μὴν οὐ τοῦτο μέγιστον, οἶμαί, φαμεν τὸ τῆς ἡδονῆς,
ἀλλὰ τὸ τοσοῦτο τοῦ νοῦ κέρδος μεθ᾽ ὅ,τι πλείστης τῆς
ἡδονῆς, ὥσπερ οἱ ἐν γαλήνης εὐκαιρίᾳ καὶ πνευμάτων
ἔαρι πρὸς πελάγη καὶ θαλάσσας ἀφέντες καὶ ἀναγόμενοι
καὶ τὰ μέγιστα πονοῦντες καὶ κατακτώμενοι κέρδη καὶ τὸ
τῆς εὐπλοίας ταύτης κάλλιστον ἔχουσιν ὄντως ἡδονῆς
παρεμπόρευμα· καὶ οἱ πρὸς τὴν ἐλπίδα τῶν μεγίστων
κάματον ἅπαντα καὶ τόλμαν κινδύνων αἱρούμενοι καὶ

as we said previously. In this way, both the mind and the pleasure are in the best possible condition, the mind by being active but also charming, the pleasure by being both vehement and chaste, as is the case with the spectacle of the sky, which we sometimes see assuming an overwhelmingly beautiful combination of colors when at noon on a sizzling summer day it suddenly pours rain, so that the moisture becomes interwoven and intertwined with the rays of sunlight above and diffracts the rays of fire and embellishes them until it creates a beautiful combination that is unexpected and extremely pleasant.

Practicing this kind of wisdom is thus not entirely without joy, and its zenith is neither austere nor discouraging, but everyone who beholds it will be able to admire its easily recognizable combination of tremendous beauty and grace. 4

Chapter 27

We are not speaking, I think, of pleasure as something very important, but of the great intellectual profit that comes from this enormous pleasure, just as those who set out and sail a ship in calm weather with favorable winds across the high, open seas, and who work extremely hard to make a profit, consider the best by-product of their journey this easy voyage, which brings true pleasure. On the other hand, as for those who in the hope of greater profit choose great effort and risk danger with no hesitation, how much

πρὸς μηδὲν ἀποκνοῦντες πόσου ποτ' ἂν πρίαιντο καὶ τίνες
ἄρα γένοιντ' ἄν, μετ' εὐφορίας καὶ ραστώνης τοσαύτης
εὐτυχοῦντες τὰ κέρδη;

2   Καὶ τὰ μὲν ἀγαθά φασιν οὐκ ἐπίηρα, παμπλείστου δ'
ἀγῶνος δεῖται. Νῦν δ', οἶμαι, τὸ τοσοῦτο τῆς παιδείας
χρῆμα ἀγῶνος μὲν ὡς οὐκ ἄρα μεγίστου δεῖται, οὐκ ἂν
μήποτε ἔγωγε ἐρῶ—μικροῦ γὰρ ἀγῶνος οὐ μέγ' ἔρχεται
κλέος, φησὶν ἡ τραγῳδία—ὡς δ' ἔρχεται τὸ τοσοῦτο μέγα
καὶ κέρδος καὶ κλέος ἀγῶνι μὲν ὡς ἀληθῶς καὶ καμάτῳ
πλείστῳ, σὺν ἡδονῇ δ' ὅμως καὶ γλυκυθυμίᾳ συμπεφυκὸς
πάνυ τοι πλείστῃ καὶ πολυεράστῳ, τοῦτ' οἶμαι καὶ δικαίως
ἂν ἐρεῖν αὐτὸς καὶ πεῖραν ἀξιῶν λαμβάνειν οὐκ ἂν
αἰσχυνθῆναι, ὡς οὐκ ἔστιν ὅστις ποθ' ἁψάμενος καὶ
μετρίως, οὐδ' ὅστις ξυγγεγονὼς ἀληθῶς τε καὶ εὐψύχως,
οὐχ ἅπαντες ἂν συμφαῖεν.

28

Χωρὶς δὲ τούτων, εἴπερ οὐ καθάπαξ φλαῦρόν τι καὶ
εὐδιάβλητον τὸ τῆς ἡδονῆς τοῦτο χρῆμα, ὡς οὐκ ἔγωγε
οἶμαι, ἀλλ' ἔστιν ὅτε καὶ οὗ καὶ ἐφ' οἷστισι δέδοται καὶ
νενόμισται καὶ οὐκ ἀπόθεσμον, ἐν τίσιν ἂν εἴη μᾶλλον ἢ
τίς ἂν ἕλοιτ' ἄλλοσέ πῃ ἢ περὶ οὗ νῦν ὁ λόγος, ἐνταῦθ' οὗ
καὶ πλεῖστόν ἐστι καὶ κάλλιστον εἰς ἀγλαΐαν καὶ τρυφὴν

would they pay and what kind of persons would they become in order to be fortunate enough to acquire this profit with such ease and facility?

They claim, of course, that what is good brings no pleasure, but requires enormous effort. As for myself, I would never deny that education does indeed demand great effort given the significance of the matter—as the tragedy says, *after a brief struggle, you can never have great fame*. I nonetheless believe that I would be justified in saying that no matter how truly great the struggle and effort required to achieve great profit and fame, it is automatically accompanied by great and highly desirable pleasure and delight. And if I were to ask someone to test the validity of my opinion, I would not be embarrassed, for no one who has tried it even for a short while or has truly engaged with it with a stout heart will disagree with me.

Chapter 28

Apart from the above, if the issue of pleasure is not entirely trivial and blameworthy, as I think it is not, but rather there are some contrary instances in which it is permitted, used customarily, and not forbidden, in what other circumstances could this mostly occur, or in what other case could a person opt for it, except for the case we are now examining, that is that of education? In this latter case, the pleasure is both great and extremely beautiful, it directs our most

τοῦ βελτίστου καὶ βασιλικοῦ μέρους, αὐτῆς τῆς ψυχῆς, καὶ
τὴν ἐξ ἐπιστήμης καὶ παιδείας τελείωσιν καὶ τοῦ νοῦ τοσαύτην ἀνθοφορίαν καὶ εὐκαρπίαν;

2   Εἰ δ’ ἀτενές ἐστι καθόλου πρὸς ἄπασαν ἡδονὴν ἡ τε-
λειότης καὶ πρὸς οὐδὲν ὁτιοῦν μαλθακὸν ὁρᾷ, καθάπερ τὰ
Γοργόνεια φάσματα, παρομαρτεῖ δ’ ὅμως αὕτη δι’ ἀδυναμίαν (ἢ οὐκ οἶδ’ ὅπως ἐρῶ), νόσημα ἀναγκαῖον καὶ φύσεως
πάθος ἄτμητον, τί οὐ μάλιστα τρεπτέον ἐστὶ τὸ τοιοῦτον
πάθος, ἔνθα δὴ λώϊόν ἐστι χρησαμένοις ἡμῖν καὶ πεπον-
θόσι, καθάπερ οἱ τέχνῃ πλέοντες ἄπαν, καὶ τἀντίπαλον καὶ
δύσνουν πνεῦμα, μεταχειρίζουσί τε καὶ τρέπουσι πρὸς τὴν
χρείαν; “Μὴ γὰρ νοσοῖμεν” καὶ ὁ ἐξ Ἀκαδημίας φησὶ λόγος,
“νοσήσασι δὲ παρείη τις αἴσθησις.”

3   “Οὐκοῦν μηδὲ ἡδυνοίμεθα καὶ τοῦτ’ ἂν ἄμεινον ἦν,”
φησὶν ὁ νῦν λόγος οὗτος—“νοσεῖν γάρ ἐστι δὴ τοῦτο κατ’
αὐτὸν καὶ οὐ παντελῶς εὖ ἔχειν”—ἡδυνομένοις δ’ οὖν
ὅμως κατ’ ἀνάγκην φύσεως ἄτρεπτον, παρείη τις κέρδους
συλλογισμὸς καὶ συναίσθησις. Καὶ πάρεστιν ὡς ἀληθῶς
ἐνταῦθα νῦν μέγιστον, ἡ τοῦ νοῦ προκοπὴ τοῖς ἐπὶ παιδείᾳ
καὶ τέχνῃ λόγων τὴν ἡδονὴν ἑλομένοις. Καὶ μὴν ὁ μὲν
τραγικός φησιν Εὐριπίδης, “εἴπερ ἀδικεῖν χρή,” τυραννίδος
πέρι, “κάλλιστον ἀδικεῖν,” ἀγνώμονα παντάπασι καὶ ἀνε-
λεύθερον λόγον ὡς ἀληθῶς εἰσενέγκας. Οὔτε γὰρ ὅλως
τἀδικεῖν οὔθ’ ὑπὲρ οὗ μάλιστά φησιν, αἱρετέον.

4   Καὶ περὶ μὲν τούτων οὐ νῦν καιρὸς λέγειν. Ὁ δ’ οὖν
ἠβουλόμην, ὡς τοῦτο μᾶλλον ἐμοὶ δοκεῖν δικαιότερον, ὡς,

important and sovereign part, the soul itself, toward splendor and enjoyment, it is brought to completion through the assistance of knowledge and education, and it leads to an important type of intellectual productivity and fertility.

Even if perfection pays no attention whatsoever to pleasure and does not cast a glance at anything weak, as if it were the Gorgonian monster, but if nevertheless pleasure itself comes along, due to a certain weakness, an unavoidable sickness (I am not sure how to put this), or a natural human emotion that cannot be erased, should we not try by any means to divert such an emotion in the direction where it will be more agreeable to us who use and experience it, just as those familiar with the art of sailing manage every adverse and inimical wind, making it favorable? The Academic doctrine says, *"Pray that we not be ill, but if we be ill, pray that sensation be left to us."* 2

"Very well, we shall feel no pleasure, and this would be better," says this very treatise—"for this is truly a sickness and not an entirely healthy state"—but for those unable to escape the feeling of pleasure by natural necessity, there ought to be some calculation of the gain and realization of their situation. In this case, there is great gain indeed, that is the intellectual progression of those who choose the pleasure linked to education and the crafting of rhetorical speeches. Indeed the tragic poet Euripides in his treatment of tyrannical power says, *"If injustice is necessary, it is best to act unjustly,"* putting forth a statement both completely irrational and inappropriate for a free spirit. For injustice is never acceptable, not even for the reason Euripides puts forward. 3

But this is not the time to discuss such issues. What I wanted to say, judging it more just, is that if it is absolutely 4

εἴπερ ὅλως ἄνθρωπον ἥδεσθαι χρὴ καὶ παντὸς μᾶλλον ἡ
φύσις ἀναγκαῖον ἕλκουσα, ἐκ σοφίας καὶ περὶ λόγους
ἡδυντέον αὐτόν τινα ἑαυτὸν ἡδονὴν πλείω τε ἢ κατὰ τἄλλ᾽
ἅπαντα καὶ πάσης ἁγνεύουσαν ὄντως καὶ ἀπηλλαγμένην
ὑγρότητος καὶ ἀωρίας.

29

Καὶ μὴν οὐ τοῦτο ἔγωγε λέγω, οὐδ᾽ ὡς ἄν τις ἄρα ὑπο-
νοήσειε—μηδ᾽ οὕτω μανείην—ὡς διά τινα νόσον ἄρα συν-
ήθη καὶ οὐ παντάπασιν ἠλλοτριωμένην τῆς φύσεως, οὐδ᾽
ἀπόβλητον τὰ τῆς σοφίας αὐτῆς σπουδαστέον—ὁδοῦ φασι,
μᾶλλον δὲ συμφορᾶς τινος, ὡς ἔοικε, πάρεργον, ὡς ἄν τῳ
δόξαι ἴσως—ἀδιαβλήτῳ τινὶ πράγματι καὶ οὐ κακῷ τὸ κακὸν
ἰωμένους κατὰ τὴν παροιμίαν, ἀλλ᾽ ὡς ἀντὶ μεγίστου καὶ
καλλίστου τοῦδε καὶ πρώτου τῶν ὅσα κατ᾽ ἀνθρώπους
εἰσὶ χρήματος ἅπαντα αἱρεῖσθαι δέον ἐπικτωμένους καὶ
σπουδῇ πάσῃ χρῆσθαι, μηδὲ τούτου φειστέον, ὡς ἔοικε,
μηδ᾽ ἀποκνητέον, καὶ εἴπερ ἄρα καθόλου νόσημα ὁτιοῦν,
ὡς ἄν τις φαίη, ἐπὶ παντὸς ἀναγκαίᾳ τινὶ καὶ ἀπαραιτήτῳ
φύσεως ἕξει παρέλκει, κἀνταῦθα δὴ παρειλκύσθω, τῆς
τοσαύτης ἐπικερδείας ἕνεκα παρεωραμένον καὶ μηδὲν
μᾶλλον διὰ τοῦτο τῆς ἐξ ἀρχῆς ἀποστατέον σπουδῆς γεννικῶς τὸ σύμπαν ἐχομένους, ὥσπερ καὶ οἱ πολύχουν, οἶμαι,
λήϊον ἀμώμενοι καὶ πολύσταχυ συνεπαμῶνται πάντως καὶ

110

obligatory that a person feel pleasure, and if nature more than anything else attracts what is necessary, then that person should get pleasure from wisdom and participation in education, since this pleasure is greater than anything else, pure indeed, and free from any sensuality or ugliness.

Chapter 29

I certainly do not say, as someone might assume—I am not so demented!—that we should pursue this wisdom because we are prompted by a common disease, which is not entirely alien to nature or abhorrent—they say that wisdom *is brought to us as a secondary purpose of our journey,* as one might think, or better by some misfortune, so it seems—in other words, I am not saying that we should be curing *evil with something that is* blameless and *not evil,* as the proverb goes. Rather, what I am saying is that it is necessary for us to choose to acquire this wisdom as the greatest, most beautiful, and principal object of everything that exists for mankind, and that we should make use of it by all means, and neither be sparing with it, as it seems, nor indolent. Even if some sickness in general drags on due to a necessary and unavoidable state of variable nature, as one might say, then may it drag on in this case; it can be overlooked on account of the great gain one will receive. Because of this, we should not abandon our initial efforts but should remain firm with absolute bravery, just as people who harvest a rich-soiled, fertile plain also harvest the destructive weeds and pests

τὰν μέσῳ, ἤν τινά που παραφύηται γῆς ἀκμαζούσης ὑβρίσματα καὶ λωβήματα.

2 Καὶ ὥσπερ ὅσοι τῶν ἐμπορευομένων ἐν πελάγεσι ναυτιῶσιν, ἅπανθ᾽ ὁμοῦ σκάφη δυσχεραίνουσι, κἂν εἰς ἀκάτιόν τις ἐμβάλῃ, ἀπαραίτητος ἡ νόσος, κἂν εἰς φορταγωγὸν μεγίστην, κἀνταῦθα ἔπεται καὶ ταὐτὸ τοῦτο πάσχουσι καὶ ναυτιῶσι πανταχῇ περιπλέοντες καὶ μικρὰ καὶ μείζω κατακτώμενοι κέρδη, ἀμείνους μέντ᾽ ἂν εἶεν ὅμως πολύ, κἂν εἰ ἐνταῦθα ναυτιᾶν ἀνάγκη πάντως, μεγίσταις ἑαυτοὺς ναυσὶ πιστεύοντες καὶ διὰ τὰς πειρατικάς, οἶμαι, ἐφόδους καὶ διὰ χειμῶνας ἅπαντας ἀντιπράττοντας καὶ πρὸς τὰ μέγιστα μᾶλλον παραβαλλόμενοι κέρδη, παραπλησίως ἐμοὶ δοκεῖν ἔχουσι καὶ οἵτινες ἀντὶ πάντων τῶν ἄλλων, μᾶλλον ἐν λόγοις καὶ τοῖς ἀπὸ τῆς παιδείας ἄρα θησαυροῖς ἥδεσθαί τε καὶ πάσχειν, ὅστις οὕτω βούλεται καλεῖν, εἵλοντο.

30

Ἀλλὰ ταῦτα μὲν ἴσως ἀνάγκῃ τινὶ μᾶλλον καὶ δρόμῳ λόγου παρήχθη νῦν εἶναι, ἐπ᾽ ἀληθείας δὲ αὐτῆς ἐξετάζοντι, τὸ μὲν τῆς παιδείας οἷόν ἐστι χρῆμα, καὶ εἴρηται μὲν ἤδη μετρίως καὶ εἰρήσεται, ὡς οἷόν τε ἑξῆς, καὶ τὰ πλείω γε ὡς ἀληθῶς παρήσομεν, οὐδ᾽ ἐφιξόμεθα. Ἡδονὴν δέ, ὡς

that happen to grow beside the wheat of the productive land, I think.

And just like merchants on the open sea, who suffer from seasickness and necessarily feel ill on board every ship, and unavoidable nausea follows them whether one puts them on a light boat or a huge cargo ship, and they will be troubled by this same nausea and will be seasick wherever they sail, regardless of the amount of profit they will make, whether much or little; but nevertheless they would certainly do much better to rely on large ships, because in that instance, I think, they could combat both pirate attacks and all sorts of adverse storms, and at the same time bring in much greater profit, although they will necessarily suffer from nausea even on ships of this type; so I think the same is the case with those who have opted to take pleasure in the words and treasures of education more than anything else, and to experience pain too, should one wish to describe it thus.

Chapter 30

But perhaps for the time being, all this has been presented out of some kind of necessity and by the course of the discussion. For the one, however, who investigates the very truth concerning the essence of education, some points have been sufficiently covered already and will be discussed, to the extent possible, in what follows. Moreover, as is true, I will leave aside and not touch upon many matters. But it

ἔοικεν, οὐ πᾶσαν, οὐδὲ παντάπασιν ὀστρακιστέον, οὐδ᾽ ἀποκηρυκτέον ἀνθρώπων, ἀλλὰ πλείστην μὲν ἴσως, τὴν δὲ οὔ.

2 Ὅση μὲν γὰρ μόνη τοῦ σώματος ἄκρατός ἐστι καὶ ἀκόλαστος, περὶ τὴν αὑτοῦ κολακείαν καθόλου σπουδάζουσα καὶ μηδὲν ὅ,τι πλέον, προσαναματτομένης τὰς κηλῖδας διιούσας καὶ τῆς ψυχῆς αὐτῆς ἀναγκαίᾳ τινὶ καὶ ἀτρέπτῳ τοῦ δεσμοῦ καὶ τῆς φύσεως ὁλκῇ καὶ παρόδῳ, ταύτην ὡς οἷόν τέ ἐστι παντὶ σθένει καὶ τρόπῳ χρῆναι φεύγειν ὡς δυσμενῆ παντάπασιν.

3 Ὅση δὲ μόνης αὐτῆς ἐπὶ θάτερα ψυχῆς ἤρτηται καὶ λογισμῷ τινι πάντως συνέζευκται, πρὸς δὴ ταύτην οὐκ ἀποδειλιατέον ὡς ἐπίβουλον, οὐδ᾽ ἀποτρεπτέον. Ἐπειδὴ γὰρ ἔνι τι προδήλως τῆς ἡμετέρας ψυχῆς ἄλογον καὶ παθητικόν, τοῦ δὲ μετὰ πρώτην εὐθὺς τὴν αἴσθησιν ἡδονή τε καὶ τοὐναντίον μόρι᾽ ἄττα καὶ τεμμάχι᾽ ἐξῆπται, φύσεως ἀναγκαίως ἑπόμενα συνεχείᾳ, καὶ διαδρᾶναι καὶ παραιτήσασθαι τὸ σύμπαν οὐκ ἔστι, χρηστέον μέν, ὡς ἔοικεν, ἀνάγκη, χρηστέον δὲ ὅμως ᾗπερ ἄρα βέλτιον, τὸ δὲ ἐστὶν οὐκ ἄλλως ἢ λόγου παιδαγωγοῦ, μᾶλλον δὲ βασιλέως δεῖσθαι, καθιστῶντος οὐκ ὀλλῦντος, καὶ οἰκονομοῦντος οὐ καταστρεφομένου, καὶ χρωμένου μὴ παρορῶντος.

4 Καὶ ἰατρὸς γάρ, ᾧ χρῆσθαι παρὸν ὅλως κατ᾽ ἄλλην τινὰ οἰκονομίαν καὶ τέχνην, οὐ τέμνειν καὶ τὸ δοκοῦν δυσχερὲς ὁπωσοῦν καθιστᾶν ἄλλως ἢ κάειν, ἀμαθὴς ἂν εἴη καὶ τέμνων ἔπειτα ἐνταῦθα καὶ κάων, ἐπεὶ κἀνταῦθα ἡ φύσις

seems that not all manifestations of pleasure should be entirely banished or denounced among men, for although its largest part is indeed banishable, another part of it is not.

The type of pleasure that is concerned purely with the 2 body and is licentious, which aims only at physical satisfaction and nothing else, while the soul itself is besmirched with the stains that pass through it by virtue of some necessary, fixed attraction and channel of communication of the natural bond between body and soul, this must be avoided as much as possible with all one's might and in any way possible, because it is extremely harmful.

On the other hand, as for the type of pleasure that is con- 3 cerned with the soul alone and is in every respect combined with some sort of rationality, one should not flinch from or avoid this as being harmful. For since there is obviously a certain irrational and passion-susceptible part of our soul, from which immediately after the initial sensation pleasure and pain are excited, resembling certain fragments and pieces that inevitably follow the continuity of nature, and since it is impossible to entirely escape or ignore them, one ought necessarily to use sensation, so it seems, although one ought to use it in the best possible manner. And there is no other way to do this than by demanding education as our teacher, or rather as our emperor, who does not destroy our affairs but arranges them, does not damage but manages them, does not disregard but uses them.

For the physician who can employ some alternative 4 method of medical treatment rather than incision or cauterization and can overcome in a different way a seemingly vexatious problem, would be stupid if he nonetheless employed incision or cauterization in this instance. For in our

οὐκ ὀλετῆρα τῶν οἰκείων αὐτῆς, ἀλλ᾽ ἡγεμόνα τὸν νοῦν καὶ ἰατρὸν ἐπεστήσατο. Καὶ γὰρ οὔτ᾽ ἀχρεῖον τὸ γεγονὸς δὴ τοῦτο καὶ παρεζευγμένον ἄλογον τῇ νοερᾷ τε καὶ λογικῇ μοίρᾳ τῇ φύσει γέγονε (πόθεν; ἤ γε πάντα ἔλλογός τε καὶ ἐνεργός) οὔτε ἐφ᾽ ᾧ καὶ ὀλέσθαι γέγονε (τοῦτο γὰρ ἔτι πω καὶ δεινότερον), ἀλλ᾽ ἵνα ὡς ἂν εἴ πως ὑποζυγίῳ τὸ κρεῖττον χρῷτο, κατατιθασσεῦον εὖ μάλα καὶ ἡνιοχοῦν πρὸς ὑπηρεσίαν, ἥντινά οἱ δόξειε λυσιτελεῖν.

31

Καὶ τὰ μέν γε καὶ μείζονος ἴσως καὶ ἄλλου λόγου καὶ νῦν οὐ καιρὸς λέγειν. Ὁ δ᾽ οὖν ἐβουλόμην καὶ ὁ λόγος ἦν, ὡς ἔστι καὶ ἡδονῇ χρῆσθαι, πρὸς τὸ βέλτιον, οἶμαι, ἐσκευασμένοις καὶ ἐπ᾽ ἔργοις ὄντως ἀρίστοις, πάσης ἀπηλλαγμένη κακοηθείας καὶ βδελλυρίας, καὶ οὐ παντάπασι καταψηφιούμεθα ταύτης ξενηλασίαν τῆς φύσεως. Συμβέβηκε δὲ αὐτῇ μάλιστα ἐνταῦθα σφόδρα τε εἶναι καλλίστη καὶ πάνυ πλείστη. Τῷ ὄντι γὰρ πολὺ τὸ ἐπαγωγὸν αὐτὴν ἔχουσαν καὶ μεγίστην ἰσχὺν εἰς τὴν φύσιν συνέζευξεν ὁ Θεὸς ἐπὶ τοῖς ἀμείνοσι πράγμασι πλείω ἑαυτῆς ἢ κατὰ τὰ ἄλλα ἅπαντα, ὡς ἂν ἀτρέπτως μάλιστα ἔχοιντο οἱ σπουδάζοντες καὶ διὰ τὸ συγγενὲς τοῦτο καὶ φίλον θέλγητρον.

case nature has rendered our mind a ruler and a physician, not a terminator of nature's possessions. For nature has not produced this creation to be useless or as an irrational associate of the logical and rational faculty (how could this be possible, given that nature creates everything in rationality and good working order?), nor was the irrational part of the soul created to act against the rational part (for this would have been even more dreadful); instead, it was created so that the best part could somehow use it as a beast of burden, taming it effectively so as to employ it for whatever service the best part considered useful.

Chapter 31

But this is the topic of another, perhaps more extensive discourse, and this is not the proper occasion to expound on the point. What I wanted to stress, however, and what was my topic here, is that those who are being prepared, I think, to achieve truly noble deeds can definitely use pleasure for their benefit. This pleasure is entirely free from malignity or wickedness, and we should not choose to banish it entirely from nature. In fact, in the present case of education, pleasure happens to be very beautiful and very plentiful as well. For, indeed, since pleasure possesses great appeal and enormous power, God has endowed nature with a portion of pleasure that is greater than the portion of all other things that aim at what is best. The result is that those who strive exceedingly hard may remain stalwart by virtue of this congenial, amiable charm.

2   Ὁρῶμεν δὲ τοῦτο μάλιστ᾽ ἐπ᾽ αὐτῆς ἀρετῆς, ὃ δὴ μόνον
ὄντως καὶ πρῶτον καὶ μέγιστον ὂν κατ᾽ ἀνθρώπους
ἀγαθόν, τὸ αὐτὸ καὶ ἥδιστόν ἐστι καὶ σφόδρα οἱ μετιόντες
ἐν ἡδονῇ τινι καὶ ῥαστώνῃ πάντως ἀρρήτῳ καὶ κόρον οὐκ
ἐχούσῃ διαφέρουσι τὴν τοῦ βίου ταύτην πρόθεσιν, οὐκ
οἶδ᾽ ὡς εἴ τινες ἄλλοι, καὶ πρότερον ἤδη εἰρημένον οὐκ
ἄλλως τις ἔχον εὑρήσει, εἰ βούλοιτο τῶν ἀνδρῶν πυνθάνεσθαι καὶ μάλιστα ἐφ᾽ ἑαυτοῦ πεῖραν λαμβάνειν.

32

Τὸν δ᾽ αὐτόν, οἶμαι, τρόπον ἔχει καὶ ἡ τοῦ νοεροῦ καθ᾽
ἡμᾶς ἐργασία καὶ παρασκευὴ καὶ τῶν λογισμῶν αὐτῶν
ὑπὸ παιδείας εὐρυθμία καὶ προκοπή, καὶ μάλιστα ὁπόθ᾽,
ὡς φιλεῖ ξυμβαίνειν, ἀρετῇ συνελθοῦσα, πάντα τἆλλα
κατὰ τὸν βίον ἐν δευτέρῳ ποιησαμένη, ἑαυτῇ ζῇ μόνη καὶ
τῇ τῶν ὄντων ἀσχόλῳ θεωρίᾳ, ὡς οὐδὲν τίποτ᾽ ἄλλο γέ-
νοιτ᾽ ἂν κατ᾽ ἀνθρώπους ἥδιον, ὅταν τις ἑαυτοῦ γενόμενος
ὅλος καὶ τῆς ἐν ταῖς βίβλοις καὶ σοφίᾳ νεύσεως καὶ τρυφῆς
καὶ συνουσίας καὶ συναγαγὼν ὡς οἷόν τέ ἐστι τῶν ἄλλων
ἁπάντων εἰς ἀκλόνητον καὶ ἄσχετον καθάπαξ ἁπάντων
καὶ ἀνέκδημον καὶ ἀμέριστον ἑδρασμὸν καὶ μονὴν ἐλευθέραν τε καὶ ἀτύρβαστον, ἔπειθ᾽ οὕτω παντάπασιν ἄδετον
καθάπερ ἐν μοναυλίᾳ ὥσπερ ἀφ᾽ ὑψηλῆς τινος σκοπιᾶς

We mostly encounter this in the specific case of virtue, 2 which by means of being the truly unique, original, and most significant blessing for human beings is also the most pleasurable. Those who participate in virtue try very hard to maintain this purpose in life to the very end, being in a state of ineffable delight and relaxation that cannot be satiated, much more so than other people. I have already referred to this before, and there is no other way one can learn about the topic, if one wishes, than to ask men about it or indeed experience it oneself.

Chapter 32

The same is the case, I think, with the function and preparation of our rational faculty, the good management and progress of our intellect that comes from the influence of education, especially when our mind, as regularly happens, after it engages with virtue, renders all other human concerns of secondary importance, and lives for itself alone, and its only activity becomes the contemplation of existing matters. There could thus be nothing more pleasant among human beings than the moment when a person turns entirely to himself and to the acceptance of, pleasure in, and discourse with books and wisdom, and focuses his mind, as far as possible, away from all other preoccupations onto a stable, utterly independent, unswerving, and undivided permanence that is also free and undisturbed. Afterward, as in a solo pipe performance, he allows his mind to be completely

ἀπόλυτον ἐπόπτην ἀφήσῃ πρὸς ξύμπαντα τὸν κόσμον καὶ
τὴν ἄπλετον οὐσίαν τὸν νοῦν, καὶ περισκοποῖτο διαίρων
ὁμαλῶς καὶ ἀλύπως τὼ ὀφθαλμὼ πάντα ἑξῆς, καταθεώμε-
νος τὰς ἀμυθήτους ἁρμονίας τῶν ὄντων καὶ συμπλεκόμε-
νος καὶ μακαρίαν ὄντως καὶ θειοτάτην ἐπαφὴν ἐφαπτό-
μενος, μὴ κατορρωδῶν ἀμέλει, μὴ κατοκλάζων, οἶμαι, μὴ
κάμνων, μὴ ξυμπίπτων μὴ καθάπαξ πρὸς τὸν ἀπέραντον
δίαυλον, ἀλλ᾽ οἷόν τινα πομπὴν ἀκύμονά τε καὶ ἔμμουσον
ταύτην καὶ πορείαν ἐκδημῶν ἀείποτε ἀνήνυτον μέν, ἄπο-
νον δέ, καὶ ἀόριστον μέν, ἡδίστην δὲ καὶ μετὰ γαλήνης
τῶν ἔξωθεν, καθάπερ ἐν ἀστασιάστῳ τινὶ καὶ ἠρεμαίῳ
πελάγει τῇ τοῦ κόσμου παντὸς οὐσίᾳ, κουφίσας τῶν ἄλλων
ἁπάντων καὶ τὰ τῆς θεωρίας ἀναπετάσας λαίφη, τὸ τῆς
διανοίας σκάφος ἐφίησι, περιπλέων πάνθ᾽ ἕκαστα καὶ ἐπι-
ξενούμενος καὶ κατατρυφῶν, ἅττα ἂν δοκῇ καὶ ἃ βέλτιστα
καὶ τὰς ἀμυθήτους τῶν ὄντων ἀσπαζόμενος καλλονάς,
κἄπειθ᾽ οὕτω καθ᾽ αἵρεσιν πᾶσαν ἐν ἑαυτοῦ κάλλιστος ἀπὸ
καλλίστων, φασίν, ἐπανιὼν οἴκαδε, ζητῇ καὶ σκέπτηται
κἂν τῷ ἑαυτοῦ συνεδρίῳ καὶ βουλευτηρίῳ τῆς διανοίας
γιγνόμενος, τἀληθὲς ἐν αὐτοῖς ἰχνηλατῇ καὶ ἀνορύττῃ,
καὶ τὸν ἐφ᾽ ἑκάστοις σύγκρατον νοῦν τε καὶ λόγον ἀνα-
λαμβάνων, τελευτῶν ἄρα καταπλήττηται καὶ θαυμάζῃ τὸν
εὑρετὴν καὶ τεχνίτην ἐν ὄντως ἀρρήτῳ τῇ συναισθήσει,
ἄρρητον αὐτίκα αὐτόθεν γλυκυθυμίαν ἀποφερόμενος.

2   Αἴ, αἴ, τί τούτου γένοιτ᾽ ἂν ἥδιον ὄντως ἀνδρὶ τῶν
ἁπάντων ἄλλο, ᾧ μὴ παντάπασι κατεκιβδηλεύθη καὶ

unfettered, and as if from a high vantage point becomes a careful overseer who observes the entire world and its boundless essence. When he opens his eyes, he can see everything in a sequence, easily and with no effort. He can see the countless harmonies of everything that exists, with which he engages; he comes into contact with something that is truly blessed and profoundly divine, with no fear or slackening, I think, without feeling fatigue or hesitation once he embarks upon this endless course. Every time he sets forth, it is as if this were an untroubled celebratory procession of the Muses, and a journey; never ending but not tiring; without a destination but quite pleasant, free of external distractions. This person has relieved the vessel of his mind from everything else and unfurled the sails of contemplation, and he throws it into the matter of the entire universe, as if onto a calm, serene sea. He sails all over, he visits and enjoys many places that he fancies and considers the best, and he embraces the countless beauties of what exists. Then, because he grows extremely beautiful himself, due to his association with what is most beautiful, as they say, he returns home as he chooses, and begins pondering and examining what he has seen, and seeks refuge in the meeting place and council chamber of his thought in order to seek out and discover the truth in what he has seen. When he retrieves the meaning and reason mingled together in every single thing and finishes his examination, he is astonished and admires the inventor and craftsman, that is God, with a truly ineffable sentiment that suddenly makes him feel ineffable pleasure.

Alas! What else could really be more pleasant than this 2 for a man whose soul has not been completely adulterated

κατενόησεν ἡ ψυχή, μηδὲ συμπλακεῖσα τοῖς τοῦ κόσμου τοῦδε λήροις καὶ μολύσμασι, κηλῖδάς τινας ἔστιν ὑφ᾽ ὧν δευσοποιοὺς καὶ μύση κακῶς προσανεμάξατο, καὶ καταγοητευθεῖσά τε καὶ καταπεδηθεῖσα, ἔστιν οἶστισι συνέφυ καὶ προσέσχεν ἄτρεπτος, ἀλλ᾽ ἀνεπιστρόφῳ παντάπασι καὶ ἀτρεμιζούσῃ διανοίᾳ τε καὶ κινήσει τοῖς τῆς σοφίας πτεροῖς αἰθεροδρομεῖ καὶ δίεισι πάντων ἀεὶ κατὰ τὴν παροιμίαν βάλλουσα ἐς μακαρίαν καὶ τρυφὴν οἵαν ἀκύμονα καὶ μὴ σεσοβημένην, μηδὲ φορτικῶς ἄρα κατέχουσαν, μηδ᾽ ἐπικτωμένην, ἀλλ᾽ ἐλευθέραν ὄντως καὶ λογικῇ φύσει πρέπουσαν καὶ διιοῦσαν ἵλεων καὶ περιλαμβάνουσαν τὴν τοῦ νοῦ χώραν καὶ τὴν λογικὴν ἅπασαν συμφυῖαν καὶ ἁρμονίαν ἀΰλῳ τε καὶ ἀλύπῳ σοφίας πνεύματι.

33

Ἀλλ᾽ ἐμοῦ τις ἂν ἴσως θαυμάσαι, τί δήποτε τοσοῦτο προειπὼν ἄρα καὶ προθέμενος, ὡς οὐ πάντα ἐκ πάντων ἐπαινέσομαι παιδείαν, ὡς οἱ πολλοὶ τῶν σπουδαζόντων τὸ χρῆμα πάνθ᾽, ὅσ᾽ ἂν οἷοί τε γένοιντο, κατεπείγονται καὶ ἀποσεμνύνουσιν, ἔπειθ᾽ οὕτως ἔλαθον ἐμαυτὸν αὐτίκα διὰ πάντων ὡς ἔπος κλεΐζων καὶ ἀνατιθεὶς αὐτῇ τὰ δοκοῦντα κάλλιστα, ἀφ᾽ ἑστίας, ὡς ἄν τῳ δόξαι, τἀναντία δρῶν καὶ περιπίπτων ἐμαυτῷ.

or become seriously ill, nor has been wickedly besmirched by some indelible stains and defilement through embracing the chattel and pollution of this world, nor has attached and fixed its attention to them as a result of its infatuation with and dependence on them? The soul of such a man, by contrast, has completely firm and stable thoughts and movement, and flies in the sky above with the wings of wisdom; it always passes through everything *until it reaches bliss,* as the saying goes, and a calm enjoyment, which is never agitated, does not hold sway over it in a vulgar manner, rendering it its own possession, but instead it is truly free and suitable for a rational nature, transcends gracefully and embraces the region of the mind, the entire rational congruence and harmony with the help of the immaterial, painless spirit of wisdom.

Chapter 33

Someone might be puzzled by me, however, since at the beginning of my treatise I said that I did not intend to extol education in all respects and by all means, as many of its students do, who rush to praise it in as many ways as they can; nevertheless, without even realizing it, I systematically glorified education straight away, and I furnished it with whatever praise I considered most beautiful *from the* proverbial *beginning,* so that I might appear to some to be acting contrary to my words and to be caught in my own snare.

2　Μάλιστα μὲν οὖν ἔγωγε τοῦτο δηλαδὴ μόνον προὔλεγόν τε καὶ προὐνοούμην, ὡς ἐπ᾽ ἀληθείας ἁπάσης εἰρήσονται οἱ λόγοι καὶ οὐδὲν ἄρα φορτικόν, οὐδ᾽ ἐπαχθές, οὐδ᾽ ἐπαινεῖν πλέον ἢ ἔδει ἐσκεύασμαι περὶ σοφίας, καθάπερ ἅπαντες εἰς τὰ παιδικὰ νομίζουσιν, ἐπαινεῖν δὲ οὐ παντάπασιν ἔγωγε ἀπεῖπον, οὐδ᾽ ἃ πρόσεστιν, οἶμαι, τῷ πράγματι καὶ προφέρειν ἀληθῶς ἔξεστι παρρησίᾳ, μὴ οὐ προφέρειν, εἴπερ ἂν οἷός τ᾽ εἴην, οὐδὲ τοῦτ᾽ ἦν ἡ ἀπόρρησις, ἀδικῆσαι τἀληθῆ καὶ φαῦλα δόξαι τε καὶ ἐρεῖν τὰ βέλτιστα, ἐπεὶ καὶ ἄλλως χάριεν ἂν ἦν ἴσως, ὦ φιλότης, εἴ γε βουλόμενός σε προτρέπειν καὶ παρακαλεῖν ἐπὶ παιδείαν καὶ τὴν τῶν λόγων ἐπιμέλειαν, ἔπειθ᾽ ἑωρώμην λοιδορούμενος αὐτὸς εἰς τὸ πρᾶγμα καὶ ἠρημένος, ἅττα ἂν δυναίμην κακῶς ἐρεῖν· καὶ τοῦτ᾽ ἦν ὡς ἀληθῶς ἂν ἀφ᾽ ἑστίας ἐμαυτῷ περιπίπτειν καὶ γελοίως ἔχειν, ὅστις ἂν ἔπειτα ὁρῴη.

3　Ἔπειθ᾽ ὅτι μάλισθ᾽ οἷς ἄρα προεῖπον, παρέμεινα καὶ τετήρηκα σαφῶς τὴν τάξιν, ὅστις ὀρθῶς, οἶμαι, ζητεῖ, καὶ πρότερον μὲν ἤδη γεγονός τε εὑρήσει τοῦτο καὶ εἰρημένον, οὐ μὴν ἀλλὰ καὶ νῦν αὖθις ἐροῦμεν.

On the one hand, all I meant to say and stress in my in- 2
troduction is that my exposition would be shaped by truth
alone, and that I would not be contriving anything vulgar or
disturbing, or praising wisdom more than necessary, as everyone usually does with regard to the objects of his passion.
On the other hand, I did not categorically refuse to praise
wisdom or to mention the attributes, I believe, that it has
and that can truly be ascribed to it when speaking frankly, if
I could do so. My refusal to praise wisdom did not mean
that I would do damage to its actual features or that I would
consider and argue that its benefits are useless. For it would
probably have been ridiculous, my dear friend, if I wanted to
urge you to engage with education and participate in intellectual activities, while I myself was seen castigating the
matter and choosing whatever I could to disparage it. This
would truly have been as if I were caught in my own snare
from the very beginning and had made myself a laughing-
stock for anyone who saw me.

I accordingly believe that anyone who explores the issue 3
properly will realize that I have remained quite faithful to
my initial statements and have carefully observed their arrangement; meanwhile he will find that now again I shall
speak in accord with what has previously been done and
said.

34

Εἰσὶ μὲν αὖ οἵ φασιν ἀθάνατον μόνον ὑπὸ παιδείας γίνεσθαι τὸν σπουδαῖον. Λείπεται γὰρ τἀνδρί, φασι, μνήμη πολυμήκης ἑξῆς καὶ κλέος ἀείζῳον, ὑφ᾽ ὧν ἔλιπε λόγων. Τοῦτό γε μὴν οὐ τοῦ σοφοῦ μόνον ἔοικεν εἶναι, ἀλλ᾽ ἀμέλει καὶ ἄλλων ἐπ᾽ ἄλλοις καὶ μικροῖς τε καὶ μείζοσι, καὶ Φειδίου καὶ Πολυγνώτου καὶ καθ᾽ ἡμᾶς Εὐλαλίου, Ζευξίππου τε καὶ Λυσίππου, εἴθ᾽ οὗτινος βούλει, οἳ δόκιμοι γεγόνασιν ἐν τέχναις αἷστισιν ἄρα καὶ ὧν ἔργα χειρῶν παραμένειν ἔχει, καὶ τὸν μὲν οἱ λόγοι, τοὺς δὲ γραφαὶ καὶ ἀγάλματα, τοὺς δ᾽ ἄλλα μηχανήματα, τοὺς δὲ οἰκοδομαί τινες καὶ νεώρια, τοὺς ἄλλο τίποτ᾽ ἄλλους παραπέμπουσι καὶ διδάσκουσι, τὸν ὅμοιον τρόπον, ὥς φασιν, οὐ θνήσκοντας.

2   Εἰ δ᾽ ἐρεῖ τις ἴσως ὡς ἄρ᾽ ἀλλ᾽ ἐκεῖνο μάλιστα ὀνησιμώτερον καὶ βιωφελέστατον, ἄλλος ἂν εἴη λόγος. Βιωφελέστατον μὲν γὰρ ὡς ἔστι καὶ ζῶντι καὶ τελευτῶντι τὸν αἰῶνα τοῦ βίου τῷ σοφῷ τοὔργον καὶ τὸ σπούδασμα, ὅ,τι ποτὲ προήνεγκεν, ἢ τὰ τῶν ἄλλων, ἔγωγε λέγω καὶ οὐκ ἄν, οἶμαί, τις νοῦν ὅλως ἔχων ἄλλως ἐρεῖ. Ὅτι δ᾽ οὐδὲν μᾶλλον αὐτῷ διὰ τὴν ἀνάγκην τῆς μνήμης ἢ τοῖς ἄλλοις τὰ σφέτερα αὐτῶν πολυζωΐας αἴτιον, ὡς ἄρα τινὲς βούλονται, τοῦτο πανάληθές τέ ἐστι καὶ τοῦτο ἦν ὁ λόγος.

Chapter 34

Moreover, there are some persons who claim that a scholar can become immortal by means of education alone. For the memory of this man, they say, persists for many years to come and his fame lives on forever on account of the writings he has left behind. But this does not seem to be an advantage that belongs to wise men alone, but it also adheres to other men under other circumstances, significant and insignificant alike, for instance Phidias, Polygnotus, our own Eulalios, Zeuxippus, Lysippus, and anyone else you like. These individuals achieved excellence in various sorts of arts, and the achievements of their hands remain eternal. The scholarly man is escorted by his writings, others by paintings and statues, various mechanical devices, buildings and dockyards, or yet something else, teaching that all skilled men are immortal in the same way, as they say.

If someone were perhaps to claim, however, that a particular one of these occupations is more beneficial and more useful in life, that would be a topic for a different discussion. For I would say that what is most beneficial to the wise person, both while he is alive and at the end of his life's course, is his own work and pursuit, whatever he has ever produced, rather than the works and pursuits of the others, and I do not think any person of sound mind would argue otherwise. It is also wholly true, and this is what I have argued, that the occupations of the wise man are not the cause of a more enduring afterlife for him than are those of other craftsmen, due to the essential nature of the commemoration that is left behind, as some people want to believe.

3   Ἐζητοῦμεν γὰρ νῦν εἶναι οὐχ ὅ,τι πέρ ἐστι κρεῖττον καὶ
λυσιτελέστατον κατὰ τὸν βίον ἀνθρώποις, ἀφ᾽ ὧν ἕκαστοι
σπουδάζουσι πραγμάτων, ἀλλ᾽ εἰ μόνον, οἶμαι, οἱ λόγοι
τὸν δημιουργὸν ἔπειτ᾽ ἀθανάτῳ μνήμῃ παραπέμπουσι καὶ
οὐ συγχωροῦσι κεῖσθαι, καὶ καθεωρῶμεν ὡς οὐδὲν ἧττον
οὐκ ἐπιλήστους, οὐδὲ θνητοὺς διὰ τὴν μνήμην ταύτην
οὐδὲ τἆλλα τοὺς ἄλλους πατέρας, ὧν εἰσιν, ἐῶσι. Καίτοι,
χωρὶς τούτων, τί τοῦτ᾽ ἂν εἴη τὸ σεμνὸν ἢ τίποτ᾽ εἰσὶν οἱ
λόγοι τῷ σπουδαίῳ μένοντες ἢ τίς ὄνησις τἀνδρὶ τῶν
λόγων, οὓς ἔλιπε, σπουδαζομένων τε καὶ τιμωμένων, ἢ τί
πλέον ἐντεῦθεν αὐτῷ ἥδεσθαι καὶ ἀπολαύειν ἢ καὶ ἄλλοις
οἷστισιν ἄρα μετ᾽ αὐτοῦ κειμένοις, ἐπ᾽ ἀγροικίας καὶ βα-
ναυσώδους τινὸς βίου τὸ ζῆν ἐξανύσασιν;

35

Ἀλλὰ ταῦτα μᾶλλον, ὡς ἔοικεν, ἐραστῶν εἰσιν οἱ λόγοι,
πάντ᾽ οἰομένων τῷ πάσχειν χαρίζεσθαι δεῖν οἷς σπουδάζουσιν. Οἷς συγγνωσόμεθα μὲν ἴσως, οὐ πεισόμεθα δὲ σωφρο-
νοῦντες αὐτοί, ἐπεὶ καὶ Πλάτωνι καὶ εἴ τινί ποτ᾽ ἄλλῳ τῶν
παλαιῶν ἐκείνων ἀνδρῶν καὶ πανσόφων περὶ φιλοσοφίας
μάλιστα ἠγώνισται, ὡς μόνον ἐν πολιτικοῖς αὔταρκες
πράγμασι καὶ τἆλλ᾽ οὐδὲν ἐνταῦθ᾽ ἅπαντα τοῦδε χωρὶς καὶ
μόνον ἐφάμιλλόν ἐστι βασιλείᾳ πρὸς ὄντως οἰκονομίαν
ἡρμοσμένην ἀνθρώπων καὶ διὰ μόνου τούτου συνελόντ᾽

For what we were now seeking to find, I think, was not 3 which of the occupations with which different people are engaged is the best and most profitable for human life, but whether it is only literary compositions that secure eternal memory for their author and do not allow him to die. I have observed that other occupations leave their creators unforgotten or immortal to the same extent, because of this memory. Still, apart from this, what is the value of such fame? In what way are the works that endure significant for the learned man, or what benefit does he get from the writings he left behind, even if subsequent generations study and honor them? Or what greater pleasure and satisfaction could he receive when his works are studied compared to other people who now lie dead along with him, having spent their whole life as rustic peasants and artisans?

Chapter 35

Such are the words of lovers, it seems, who believe that they should offer everything to their objects of desire because of their passion for them. We could perhaps pardon them, but we shall certainly not be persuaded by what they say, if we are sensible. For Plato and anyone else from that group of extremely wise ancient men struggled to prove that philosophy in particular is the only thing that stands on its own in the community, that everything else is useless without it, that it alone is equal to kingship as regards the proper management of men, and in short that only through

ἐρεῖν ἅπαντ᾽ ἂν ὀρθοῖντο τοῦ βίου πράγματα καὶ καλῶς
ἄγοιντο, παρόντος τε καὶ ἐπιστατοῦντος, ἀπόντος δ᾽
οὐκέτ᾽ οὐδ᾽ ὁτιοῦν, ἀλλ᾽ ἅπαν τοὐναντίον, καὶ λῆρος καὶ
ἀηδία καὶ οὐδὲν ὑγιές, οὐ πεισόμεθα μὲν πάντως ἐπιχει-
ροῦντι καὶ βουλομένῳ, κἂν ὅτι πλεῖστον βιάζηται δια-
λεκτικαῖς ἀνάγκαις τισὶ καὶ δεσμοῖς, γνωσόμεθα δὲ ὅμως
καὶ συγγνωσόμεθα, διὰ φιλαυτίαν οὕτως ἐπειγομένῳ
σφόδρα καὶ οἷς διὰ παντὸς ἐσχόλασε τοῦ βίου συνηγο-
ροῦντι, ὡς ἂν ἀμέλει δοκοίη τὰ βέλτιστα καὶ τῶν ἄλλων
ἀμείνω πάντων ἐξελέσθαι καὶ μή τις, οἶμαι, νεμεσῆσαι
καταγνοὺς ἀργίαν τἀνδρὸς καὶ βίου καὶ πολιτείας πάσης
διὰ τὴν αἵρεσιν ταύτην ἀπραξίαν.

2   Πρὸς γὰρ ταύτην, ὡς ἔοικεν ἄρα, τὴν ἀνάγκην φιλονει-
κεῖν ᾤετο χρῆναι καὶ ἀποδεικνῦναι πάνθ᾽ ὁμοῦ πράγματά
οἱ προσόντα διὰ φιλοσοφίαν καὶ οὐδὲν μὴ εἶναι πρὸς ὃ μὴ
παρεσκευάσθαι, μηδ᾽ ἔχειν δύναμιν ταύτην, μὴ τυγχάνου-
σαν δὲ τῶν πραγμάτων δι᾽ ἀπειρίαν αὐτὴν τῶν πολλῶν
φευγόντων καὶ ἄγνοιαν καὶ δυσβάστακτον ἐπιστασίας ὀρθῆς ὄγκον, ἀποστρέφεσθαι καὶ ἰδιοπραγεῖν, μυσαροῖς καὶ
τετυφωμένοις ἔθεσιν ἀξιοῦσαν μὴ συμφύρεσθαι.

the presence and assistance of philosophy can human life be set straight and our affairs take their proper course; that without its presence nothing goes well, but everything is reversed, is rubbish, disgusting, and unsound. Yet no matter how exhaustively he made all these arguments through the use of dialectical power and charm, attempting to prove what he wanted, we will not be completely persuaded, but we will understand and make allowance for Plato's position, because he is much motivated by self-love and defended the areas to which he devoted his entire life, in order to produce the impression that he had chosen the best course in comparison to everyone else, and so that no one would feel displeased and accuse Plato of inactivity and utter abstention from political life brought about by this choice of his.

For, so it seems, it was this accusation he thought he had 2 to challenge, and to prove at the same time that thanks to philosophy he had numerous qualifications and there was no situation he was not prepared to handle and for which he did not possess this capacity. But his capacities did not always achieve their targets, because many people, due to inexperience, ignorance, and the intolerable burden of honest authority, turned their back on Plato's abilities, as a consequence of which Plato limited himself to his private activities and did not allow his capacity to be confounded by the abominable and insane customs of his age.

36

Ἀλλὰ ταῦτα μέν ἐστιν, ὡς ἔφαμεν, λόγοι μόνον μὴ δε-
δοκιμασμένοι, μηδὲ πεῖραν ἐν τοῖς πράγμασι δόντες, καὶ
κάλλιστα μὲν εἴρηνται καὶ πάνυ τοι σεμνῶς, φύσιν δ' ὅμως
οὐκ ἔχει τινὰ τελευτῆσαί τε καὶ πραχθῆναι, ἐπεί, εἴ πως
ἄρα ἐνῆν, ἀδύνατον ἂν ἦν, ὥς γέ μοι δοκῶ, μὴ καὶ καιροῦ
τυχεῖν τινος εἰς φορὰν ὅλως καὶ διὰ τῶν πραγμάτων ἐπί-
δειξίν τινα εὑρεῖν καὶ πάροδον, εἰς τοσοῦτον ἤδη παρελ-
θόντα τὸν χρόνον. Ἐπεὶ δὲ λοιπὸν οὔτε πω καὶ νῦν γέγονεν οὔτε μήποτε γενήσεται—δῆλον γὰρ ἀναμετρουμένοις
καθόλου τἀνθρώπινα—ἡ διὰ τὴν τούτων ἀτυχίαν τῶν
πραγμάτων καθάπαξ ἀποχώρησις, ἤν τις τοῦτ' ἀξιοῖ,
κατάλυσίς τις ἔοικε τῷ ὄντι εἶναι τοῦ μεγίστου τε καὶ καλλίστου μέρους φιλοσοφίας, τοῦ πολιτικοῦ.

2   Ἐφιεμένῳ γὰρ πραγμάτων ἀνηνύτων καὶ μὴ ἄλλως
συμπλεκομένῳ, λείπεται παντελὴς ἀπραξία. Καίτοι μάλιστα ἔγωγε ᾤμην καὶ νῦν οἴομαι πολιτικὴν ἐφίεσθαι μὲν
τῶν εἰκότων καὶ σφόδρα ἐπὶ μεγίστων τε καὶ καλλίστων
ἐξεῖναι δείκνυσθαι καὶ κατορθοῦν, οὐ μὴν ἀλλὰ μὴ τυγ-
χάνουσαν, οἶμαι, ὡς ἄρα ἔξεστι πράττειν, τοῖς παροῦσι
χρῆσθαι καὶ παρεσκευάσθαι πρὸς ἅπασαν χώραν καὶ οἵαν
τ' εἶναι πρὸς ἅπασαν ὕλην, ὥσπερ ἄρα καὶ κυβερνητικὴν
ὁρῶμεν οὐκ ἐν εὐφορίᾳ πνευμάτων ἐνεργὸν μόνον, ἀλλὰ
καὶ πρὸς ἅπασαν ὥραν καὶ τύχην οὐκ ἐρραστωνευμένην,
οὐδ' ἀτόλμητον.

Chapter 36

But these, as we said, are merely words that have undergone no scrutiny nor been tested in practice, and although they are formulated in an elegant and quite noble way, it is still by nature impossible to accomplish or fulfill them. For if such a possibility somehow existed, it seems to me that it would have been impossible for someone not to find the right opportunity to fulfill them completely and to discover through deeds some demonstration or proof, given that so much time has now elapsed. Since they have neither been fulfilled until today nor will they be fulfilled in the future—this is obvious to anyone who considers human affairs in their entirety—complete withdrawal from social life on account of the failure of these issues in fact appears to be, were one to consider this, a kind of dissolution of the greatest and most beautiful part of philosophy, namely politics.

For absolute inactivity is all that is left to the person who   2
seeks impossible ventures and remains otherwise uninvolved. As for myself, I strongly believed in the past and continue to believe now that politics seeks what is proper and is able to show itself and succeed in the most important and crucial cases. I also believe that even when politics fails to operate properly, it employs the means at its disposal and prepares to confront any situation and any case, so far as it can. This is what we see happening with the art of helmsmen, who do not only function amid favorable winds, but remain vigorous and brave under any weather conditions or circumstances that might occur.

3   Πολλάκις δὲ αὐτὸς εἴκασα, κατασκοπούμενος ἐν
ἐμαυτῷ τὴν πολιτικὴν ταύτην ἀρετὴν καὶ ὅση ψυχῆς κατ-
όρθωσις, εὐφημίᾳ μὲν ἁπάσῃ πάντων τιμώντων καὶ λόγοις
μὲν ἐντελῶς ἀποδεδειγμένην τε καὶ ἀνευρημένην, οὐδέπω
δὲ ὡς ἀληθῶς καὶ τήμερον παντάπασιν ἔν τισιν ἐγνωσμένην,
μηδ᾽ ὅντινα ἄρα τῶν ἐξ ἀρχῆς ἄνθρωπον παντελῆ κατειρ-
γασμένον ταύτην καὶ κτησάμενον καὶ κατηνυκότα πάντων
τῶν ἑαυτῆς ἀμείωτον, καὶ εἰ μάλιστα ξυνεώρακε καὶ κατα-
μεμέτρηκεν ἐξειπὼν εἰς ἀκρίβειαν, παραπλησίως ἔχειν,
ὥσπερ ἄρα καὶ περὶ τὸ σωματικὸν τοῦτο κάλλος τόδε συμ-
βαῖνον ὁρῶμεν, ὃ ζωγραφοῦσι μὲν καὶ καταρρυθμίζουσιν
ἐντελῶς οἱ λόγοι, κτήσασθαι δὲ ἢ τοιοῦτο κατιδεῖν ἔν τινι
οὐχ οἷός τ᾽ ἄρ᾽ οὐδεὶς γέγονεν οὔτ᾽ ἔγνωμεν ἀλώβητον
ὁτῳοῦν παρόν, ἔστι δὲ ὅμως κάλλος ἐν ἀνθρώποις καὶ
πλεῖστον, εἰ καὶ μὴ πλῆρες καὶ πλεῖον ἄλλο ἄλλου.

4   Καὶ πολιτική τις, οἶμαι, ἀρετὴ πάντως ἔστι καὶ νοῦ καὶ
ψυχῆς εὐδοκίμησις, εἰ καὶ μὴ παντέλεια καὶ ὡς ἄρ᾽ οὐδεὶς
παντάπασι μὴ νεμεσήσαι· ξυμβαίνειν δὲ ταῦτα οὐ διά τινα
ἀναγκαίαν καὶ φυσικὴν ἀνυπαρξίαν, ὡς ἤδη τινὲς ἐνόμισαν, τἀγαθοῦ, ἀλλὰ διὰ τὸ τῆς ὕλης ἐμοὶ δοκεῖν, περὶ ἣν
ἀνάγκην ἔχει ἀρετή τε πᾶσα καὶ πρᾶξις καθορᾶσθαι, δυσ-
άγωγόν τε καὶ πολύνοσον καὶ πάντως πρὸς ἡντιναοῦν τῆς
συμμετρίας ἁμαρτίαν εὔτροπον.

I often drew inferences and examined carefully within 3
myself this political virtue and the extent to which it re-
forms the soul. Everyone honors it with great praise, and
they elaborate and describe it with detailed words, even
though until today it is truly impossible to discern it in anyone in its entirety, nor from the beginning of time did anyone succeed in employing it perfectly, possessing it fully, or
accomplishing it without being deprived of all its assets; and
if someone has closely examined and assessed this, he could
describe it with due precision, behaving much as we see
happening in the case of physical beauty: words can represent it and describe it in detail, yet no one has managed to
acquire it or to encounter something similar in another person, and we all know that beauty is not entirely faultless.
Despite this, beauty is a most important attribute among
mankind, even if it is imperfect and greater in one case than
in another.

I think that political virtue is assuredly the progress of 4
mind and soul, even if it is not absolutely perfect, as a consequence of which no one is completely immune to castiga-
tion. This happens not because good things do not exist by
necessity and by nature, as some people thought, but because of the fact, as I think, that the matter, in relation to
which all virtue and actions are by necessity considered, is
indomitable, liable to many aberrations, and, certainly, susceptible to every sort of entropy.

37

Τοιγαροῦν οὔτε κυβερνητικὴν οὔτε στρατηγικὴν οὔτ᾽ ἰατρικὴν οὔτ᾽ ἄλλην ἅπασαν ἢ τέχνην ἤ τινα ἄσκησιν καὶ ἐμπειρίαν εὑρήσει τις ἐντελῆ καὶ πρὸς τὰ σφέτερα αὐτῆς καθάπαξ καὶ ἐπὶ πάντων εὔδρομον, ἀλλὰ δι᾽ ἣν εἴρηται νῦν ἀνάγκην, ἐλλείπει καὶ πάντως ἔστιν ἐφ᾽ οἷς ἥττηται καὶ βουλομένοις ἐπιτιμᾶν τε καὶ καταμέμφεσθαι χώρα λοιπὸν ἐξέσται καὶ οὐκ ἂν ἔπαινός τις ἄκρατος εἴη κατὰ παντὸς ἀνδρός τε καὶ τεχνίτου καὶ πράγματος, ἀλλ᾽ οἱ μὲν ἄρα χρηστοὶ πάντα ἐπαινοῦσι καὶ πρὸς οὐδέν εἰσιν ἐπαχθεῖς, οὐδὲ βασκαίνουσιν, οὐδ᾽ ἐπιτιμῶσι, φιλανθρωπίᾳ τινὶ καὶ φύσεως εὐκολίᾳ μήτε βουλόμενοι μήτε περινοοῦντες ἀηδές τι καὶ φλαῦρον.

2   Οἱ δ᾽ ἀκριβέστεροι τῶν ἀνθρώπων καὶ σώφρονες ἄγανται μὲν καὶ καταμεμετρήκασιν, ἢν ἄρα τὰ πλείω τῆς κρείττονος καὶ ἀνεπιτιμήτου μοίρας καὶ ἀρετῇ καὶ λόγῳ κεκόσμηταί τῳ προσόντα, πάντα δ᾽ οὐ ζητοῦσιν, οὐδ᾽ οἴονται μὴν ἐξεῖναι, κατανενοήκασι δὲ ὅμως καὶ μετρίως ἔχουσι καὶ ξυγκεχωρήκασιν, ἢν ἄρα καὶ θατέρου μέρους τῆς ἐναντίας ἰδέας, ὥσπερ ἀναγκαῖόν τι μοιρίδιον κρᾶμα καὶ ἀπαραίτητον, φύσεως ἐνδείᾳ λώβημα συμβέβηκεν εἵλκῦσθαι, μὴ πάνυ δέ τοι πλεῖστον ᾖ, μηδὲ μάλιστα ἰσχύον.

Chapter 37

Accordingly, no one will find that the craft of steering, generalship, or medicine, or any other craft, activity, or skill is perfect and swiftly attains its goals in every case, but due to the necessity just mentioned they are wanting and assuredly fall short in certain respects, so that there will be room for anyone who wishes to castigate and blame them in the future. Nor would there be unmixed praise for a person, craftsman, or object, but good men praise everything and are aggrieved with nothing, and they feel no envy and find no fault, because their humanity and good temper mean that they do not wish or consider anything disagreeable or trivial.

Those who are more scrupulous and prudent, however, 2 express admiration and ponder whether the main portions of a superior and blameless fate are adorned in a person by the presence of virtue and reason, but they do not investigate everything or even consider this investigation possible. At the same time, they show understanding, moderation, and forgiveness if, with a person partaking in the opposite condition, a flaw happens to derive from the deficiency of nature, like a necessary and unavoidable admixture that determines our destiny, so long as this flaw is not too prevalent or particularly powerful.

38

Οἱ δὲ πολλοὶ τῶν ἀνθρώπων καὶ σφόδρα εἰσὶν αὐθάδεις καὶ τολμηροὶ καὶ κακοπράγμονες καὶ ἐπαχθεῖς καὶ κακοήθεις τῶν ἀλλοτρίων κριταὶ καὶ πρὸς πάνθ᾽ ὁμοῦ πράγματα καὶ ἀνθρώπους δυσνούστατοι καὶ κακόφρονες καὶ πάνυ τοι χαίρουσιν ἀηδῶς ἅπαντα πραττόμενα καὶ ἅπαντα ἀηδῶς ἀκούοντα καὶ λέγουσιν οὕτως αὐτοὶ μάλιστα καὶ καταμέμφονται ὡς ἥδιστα σφίσιν, ἁπάντων δὲ μόνα τὰ κακῶς ἔχοντα ζητοῦντες καὶ λελωβημένα, ἀείποτ᾽ ἀφθονίαν ἔχουσι βλασφημεῖν καὶ πάντως οὐδέποτ᾽ εἰσὶν ἐνδεεῖς ὧν ἐρῶσι καὶ οὐδένας λοιπὸν ἐῶσιν οὔτ᾽ ἀνθρώπους οὔτ᾽ οὐδὲν ἐπιτήδευμα τωθασμοῦ καὶ χλεύης τινὸς καὶ καταδρομῆς κρείττω, ἀλλ᾽ ἅπαντα μὲν ἀεὶ βούλονται σφόδρα καὶ ξυννοοῦσιν εἶναι φαῦλα, λέγουσι δὲ ὅμως κακῶς καὶ πλεῖν ἢ νοοῦσί τε καὶ βούλονται, πράττοντες, ὡς ἔοικεν, ἕκαστος τὰ σφέτερα αὐτῶν κρείττω δοκεῖν καὶ σφίσι λοιπὸν ὡς βελτίστοις προσέχειν ἢ μάλιστ᾽, οἶμαι, πρὸς τὰ οἰκεῖ᾽ ἀτυχήματα τοῦ καλοῦ καὶ ἁμαρτίας ξυνηγοροῦντες ἑαυτοῖς, ὡς ἁπάντων παραπλήσι᾽ ἐχόντων τε καὶ πασχόντων καὶ οὐδὲν ἐν ἀνθρώποις ὅλως ἀνεπιτίμητον.

2   Καὶ καθάπερ αἱ μεμψίμοιροι φύσει καὶ βάσκανοι γυναῖκες ἀείποτ᾽ ἀλλήλαις ἐντυγχάνουσαι καὶ συγγινόμεναι, σφόδρα ἔπειτ᾽ ὄπισθεν αἰτιῶνται καὶ κατηγοροῦσιν ἄλλη ἄλλης, τὰ καὶ τὰ φασὶ κατὰ τοῦ προσώπου, τὰ καὶ τὰ πρὸς τὴν ξύμπασαν τοῦ σώματος ἄρα φυήν, καὶ πάντως ὁτιοῦν λαμβάνουσι καὶ διαλοιδοροῦνται, αἱ πλείους ἐμοὶ δοκεῖν

Chapter 38

Most people are extremely stubborn, reckless, wicked, burdensome, and malicious judges of their fellow men; they are similarly ill-disposed and malignant against everything and everyone; they take great pleasure in all unpleasant deeds and in everything disreputable, and they themselves talk like this incessantly and take great pleasure in criticizing others. They only want what is base and shameful from everything, they always have an abundance of targets to scoff at, and they never lack something they love to mock. They accordingly let no person or pursuit rise above ridicule, jests, and invective, but they always want and believe everything to be terrible; their accusations, however, surpass what they think and desire, and they do this, apparently, because each of them considers his own achievements to be superior, so as to henceforth attract the attention of their fellow men to them as the best. More than anything else, they act like this, I think, in order to plead their own cause with regard to their personal moral mistakes and failures, since everyone is in the same condition and suffers from the same problems, and nothing in human affairs can be wholly free from criticism.

They are precisely like women who are by nature 2 faultfinding and envious, and who constantly meet up and converse with one another, but nevertheless afterward blame and hurl accusations at each other behind their backs and say thus and such regarding the woman's face or entire bodily appearance. They always discover some flaw to make fun of, although I think that most of them are more ill-

πάνυ τοι αἰσχίους οὖσαι, ὡς ἀληθῶς σπουδάζουσαι μή τι δοκεῖν ἀστεῖον ὅλως εἶναι καὶ χάριν ἡντινοῦν καὶ ὥραν ἀνεμέσητον, τὸν αὐτόν, οἶμαι, τρόπον οἱ πλείους τῶν ἀνθρώπων πρὸς τἀλλότρια βλέπουσιν ὀξὺ φαῦλα καὶ σφόδρα περινοοῦντες καταιτιῶνται καὶ προφέρουσιν ἡδέως, ὡς ἂν ἄρα μὴ δοκοῖεν αὐτοὶ κακῇ μόνοι μοίρᾳ συνόντες, ἀλλ' ἀμέλει πάντες ὁμοῦ καὶ μηδαμῶς ὂν ἐν τῇ φύσει τὸ τοῦ καλοῦ πλῆρες, ἀλλά τινα πλάνην οὖσαν τὴν εὐφημίαν καὶ ζήτησιν τἀγαθοῦ καὶ σύνθημα ἀνθρώπων καὶ λόγον ἄλλως.

39

Τοιγαροῦν ἅπαντα καταμέμφονται καὶ περιτρέπουσι καὶ οὐδὲν ὅ,τι σφίσι παρεῖται μὴ οὐ κακῶς λέγειν χρῆναι καὶ μάλιστα κατεπείγονται τοῦθ' οἱ φαῦλοι καὶ δρῶσιν ἐπὶ τοὺς σπουδαίους καὶ νομίζουσιν ἅπαντα λῆρον εἶναι καὶ οὐδὲν ἱερόν, ἤν τινά που ἴσως κατασκέψωνται τύχης ἀωρίαν καὶ νόσημα ξυμβὰν ἀνάγκῃ τινὶ δυσκόλῳ, σφόδρα ἀντιλαμβανόμενοι καὶ ἐπιτιμῶντες, οἱ δειλοὶ κατὰ τῶν ἀνδρείων, οἱ μικρολόγοι κατὰ τῶν ἐλευθέρων, οἱ ἀκόλαστοι κατὰ τῶν σωφρόνων, οἱ πάντα ἀπαίδευτοι κατὰ τῶν πεπαιδευμένων, οἱ συκοφάνται κατὰ τῶν ἀστείων καὶ εὐγενῶν.

favored than the women they accuse. In fact, they are trying to show that nothing is absolutely beautiful and that anything graceful and attractive has an aspect worthy of reproach. I think that most people observe the flaws of their fellow men with a similarly sharp eye and examine them very carefully and criticize them and happily disseminate the criticisms, so that they may not appear to be the only ones linked to a bad fate, but that everyone else also appears bad along with them. To put it in a few words, they want to show that nothing entirely good exists anywhere in nature, and that the praise of and search for goodness is merely an illusion, a construction of men, a term without meaning.

Chapter 39

They therefore reproach and undermine everything, and there is nothing about which they do not feel a need to express their censure. This is what base men in particular rush to do against decent men, they think that everything is folly and consider nothing holy; whenever they happen to spot a chance anomaly or defect caused by some troublesome necessity, they vehemently attack and censure it: cowardly people rail against brave ones, the captious against the magnanimous, the licentious against the prudent, the utterly uneducated against the educated, slanderers against decent, noble persons.

2   Καὶ τοίνυν, ὡς ἤδη νῦν εἴρηται, εἰς ἅπαντα ἔπεισιν
ἀναιδῶς, καὶ τὰ κάλλιστα, ἡ βασκανία καὶ κακοήθως παντὶ
σθένει δεῖν οἴεται μάλιστα ἐπιτίθεσθαι καὶ κατελέγχειν καὶ
οἷός τέ ἐστιν ἕκαστος ἄρα τῶν πολλῶν τε καὶ πάνυ φαύλων
τὰς τῶν ἀγαθῶν ἀνδρῶν εὐφημίας περιτρέπειν, κἂν ὅτι
μάλιστα ὦσιν ἀληθεῖς τε καὶ πρόδηλοι, λυμαινόμενος
ὁπωσοῦν καὶ πράττων μὴ παντάπασιν ὡς βελτίστοις καὶ
κατηνυκόσι προσέχειν τὸν νοῦν, οὐδ᾽ ἔστιν, ὡς ἀείποθ᾽
ὁρῶμεν, ἔπαινον ὁντιναοῦν ἀλώβητον εὑρεῖν, ἀλλ᾽ ἐκ-
πολιορκεῖται καθάπαξ ἀσπόνδῳ πολέμῳ καὶ πολυμηχάνῳ
τε καὶ κακοσχόλῳ καὶ παμπληθεῖ στρατοπέδῳ τῆς ἀρετῆς
ἡ τιμὴ πάντοθεν ἐκκρούοντι καὶ καταγνῦντι.

40

Ταῦτ᾽ ἄρα οὐδ᾽ ὁ περικλέϊστος ἀνὴρ ἐφ᾽ ὁτωοῦν καὶ
κατωρθωκὼς μάλιστα καθόλου δύναιτ᾽ ἂν περιγενέσθαι
καὶ παρελθεῖν ἅπασαν ἐπίβουλον καὶ βούλησιν καὶ γλῶτταν κακουργοῦσαν καὶ ὁ πλείστοις πάνυ τοι πολλοῦ τινος
ἄξιος εἶναι δοκῶν ἀρετῆς δή τινος χάριν καὶ δοκίμου τέ-
λους καὶ πλείστοις ὅσοις ὁσημέραι περιαντλούμενος τοῖς
ἐπαίνοις, ἔστιν ὅμως ὑφ᾽ ὧν ἀκούει κακῶς καί τινες ἔδοξαν
ἄρ᾽ ἐνίοτε καταδραμεῖν εὐκαίρως τἀνδρὸς καὶ παντάπασιν
οὐκ ἀπέτυχε χώρας ἡ βλασφημία οὔθ᾽ ἡδονῆς τινος

As I have already said, therefore, envy shamelessly at- 2
tacks everything, even what is most beautiful, and believes
that it must assault everything maliciously with all its might,
and disgrace it, and every member of this numerous crowd
of extremely wicked men does his best to undermine the
praises spoken in favor of good men, even if they are genuine and quite obvious, so that he causes harm and succeeds
in having other people not turn the slightest attention toward the best and most accomplished individuals. As we see
on every occasion, it is impossible to find any sort of irre-
proachable praise, but the honor of virtue is entirely besieged in an implacable war by a resourceful, malicious, and
multitudinous army, which surges forth from all sides and
batters against its walls.

Chapter 40

For these reasons, even the most renowned man who has
achieved a great deal in one respect could by no means prevail and evade every treacherous intention and knavish
tongue. Even the person who is considered by most people
to be extremely worthy due to his excellence and notable
performance, and who is inundated with much praise on a
daily basis, will doubtless be castigated by someone. Some
attackers occasionally appear to have inveighed against this
man at just the right moment, and their insults do not entirely miss their mark, and cause some pleasure to those
who hear them. The very person whom some have exam-

ἀκουόντων, καὶ ὃν λογιζόμενοί τινες καὶ καταμετροῦντες ἄγανται καὶ προφέρουσιν εἰκόνα καὶ τιμὴν φύσεως, ἕτεροι καταμέμφονται καὶ προβέβληνται καὶ κηρύττουσι καὶ ἀπελέγχουσιν εὖ μάλα τἀληθὲς ἀδικεῖσθαι καὶ τὰ μὴ ὄντα δοκεῖν τε καὶ θαυμάζεσθαι.

2   Καὶ μὴν ἔθ' ὁ παντάπασιν ἀναιδής τις εἶναι δοκῶν καὶ ἀνάρμοστος καὶ λελωβημένος ἀμέλει καὶ στιγματίας οὐ συνηγόρων καθάπαξ, οὐδὲ χρηστολογούντων ἀνδρῶν οὐκ ἀπέτυχεν, οὐδὲ κατακεκλήρωται καὶ παρεῖται συγκεχωρημένος παντελεῖ λοιπὸν κακῇ μοίρᾳ κατὰ τὴν Σικελικὴν παροιμίαν ἀπαίσιός τις ἐν λατομίαις, οὐδ' ἄρ' Ἀθήνησιν ἐς τὸ Κυνόσαργες κατακεκλήρωται συντελεῖν.

41

Οὕτω πολλή τις, ὡς ἔοικεν, ἀπιστία τἀγαθοῦ περιχωρεῖ καὶ οὔτ' εἰ ἔστιν οὔθ' ὅπερ ἐστὶ κατ' ἀνθρώπους, μάλιστ' εὐπετῶς καὶ ῥᾳδίως ἔχομεν ὑποδεῖξαι καὶ ὁρίσασθαι, ἀλλ' ἄνω τε καὶ κάτω καὶ πάντῃ πάντα περιτρέπεται καὶ περὶ τῶν αὐτῶν ἀνδρῶν ἐν ταῖς αὐταῖς σχεδὸν πράξεσι τἀναντιώτατα μάλιστ' ἀείποτε δοκοῦμέν τε καὶ ἀκούομεν, πολλοῖς μὲν ἐπαινουμένων, πολλοῖς δὲ βλασφημουμένων, καὶ νῦν μὲν ἀγαθῇ τετιμημένων δόξῃ, νῦν δὲ ἀπεστραμμένων ὡς παντάπασιν ἀνονήτων καὶ οὐδὲν ἱερῶν καὶ οὐδεμία παρ' ἀνθρώποις οὐκ ἔστι περὶ ὁτουοῦν συμφωνία, οὐδὲ

ined and carefully evaluated, and whom they admire and bring forward as an honorable example of human nature, others severely castigate and attack, and make public announcements and make it clear that truth is treated unjustly and that nonexistent qualities are held in repute and admired.

On the other hand, a person who appears utterly ruth- 2 less, unfit, patently dishonorable, and a culprit never seems to lack an advocate or someone to speak kindly of him. His lot is not complete misfortune, nor does he allow himself to yield to it like a miserable slave *in the mines,* in the words of the Sicilian proverb, nor is he doomed to end up like a bastard child *at Kynosarges* in Athens.

Chapter 41

So great, it seems, is the disbelief surrounding what is good, that we cannot very readily or easily prove or determine whether it actually exists or precisely what it is among men, but everything is turned on its head in many ways; with regard to the same people and on the basis of approximately the same deeds, we constantly form and hear quite contradictory evaluations, since these same persons are sometimes praised by many but at other times criticized by many; at times they are honored with sublime fame, while on other occasions they are rejected as utterly useless and unholy individuals, and there is no agreement among men

θέλησις, οὐδὲ κρίσις ἄρα κοινή, ἀλλ' ἃ τοῖσδ' ἀρέσκει καὶ
πρόσκεινται καὶ προσέχουσιν εὖ μάλα, τοῖς δὲ οὔ, καὶ ἃ
τοῖσδε αὖθις ἥδιστα, πολλῷ μᾶλλον ἐκείνοις κατωλιγώρηται.

2   Καίτοι τί λέγω; ἃ νῦν νομίζομεν, ἔπειτ' ὀλίγον ὕστερον
οὔ, οὔθ' ἡμῖν αὐτοῖς αὖθις ξυνδοκεῖ καὶ ἀπανδάνει τὰ πρὶν
κάλλιστα καὶ παρεώραται καὶ οὐδὲν εἰς τέλος ἡδὺ οὔθ' ὃ
φέρειν οὔτ' ἐπαινεῖν ἀείποτε δὴ καὶ πάντ' ἔχομεν, ἀλλ' ἢ
μεταβάλλομεν ἡμεῖς ἢ μεταβέβληται καὶ ἢ τὰ μὲν εὖ, τὰ δ'
ὡς ἑτέρως ἔχει, ἢ τὰ μὲν νοσοῦμεν ἡμεῖς, τὰ δ' ὑγιῶς τε
καὶ ὀρθῶς ξυνεωράμεθα.

3   Χαλεπαίνουσι δὲ πρὸς δούλους δεσπόται καὶ ὅλως τοὺς
ὑπὸ χεῖρα καὶ κακῶς ἀεὶ λέγουσι καὶ μεμψιμοιροῦσι καὶ
οὐδέν εἰσιν ἡδεῖς, οὐδ' εὔκολοι. Καὶ μὴν ἔτι δοῦλοι πρὸς
δεσπότας ἅπαντα κρύφα διαλοιδοροῦνται κακουργοῦντες
καὶ ὑπολογιζόμενοι καὶ καταιτιῶνται πάνθ' ὁμοῦ γιγνόμενα
πράγματα, τὰ μὲν δικαίως, ὡς ἔοικε, τὰ δὲ φυσικῇ βασκανίᾳ, καὶ ἄλλως, ὥσπερ ἅπαντες ἄνθρωποι, τἀλλότρια
καταμέμφονται, μὴ τῶν σφετέρων ἐπιστρεφόμενοι, καὶ τὰ
μὲν τῶν ἄλλων, ᾗ δὴ χεῖρον εἴρηται ἢ ἔχει ἢ ὅλως ὁπωσοῦν
ἀκαίρως καὶ δυστυχῶς εἴργασται, ταχύτατα σφόδρα ξυν-
εῖδόν τε καὶ κατανενοήκασι καὶ προσέσχον μάλα τὸν νοῦν
καὶ κατέδραμον ὅλως ἐπὶ γλώττῃ καὶ ἀκοῇ πάσῃ καταπομ-
πεύοντες καὶ βδελυρῶς καταμωκώμενοι, τὰ δὲ σφέτερα
αὐτῶν οὐ ξυνορῶσιν οὔθ' ὅλως καταλογίζονται καὶ ὑπο-
νοοῦσι καὶ δεδίασι, παραπλήσι' ἴσως ἢ καὶ χείρω, οὐδ' ἔτι

on either topic, no goodwill, no common judgment. What some people like, welcome, and pay great attention to, others do not want; while on the other hand, what some people consider most pleasing, others despise even more.

But what am I saying? That which we now believe, after 2 some time we reject, while beautiful objects we previously were fond of and that pleased us, we later on disregard. Nothing continues to bring pleasure right up to the end, nor can we always endure or praise anything entirely. Either we change it, or it is changed; and it either turns out to some extent well, but to some extent otherwise, or we are partially sickened by these things, and partially pay attention to them in a healthy and proper manner.

Masters grow angry with their slaves and with their sub- 3 ordinates in general, and always belittle and criticize them, without ever being agreeable or easygoing. The slaves, meanwhile, make secret fun of their masters, and contriving wickedness of all sorts, they reckon the situation up and blame them for everything that happens, sometimes rightly so, it seems, but at other times driven by their innate envy; and on top of this, like all men, they expose the shortcomings of other people without realizing their own. They very quickly acknowledge and fully comprehend mistakes made by others, be they bad words, bad deeds, or any other untimely and unfortunate activity; they turn all their attention to such mistakes, rush to scoff at them so that everybody talks and learns about them, and make fun of them in a truly disgusting manner. Yet they do not see their own mistakes, nor do they fully recognize, suspect, or worry about them, although they are presumably the same as those of other people or even worse. They do not yet see what sort of

πω ξυνιᾶσι τίνες ἄν ποτ᾽ εἶεν αὐτοὶ ἢ τίποτ᾽ ἄρα καὶ
δράσαιεν ἢ ὅπως ἂν διαθεῖντο, ταὐτὰ βουκολοῦντες κατὰ
τὴν παροιμίαν καὶ τῶν αὐτῶν ἡμμένοι καὶ παραπλησίων
ἔργων τε καὶ πραγμάτων καὶ γενόμενοι λοιπὸν ἐργάται
πράξεων αὐτοί, ὧν ἐπὶ τοὺς ἄλλους ᾐτιάσανθ᾽ ὡς ἂν μὴ
καλῶς εἰργασμένων, μηδ᾽ ἠνυσμένων.

4   Καὶ τὰ μὲν ξένα κομιδῇ βαρεῖς τε καὶ φορτικοὶ κρίνουσι
φαῦλα καὶ παραφέρουσι καὶ προφέρουσιν εὐθαρσῶς ἀεί-
ποτ᾽ εἰς αἰτίασιν ἀναίδην καὶ πλατεῖ στόματι, ὡς δή τινες
ἄρ᾽ ὄντες αὐτοὶ σεμνοὶ σεμνῶς, παντάπασιν ἀρτιουργοὶ
καὶ ἀλώβητοι καὶ πᾶσαν ἀποδραπετεύσαντες ἁμαρτίαν καὶ
πάνθ᾽ ὧν ἂν ἅψαιντο καθάπαξ ἄνοσοι καὶ ἐργατικώτατοι,
ἀγνοοῦσι δὲ τὰ οἰκεῖ᾽ αὐτῶν ἐντεῦθεν μᾶλλον ἢ τἀλλότρια
ἐμπλέκοντες τῇ ἐπηρείᾳ ταύτῃ καὶ δυσχρηστίᾳ τοῖς καλῶς
ἔπειτ᾽ αὐτὰ σκοπουμένοις, παραπλησίως ἴσως ἢ καὶ χεῖρον
ἔχοντα, καὶ σφόδρα αὐτοὶ τῶν σφετέρων ἐπαχθεῖς ἐλέγχονται κατήγοροι καὶ κριταὶ καὶ δύσνοι μάλιστα πρότερον ἢ
τῶν ἀλλοτρίων καὶ ὧν ἐν νῷ εἶχον, ὥστε οὐ τὸν οἴκοι
πλοῦτον, φαίη τις ἂν κατὰ τὴν παροιμίαν, ἀλλ᾽ ὡς ἀληθῶς
τὴν ἔσω πενίαν κατ᾽ αὐτοὺς καὶ νόσον ἐκτραγῳδοῦσι καὶ
κακοὶ κακῶς προφέρουσι, σεμνολογοῦντες μέν, ἀλλ᾽
ἁλισκόμενοι, καὶ φρόνημα μέν, ὡς δοκοῦσι, μέγιστον ἐπιδεικνῦντες καὶ προβαλλόμενοι, ἡττημένοι δὲ πάνυ τοι ἔν-
δον ἐν σφίσιν αὐτοῖς καὶ ταπεινοὶ καὶ παμμόχθηροι.

people they are, how they might perhaps have reacted, or what route they would have followed had they tended to the same matters, as the proverb says, as the people they censure, and had they been engaged with the same or similar tasks and issues, thus becoming themselves agents of the activities they censure others for not undertaking properly or not accomplishing at all.

Grievous and vulgar as they are, they regard the affairs of 4 other people as entirely bad, and they make these allegations and pronounce them with no hesitation, always shamelessly and in a loud voice, as if they themselves were majestically majestic, conducted all their affairs successfully with no errors, avoided every single mistake, and were thoroughly sound and most industrious in every activity they engaged in. They do not realize, however, that they eventually hurl this abuse and distress against their own shortcomings rather than those of others, which to the mind of anyone who will examine the situation carefully are presumably the same or worse than those of others. They are deeply disgraced by being grievous accusers and ill-affected judges first and foremost of their own disadvantages rather than of those of others and of the persons they were determined to expose. Someone could thus say, in light of the proverb, that they do not really expose *the wealth of their household* but in fact their inner poverty and sickness, and they publicize the fact of their wretchedness in a wretched manner. They speak solemnly but are caught in their own trap; they think that they can put on display and promote their proud spirit, but they are in fact defeated inside themselves, being worthless and thoroughly wicked.

5 Ὥσπερ δὴ καὶ Διογένης τοὺς κατ᾽ αὐτὸν κομπώδεις καὶ ἀλαζόνας τοῖς κεχρυσωμένοις εἴκασε βέλεσιν, ἃ δὴ λαμπρὰ πάντως ἔξω δοκοῦντα καὶ προδεδειγμένα, σίδηρός εἰσι τἄνδον καὶ ἴσως ἰοῦ πλέως, ὡς δὴ καὶ οὗτοι σφόδρα μεγαληγορίαν τινά, τῶν ἀλλοτρίων ἐπόπται, προδείκνυνται καὶ καταιτιῶνται τἄλλα σεμνοί, λελήθασι δὲ τὰ ἑαυτῶν σφόδρα ἔσω νενοσηκότα καὶ δυστυχῆ φέροντες.

42

Πεφύκασι δ᾽ εἰς τοῦτο τῶν ἀνθρώπων οὐκ ὀλίγοι τινές—οὐδ᾽ εὐαρίθμητοι—ἀλλ᾽ ἅπαντες σχεδόν εἰσι τῶν ἀλλοτρίων ἐπαχθεῖς ἔργων τε καὶ πράξεων ἐπιγνώμονες καὶ νεμεσηταὶ καὶ οὐδεὶς ὅστις οὔ, οὐδ᾽ ἴσός ἐστιν αὐτῷ καὶ τοῖς ἄλλοις. Καίτοι καὶ τοῦτό γ᾽ ἐνίοτε διὰ βασκανίαν οἱ φαῦλοι καὶ χείρους κατὰ τῶν βελτιόνων καὶ ἀστειοτέρων ἀνδρῶν βούλονται καὶ οὔτε φασὶν οὔτ᾽ οἴονται ἄμεινον ἐκείνους ἔχειν τι μεταχειρίσαι, περὶ ὧν ἀμέλει σπουδάζουσιν, ἢ κατὰ σφᾶς αὐτούς, ἀπιστοῦσί τε ὅλως ἀεὶ καὶ τἀναντία λέγουσιν, ἢν ἄρα περὶ αὐτῶν ἀρετὴν ἡντιναοῦν καὶ δοκίμησιν ἠνυσμένην πυνθάνωνται, ἥν, οἶμαι, μὴ ξυνίσασι σφίσι δεδυνῆσθαι.

2 Ἃ γὰρ δὴ καὶ σφᾶς ᾠήθησαν κατειργάσθαι, μόγις μὲν ἴσως, ἀλλ᾽ ὅμως καὶ τοῖς ἄλλοις κατατίθενται καὶ ξυγχωροῦσιν, ἃ δὲ μή, βασκαίνουσιν ὡς ἔπειθ᾽ οἷόν τέ ἐστι τοῖς

Just as Diogenes used to compare those of his contempo- 5
raries who were arrogant and boastful to gilded arrows,
which on the outside appear quite splendid and beautiful,
but whose interior is iron and perhaps full of rust, so too
these overseers of the mistakes of others talk big and with a
pompous look inveigh against the mistakes of others, but
unbeknownst to them, their internal condition is profoundly diseased and wretched.

Chapter 42

Many people—not a small number—are naturally disposed toward this condition, but nearly all of them are unpleasant critics and arbiters of the works and deeds of other
persons, no one is an exception to this rule, and no one is
willing to consider himself equal to others. Nonetheless,
envy sometimes drives wicked, evil people to wish to hurl
this evil as well upon those who are better and more cultured than they are themselves; they do not admit or believe
that the latter can accomplish anything better than they can
in their area of expertise. They generally express disbelief
and always advance objections, if they find out about some
virtuous deed or achievement, which they know, I think,
that they cannot themselves attain.

For what they believe they have also accomplished, they 2
necessarily acknowledge and accept, even with difficulty,
that other people can accomplish as well. But as for what
they are unable to accomplish, they grow jealous against the

ἀρίστοις, καὶ τῆς φύσεως αὐτῆς κατεξανίστανται καὶ κατηγοροῦσιν ὡς οὐκ ἐξὸν ὅλως καὶ περιτρέπειν παντὶ σθένει
χρῆναι νομίζουσι καὶ καταμετρεῖν εἰς ἑαυτοὺς ὅρους, ἅ τ᾽
ἔξεστιν ἅ τε μή, καὶ τὸ μὲν κατ᾽ αὐτοὺς δοκεῖν σπουδάζουσι
παντέλειον, ἢν δέ τι καὶ πλέον ἀκούωσι, τοῦτο μὴ σωφρο-
νεῖν, καλοῦσι δὲ τὸ μὲν φύσεως καὶ πέρας ἀνθρώποις αὐτό,
τὸ δὲ ἄλλο τι λοιπὸν καὶ δαιμόνιον καὶ κατοχήν τινα καὶ
μανίαν.

43

Πάσχουσι δὲ τοῦθ᾽, ὡς ἔοικεν, οὐχ οἱ ἄλλοι μόνον
ὁμότεχνοι πρὸς ὁμοτέχνους καὶ συνασκηταὶ πάντως ἡντιναοῦν αἵρεσιν, ἀλλ᾽ ἥψαθ᾽ ὡς ἀληθῶς ἡ νόσος αὕτη σφόδρα
καὶ τῶν ἐν λόγοις. Ὃ καὶ πολλάκις ξυνορῶν ἐν ἐμαυτῷ
κατεθαύμασα καὶ λελύπημαι τὴν κοινὴν ἁμαρτίαν σοφίας,
ὥσπερ τἄλλ᾽ ἅπαντα, καὶ τύχην καὶ ὅπως ἀεὶ βάλλομεν
ἕκαστος ἀλλήλους ἐκ τἀφανοῦς σπουδῇ καὶ προθυμίᾳ
πάσῃ καὶ καταστρέφομεν, τὸ κράτος ἑαυτοῖς μόνοις ἅπαντες κατακληροῦν ἀγῶνα προτιθέμενοι, καὶ ἀλλήλων τὰ
χείρω καθορῶντες καὶ καταμωκώμενοι, τὰ ἡμέτερα λοιπὸν
αὐτῶν ὡς, οἶμαι, ἔχει καὶ αὐτὰ παραπλήσι᾽, οὐχ ὁρῶμεν

best persons, because these people are able in their turn to accomplish this, and they revolt against nature itself, affirm that this cannot possibly happen, and assume that they must vigorously knock down the accomplishments of others and measure what can and cannot be done by their own standards. They rush to show that their own accomplishments are perfect in all respects, but if they hear that something better has been done, they claim that this is the result of stupidity. They call their own accomplishment a product of nature and the culmination of human success, whereas the achievements of others are the result of demonic possession and madness.

Chapter 43

It seems that it is not only artisans who suffer from this envy with regard to their fellow artisans, and in general collaborators in any enterprise whatsoever, but that this sickness has in fact infected scholars to a large extent as well. I recognized this many times in myself and I was astonished and distressed by this common affliction and the misfortune that affects wisdom as well as everything else. I was also distressed to see how we constantly attack each other in secret with great zeal and enthusiasm, and are destroyed, all of us maintaining that only we ourselves have been accorded distinction in the contest, whereas we see only the worst in other people and laugh at them, without seeing, I think, that each of us is in the same position. We suffer from

ἕκαστος καὶ νοσοῦμεν μὲν τὰ οἰκεῖα, νοσοῦμεν δὲ τἀλλότρια, πλεῖν ἢ ἔχει κρίνοντες ἀμφότερα, τῇ μὲν φιλαυτοῦντες, τῇ δὲ βασκαίνοντες, τοσαῦτ᾽ ἐπαινοῦντες τῶν
ἄλλων, ὅσα προδήλως τῶν ἡμετέρων ἥττηται καὶ παρ᾽ ὧν
οὔτ᾽ ἐκείνοις οὐδὲν πλέον, ὡς ἔοικεν, οὔτε τοῖς χαριζο-
μένοις ἡμῖν ἡτισοῦν ζημία μὴ βέλτιον ἐκείνων ἔχειν.

2   Καὶ τοσούτου μέχρις ἐπαινοῦμεν, ὡς ἔπειτ᾽ ἐξεῖναι καὶ
μείζους αἰτίας προσάπτειν, καὶ παρασκευὴν ἀνύποπτον,
οἶμαι, ποιούμεθα τῆς ἐν νῷ κακοηθείας τὴν δοκοῦσαν ταύτην εὐκολίαν καὶ τὸ μέτριον τῆς εὐφημίας, πάντ᾽ ἔχει,
φάσκοντες, εὖ, τὰ καὶ τὰ ὅμως εἰ προσῆν, ἀναίτιον παντάπασι τοὔργον ἂν ἦν, καὶ παρεντίθεμεν ἴσως, ἃ μὴ προσόντα
μεγίστην ἐπιδήλως δείκνυσι τὴν ζημίαν καὶ τὴν αἰσχύνην,
καὶ λογιζόμεθα τοῦ λοιποῦ δὴ κρείττους πολλῷ δοκεῖν, ἃ
μὴ καλῶς ἔχει, κατανενοηκότες αὐτοί.

44

Ἀξιοῦμεν δ᾽ ἀείποτε καὶ σπουδάζομεν μέγιστον ἐν βίῳ
καὶ κάλλιστον δοκεῖν εἶναι τὸ χρῆμα τοῦτο σοφίας καὶ
ἀντὶ πάντων, εἴ τῳ παρείη, καὶ πολὺς ὁ περὶ τούτου λόγος
καὶ μέγιστος ἀγὼν καὶ οἷός τέ ἐστιν ἕκαστος ἐνταῦθα
μάλιστα φιλαυτεῖν τε καὶ κινδυνεύειν καὶ παραβάλλεσθαι
πρὸς ἅπαντ᾽ ἄνθρωπον, ἢν ἄρα μὴ πείθοιτο· ἐπισκεπτόμε-
νοι δὲ καὶ φιλοκρινοῦντες ἑκάστοτε πάντας, ὅσοι καθόλου

our own affairs, but we also suffer from the affairs of others, in both cases forming judgments beyond our abilities, in the former case due to self-love, in the latter due to envy. With regard to the achievements of others, we praise only those that are clearly inferior to our own and from which no good will come for them, it seems, nor will any harm whatsoever come to us who grant this concession.

And we praise just far enough that it will later be possible 2 to raise greater accusations. In my view, we produce this apparent clemency and moderate praise as an unsuspected intrigue of our malicious minds; we claim that everything is fine, but if thus and such were added, the achievement would be absolutely perfect, and we list precisely those items whose absence clearly shows that the work is utterly faulty and shameful. So from this point onward we consider ourselves far more excellent, because we spotted on our own the weaknesses of our peers.

Chapter 44

We constantly believe and try to show that wisdom is the most significant and beautiful possession in our life, and that if someone possesses it, he needs nothing else. There has been much discussion and intense debate about this matter, and with wisdom in particular every person can have self-confidence, take risks, and enter into competition with anyone who is unpersuaded. But every time we examine and make careful judgments of all the individuals who engage

περὶ τοὺς λόγους ἔχουσι καὶ φιλοπονοῦσι κοινόν, φασιν, ἄεθλον, εἰ δὲ βούλει, κοινόν τινα τοῦτον Ἑρμῆν, πάντ᾽ οἰόμεθα τρόπον κολούειν ἑκάστου τὴν δόξαν καὶ ἀποφλαυρίζειν πάντως ὁτιοῦν, ὡς μὴ καλῶς ἄρ᾽ ἔχοντος, καὶ ἥδιστ᾽ ἂν ἔχοι πάνυ τοι, εἰ μὴ πλείστου ἄξιος μήτ᾽ εἴη τῶν ἄλλων, μηδὲ δοκοίη μηδείς, κέρδος τοῦθ᾽ ἑαυτοῖς τιθέμενος ἕκαστος, ὡς ἂν δὴ μόνος τις αὐτὸς νομίζοιτο παντέλειος καὶ μόνος τἀγαθὸν ἔχων καὶ βαθύγειον καὶ πολύχουν καὶ παμφόρον, οἶμαί, τινα σοφίαν καρπούμενος, καί, ἃ λιμώττουσιν ἕκαστος, σφόδρα εὔπορος ὤν, ἐν οἷς γε τοὺς ἄλλους δηλαδὴ ξυνορῷ καὶ κατελέγχοι λειπομένους τοῦ καλλίστου καὶ παραγομένους ὑπ᾽ ἀμαθίας ἀμέλει καὶ παραθέοντας, αὐτὸς ἔπειθ᾽ ἱκανὸς ὤν, ὡς ἔοικε, μόνος ἱκνεῖσθαι καὶ χρῆσθαι, ἅτε κατανενοηκὼς ᾗ τε καλῶς ἔχει καὶ ᾗ μή.

2 Ἀγνοοῦμεν δ᾽, ὡς ἔοικε, πρῶτον μὲν τοσαύτην ὀλιγότητα τῆς σοφίας βουλόμενοι καὶ κατηγοροῦντες καὶ σπουδὴν ταύτην διὰ τὴν τοσαύτην ὀλιγότητα πάντως ἀποδεικνῦντες ἐμοὶ δοκεῖν ἀνήνυτον, ἔπειτ᾽ ὀλίγου τινὸς ἄξιον, ὃ πάντων ἀντάξιον εἶναι βουλόμεθα, προδήλως πράττοντες δοκεῖν. Εἰ γὰρ δὴ τοῦτο πανάληθες καὶ πρόδηλον—ὡς οὐκ οἶδ᾽ εἴ τι τῶν ἄλλων ἁπάντων—ὡς ἕκαστα τῶν πραγμάτων ἐκ τῶν μετιόντων αὐτά, μᾶλλον δὲ τῶν ὅλως μετασχόντων κρίνεται καὶ θαυμάζεται διά τινα τῶν ἀνδρῶν πάντως ἀστειότητα καὶ εὐχρηστίαν, ἕκαστος δ᾽ ἡμῶν οὐδένα τῶν αἱρεσιωτῶν καὶ ὁμοτέχνων πλείστου

with education and compete in the same contest as we do or, if you will, *share in our luck,* as they say, we assume that we should discredit everyone's fame however we can and disparage his activities in every way possible, as if there were no good in them. It would be a source of great satisfaction, if no one was or appeared to be more worthy than anyone else, and everyone would consider this a personal advantage, in that he who reaps the harvest of deep-soiled, fertile, fruitful wisdom would alone, I believe, be taken to be utterly perfect, the sole possessor of this blessing. In addition, while everyone else starved, he would be well provided for in the aspects in which he looks at others and censures them for lacking what is most important, that is, wisdom, and for being misled and gone astray as a consequence of their ignorance, while he alone would be capable of achieving this most important thing and of using it, it seems, because he has completely understood what is good and what is not.

When we want wisdom to be thus restricted, and chide 2 those who do not support this idea and exhibit profound eagerness for this restriction, we do not realize, I think, first of all, that we demonstrate that wisdom is utterly unachievable, and second that the very thing we patently want to show through our deeds to be worth just as much as everything else combined, is worth very little. For if it is absolutely true and more than obvious—and I am not conscious that a more fitting example exists—that every situation is judged by those who pursue it, or rather those who have participated deeply in it, and that this situation is admired due to the culture and abilities of its followers, it is likewise true that when one of us attempts to constantly show that none of his peers in their chosen profession or fellow artisans is

ἄξιον ἀείποτε πειρᾶται δεικνῦναι καὶ κατελέγχειν, περίεισι
δ᾽ εἰς αὑτόν τινα τὸν βουλόμενον ἀεὶ παρὰ τῶν ἄλλων
ταὐτὸ τοῦτο, ὥσπερ δή τις κοινὸς ἔρανος τῆς τέχνης, συλ-
λογίσασθαι δὴ τοῦ λοιποῦ χρή, τίνα δή ποτε θύραν καθ᾽
ἡμῶν τε καὶ τοῦ μεγίστου χρήματος τῆς σοφίας ἠνοίξαμεν
τοῖς φιλοσκώμμοσιν ἐπεγγελᾶν τε καὶ διαλοιδορεῖσθαι
πλατεῖ στόματι, ὡς ἄρ᾽ οὐδὲν ὄντα τὰ καθ᾽ ἡμᾶς ἄλλο
πράγματα ἢ λῆρόν τινα μόνον ὡς ἀληθῶς καὶ βασκανίαν
καὶ οὐδὲν ἱερὸν ὅλως οὔθ᾽ ἓν τοῦτο μόνον χρήσιμον μεταχειρίσαι, ὅπως ἂν εἴη τις αἰδὼς παρὰ τὸν βίον καὶ χώρα τῷ
συστήματι.

45

Ἀλλ᾽ ἔγωγ᾽ ἴσως ἐμαυτοῦ χάριν, ὦ φιλότης, οὐκ ἂν ἐπι-
τιμῶν εἴην δίκαιος τοῖς οὕτω διὰ φιλαυτίαν ἀλόγιστον
οὐ μόνον ἑαυτοὺς καταισχύνουσι καὶ καταστρεφομένοις,
ἀλλὰ καὶ τῷ καλλίστῳ καὶ πολυεράστῳ σφίσι σπουδάσμα-
τι, τῇ παιδείᾳ, λυμαινομένοις πρὸς τὴν ἐν ἀνθρώποις ὑπὸ
τῶν πολλῶν εὐδοξίαν.

2   Καὶ γὰρ καὶ πρότερον εἶπον ἀρχόμενος καὶ νῦν ταὐτὸ
τοῦτ᾽ ἐρῶ, ὡς ὄφελον μὲν μήποθ᾽ οὕτω διατεθῆναι,
ἀπετράπην δ᾽ ὅμως τῶν λόγων ἐν ἄλλοις, ὡς ἄν τῳ δόξαι,
πράγμασι, καὶ ἧς ἄρα πρότερον, οὐκ οἶδ᾽ ὡς εἴ τις τῶν
ἄλλων, ἠράσθην σφόδρα ἐν αὐτοῖς εὐκλείας καὶ ἥλων
παντάπασιν ἐμμανῶς, καὶ αὐτὸς οἶσθα, περιφρονήσας ἐπιδήλως καὶ τοῖς ἄλλοις σπουδάζουσιν ὑπεκστάς, προει-
λόμην ἄττα δὴ καὶ νῦν εἰμί.

worth much, and attempts to disgrace them, this is always redirected from the others toward the very person who seeks it, as if it were a free gift of our craft available to everyone. We must therefore consider the gate we opened to those who are fond of scoffing, so as to allow them to laugh at and freely insult both us and the most important possession in the world, wisdom, by saying that our issues are nothing else but in fact some trifle or malignity, not revered at all but useful only for a single purpose, namely to help us procure some respect in our life and some living space for our community.

Chapter 45

But for my own sake, dear friend, I would not be fair if I castigated those who due to their irrational self-love do not merely embarrass and destroy themselves but also dishonor the most beautiful pursuit, which they much desire, namely education, at the expense of the good repute it enjoys among most people.

Although I said it before in my introduction, I shall now 2 repeat the same point: I wish that matters were not disposed this way, but since they are, I turned my attention from intellectual pursuits toward different occupations, as anyone can see. And the fame from education, which as far as I know no one in the past loved more than I did, and by which I was madly captivated, this fame I came to openly despise, as you know yourself, and making way for other scholars I preferred instead the activities in which I am currently engaged.

3   Κατωλιγωρηκὼς οὕτω δὴ λοιπὸν ἀναίδην τοῦ πράγματος καὶ καταπροέμενος, χαλεπὸς οὐκέτ᾽ ἂν εἴην, οὐδὲ δυσ-
χεραίνοιμι τοῖς ὁτιοῦν εἰς αὐτὸ καθυβρίζουσι καὶ λυμαινομένοις, οὔτ᾽ ἐμαυτῷ συνηγορῶν ἴσως ἤδη—πῶς γάρ; ὃς
ἐν ἄλλοις ἔχω νῦν εἶναι—οὔτ᾽ ἀνάγκην βοηθείας τινὸς
ἔχων καὶ συμμαχίας εἰς τοὔργον, ὅπερ ἐκ πολλοῦ παρεῖδον,
ἕτερα ἀνθελόμενος καὶ προσέχειν ὑπ᾽ ἀνάγκης, οἶμαί, τινος ἀτρέπτου τὸν ἅπαντα βίον ἀμέλει προηγμένος.

4   Οὗ δὴ χάριν ἄρ᾽ ἔγωγε καὶ μέσην αὐτὴν δέδηγμαι τὴν
καρδίαν καὶ μεμνημένος οὐκ ἔχω φέρειν, ὅπως, ἐν αὐτῷ
μέσῳ πλῷ τῆς σοφίας καὶ ἴσως οὔρια πλέων, ἀθρόον, οὐκ
οἶδ᾽ ὅπως, πρύμναν ἐκρουσάμην, καὶ τρέχων ἄλλην, ἄλλην
δὴ μεταβέβληκα. Ἔπλεον μὲν γὰρ εὖ μάλα δὴ καὶ προὐθυ-
μούμην ἀνύτων τὸν τοῦ βίου σκοπὸν περὶ τοὺς λόγους
αὐτούς· ἔπειτα ἐξαίφνης, ὥσπερ ἑκουσίῳ τινὶ καὶ χειροποι-
ήτῳ χρησάμενος ἀντιπνοίᾳ, ναυαγεῖν εἱλόμην καὶ προσ-
ταλαιπωρῶ μὲν ἔτ᾽ ἀμέλει ζητῶν ἄρα καὶ πλανώμενος
ἐκεῖνον τὸν ἔρωτα—μὴ γὰρ οὕτω δὴ μανείην, ὡς παντάπασιν ἀφεῖσθαι τῶν καλῶν παιδικῶν—οὐκ ἔχω δ᾽ ὅμως ὅστις
ἂν καὶ γενοίμην, οὐδ᾽ ἀσφάλειάν τιν᾽ εὑρίσκων, οὐδ᾽ ἐφ-
ικνούμενος, ὥσπερ ἐξ ἀρχῆς ὥρμησα, ἀλλ᾽ ἀνάγκη πάντως
ἀπαραιτήτῳ συνὼν ἑκάστοτε δυσχερείᾳ κατανλεῖσθαι
μυρίᾳ καὶ πρὸς κύματα διαμιλλᾶσθαι καὶ χειμῶνα φροντίδων ἄλλοτ᾽ ἄλλων, ὧν τὸ μὲν παρῆλθεν ἤδη, τὸ δ᾽ ἀεὶ
καταλαμβάνει κατὰ τὴν παροιμίαν καὶ οὐκ ἐῶσιν ἀτρεμεῖν
ὅλως, οὐδ᾽ ἅπτεσθαι μήν, οὐδ᾽ ἐπιχειρεῖν, οἶμαι, πρὸς ἅ τις
ἂν ἐρῴη μάλιστα καὶ νοῦν ἔχοι.

Given that I so shamelessly neglected and abandoned 3 education this way, I should not be harsh with or distressed by those who insult and dishonor it, nor perhaps should I defend myself—how could I, who now have other interests, do that?—nor do I need any help or support for an activity I abandoned long ago, choosing other activities instead and being induced by some inflexible force, I think, to devote my whole life to this.

This has accordingly gnawed away at the core of my 4 heart, and I cannot bear to recall how I somehow suddenly backed water, changed direction, and followed a completely different route, while I was in the midst of my voyage toward wisdom and was sailing with favorable winds. That was a pleasant journey, and I desired to locate the purpose of my life around education itself. Then suddenly it was as if I encountered an adverse wind, which I myself welcomed and engendered. I chose to sink and I am now still wandering around and suffering hardships as I seek to find my old love again—for I am not so insane as to completely forget my youthful passion. And yet, I do not know who I should be, I cannot find any kind of security, nor can I return to the point from which I started initially. To the contrary, I live with some constant, inevitable constraint to be exhausted by myriad problems and battle against waves and storms that arise from different anxieties each time. As soon as one dangerous wave has passed, another always overtakes me, as the proverb says, and I think that they do not allow me even a moment's respite or let me engage in or attempt the activities I love most and toward which I am inclined.

46

Τῷ ὄντι γὰρ πολλή τις ἔοικεν ἀνωμαλία καὶ ζάλη κατ-
έχειν τῶν ἐλλογίμων καὶ πεπαιδευμένων ἐκείνους ἀνδρῶν,
ὅσοι τοὺς λόγους λειποτακτήσαντες, φέροντες ἑαυτοὺς
ἐνεχείρισαν κοσμικαῖς, οἶμαί, τισι μικρολογίαις καὶ θορύ-
βοις καὶ πράγμασιν, οἷς ἀεὶ παραμένειν ἀνάγκην ἔχουσιν
ἄτρεπτον καὶ τὸν πλεῖστον καταδαπανᾶν καιρόν τε καὶ
νοῦν.

2   Παντάπασί γε μὴν οὐκέτ᾽ ἀπέστησαν τῆς περὶ τοὺς
λόγους κατοχῆς ἐκείνης, οὐδὲ ξενηλασίαν τινὰ παντελῆ
τῶν προτέρων ἐκείνων εὐγενῶν εἵλοντο λογισμῶν, ἀλλὰ
δοκοῦσιν ὅμως κἀνταῦθα ἠσχολῆσθαι καὶ νέμειν ὁτιοῦν
μέρος καὶ μὴ καθάπαξ ἀνήροτον, μηδ᾽ ἀκατέργαστον ὑπὸ
παιδεύσεως τὴν τῆς διανοίας καταλείπειν χώραν, παρα-
πλήσιον ἐμοὶ δοκεῖν ὥσπερ οἱ βαθύγειόν τινα καὶ λιπαρὰν
πεδιάδα σφετέραν καταχερσώσαντες καὶ συγχωρήσαντες
ἐξυβρίσαι παντελῶς καὶ ὑλομανῆσαι τῶν ἀνονήτων καὶ
πρὸς ἅπαντα ἀσυντελῶν ἐκφύσεων, ἔπειθ᾽ ὅμως ἐπὶ τούτοις οὐκ ἀποκνοῦντες, οὐδ᾽ ἀποτρεπόμενοι καταβάλλειν
τε καὶ συμφύρειν αὐτοῖς εὐγενῆ καὶ χρήσιμα σπέρματα,
ἐπεὶ τί ποτ᾽ ἂν καὶ γεωργήσειε νοῦς ἐκεῖνος ἀστεῖον, ὃς
συμπεπίληται μὲν πλείστοις ὅσοις ἐπαχθίσμασι καὶ κατηγ-
χόνισται φροντισμάτων ἀγεννῶν καὶ λήρων, οὐκ οἶδ᾽ ὧντινων, κατατέμνεται δ᾽ αὖθις εἰς μυρίαν ἀηδίαν καὶ νῦν μὲν
ἕλκεται δὴ πρὸς πολιτικά ἄττα, φροντίδα μεγίστην ἔχων,
ὅπως ἡδύς τις καὶ μὴ παντάπασιν ἀνάρμοστος δοκοίη, εἰ

Chapter 46

For indeed enormous disquiet and distress seems to trouble prominent and educated men who have abandoned their studies and entrusted themselves at full speed to worldly problems, tumults, and trivial difficulties, I think. They are forced to remain constantly engaged with them and spend most of their time and intellectual energy on them.

They have, of course, never relinquished their old passion for education, nor have they chosen to banish their previous noble thoughts completely, but even in their current situation they seem to be concerned with them and they still offer them a portion of their attention without leaving the land of their intellect entirely uncultivated or unaffected by education. I think the case is the same with people who have allowed their deep-soiled and fertile field to dry out and thus to be overluxuriant and overgrown by useless weeds that sprout with no purposeful reason; nevertheless, without hesitating or turning away, they sow and scatter well-bred and useful seeds among them. What cultured product could that mind cultivate, a mind that is on the one hand oppressed by so many burdensome issues and strangled by sordid and foolish troubles of one sort or another, but on the other hand divides its attention among myriad disgusting things? The person who has a mind of this sort is sometimes dragged into duties regarding the state, taking the greatest care to be pleasant and not appear completely

δὲ μή, πάντως οὔτ' αὐτὸς οὔτε τὰ φίλτατα λοιπὸν χαιρήσει,
νῦν δὲ καταδεδαπάνηται καὶ προστέτηκε τοῖς οἴκοι, πολυ-
μέριμνον ἀεὶ διεξιὼν χορηγίαν καὶ μελέτην νεουργῆ καὶ
τρόπον ἀνορύττων ἑκάστοθ' ὄντινά οἱ δοκεῖ ξυνοίσειν
πρὸς ἀνενδεῆ τὴν χρείαν.

3   Ταῦτα γὰρ οὔτ' ἀποθέσθαι τοῦ λοιποῦ ἔξεστιν, ὅτῳ δὴ
καὶ ξυμβέβηκεν ἐφ' ἅπαξ συμπλακῆναι καὶ βίοτον ὄντινα
ἄρα ἑλέσθαι καὶ ξυνοικίαν καὶ διαδοχήν τινα παίδων, οὔτε
μετρίως οὔθ' ὅλως συμβατικῶς ἔχει τοῖς ἐλλογίμοις πρὸς
τὸν ἐξ ἀρχῆς σκοπόν, ἀλλ' ἀεὶ ζημίαν ἐμποιοῦσι τῷ νῷ
πλείστην καὶ τοῦ μεγίστου κτήματος ἀφαίρεσιν, τοῦ καιροῦ, διὰ τὴν ἐν αὐτοῖς συνεχῆ καὶ ἄτρεπτον μέριμναν καὶ
ὡς ἂν δή τινες λῶβαι ἀνθρώπων τῶν γε τοιούτων καὶ
κῆρες γίγνονται, τὸν λογισμὸν ἐνεχυράζουσαι καὶ τῶν
καλλίστων ἀφαιρούμεναι τοὺς προτεθειμένους καί, προσ-
αυξῆσαι δέον, ὑποτέμνονται καὶ τὰς εὐγενεῖς αὐτοῦ
βλάστας ἀποκείρουσιν ὡς ἀληθῶς ἑκάστην ἐν χρῷ καὶ
πάσας γε ἐπιφύσεις ἀκολουθούσας τῇ μονῇ καὶ ἀρδείᾳ τῆς
ἐπιστήμης ἐκθλίβουσι καὶ πρὸς τὰ κάλλιστα καὶ μέγιστα
ὡρμηκότα τὸν νοῦν χειμάρρου τρόπον ἑτέρωσε κακο-
τέχνως τρέπουσι τὴν φοράν, εἰς βαναυσώδη καὶ ἀνελεύθε-
ρον διατριβὴν μετοχετευσάμενοι.

4   Καὶ μὴν καὶ τοῦτο πολλάκις ᾠήθην, ὡς οἱ τοιοῦτοι
δὴ φροντισμοὶ καὶ τὰ κατὰ τὸν βίοτον ἀναγκαῖα ταῦτα
μεριμνήματα καὶ λογίσματα, ὥσπερ ἐπιστάται τινὲς βάσκανοι καὶ αὐθάδεις καὶ τυραννικοί, παντάπασιν ἀμβλώσαν-
τες καὶ ἐπιφράξαντες τὸ τοῦ νοῦ μεγαλοφυὲς καὶ περὶ τὰ
κρείττω μεγαλουργόν, κατέλιπον ἀργόν, καθάπερ οἵ τινα

unseemly, for otherwise neither he nor his relatives will have any joy. At other times, he is entirely consumed and worn away by household cares, looking all the time for supplies with great anxiety, contriving novel plans, and digging up any sort of method he thinks will meet the needs of his family sufficiently.

For anyone who at some point in the past has enmeshed himself in these problems and opted for family life, marriage, and children cannot escape them thereafter. Nor can scholars return to their initial goals either to a modest extent or entirely, but their cares constantly distract their mind considerably and deprive them of their most valuable possession, namely time, due to their continual, intractable concerns. These concerns become a kind of leprosy and disease at least for such men and take hold of their mind and deprive those who have undertaken these obligations of what is best. In addition, even if the mind should expand, they arrest its development and truly cut each of its noble offshoots from its very roots and oppress any growth that might have ensued from the presence and flow of knowledge. Although the mind rushes like a torrent toward the most beautiful and significant deeds, these cares cunningly shift its course in the other direction and divert it into a servile, base lifestyle. 3

In addition to this, I often thought that cares such as these, as much as the inevitable concerns and worries about life, blind our mind completely like envious, arrogant, and tyrannical overseers, and impede its genius and its ability to perform greater deeds, and make it sluggish, like bad 4

δὴ εὔγεων καὶ εὐδαίμονα χώραν, ὀρφανῶν παίδων ἐπίτρο-
ποι κακοὶ χέρσον ἀτημελήτως καὶ δυσνοϊκῶς ἀπεργασά-
μενοι.

<h1 style="text-align:center">47</h1>

Τοιγαροῦν πόλεμός τις ἐντεῦθεν ἐμοὶ δοκεῖν εἶναι καθάπαξ ἄσπονδος καὶ ἀκήρυκτος πρὸς τὴν λογικὴν ἐργασίαν
τε καὶ φύσιν καὶ σφόδρα λυμαίνεται πρὸς τὴν ἀκμὴν
ταύτης καὶ εὐεξίαν, καταστενούμενος παντὶ τρόπῳ καὶ
καθειργνὺς ταύτην καὶ ἐκπολιορκῶν, μὴ προσάπτεσθαι
τῶν σφετέρων καὶ ξυντεινόντων, καθάπερ οἱ τὰ τῶν πολεμίων δῃοῦντες χωρία καὶ τόν τε σῖτον καὶ τὸν ἄλλον
καρπὸν φθείροντες, ὃς ἀφεθεὶς μεγάλη τοῖς κεκτημένοις
ὄνησις ἂν ἦν, καὶ παντελῶς ἀπογινώσκειν καταναγκάζον-
τες καὶ σφίσι προσέχειν.

2   Πεπείραμαι δὲ καὶ αὐτὸς καὶ κατανενόηκα τοῦθ', ὥσπερ
δὴ καὶ ἄλλος τις, σφόδρα καὶ πάνυ μὲν ἠβουλόμην παν-
δέξιός τις εἶναι καὶ ἀμφότερα ὡς ἀληθῶς ἐξαρκεῖν καὶ
πρὸς οὐδέτερον ἐνδεῖν μήθ' ὅλως περιτρέπεσθαι προσρέ-
πων ὁτῳοῦν ἑνὶ τούτων ἢ δεῖ πλέον. Καὶ μὴν ᾤμην οὕτω
γε πρότερον ἐξεῖναι καὶ οὕτω δὴ σαφῶς μετετιθέμην
ἄρα καὶ προσηπτόμην πολιτικῶν δή τινων τούτων, ὧν
νομίζομεν, καὶ ἀναγκαίας ἐνταῦθα λοιπὸν κτήσεως καὶ
συνδιαγωγῆς φιλτάτων καὶ μοίρας, ὡς οὐκ ἀφεξόμενος,

guardians who are so careless and wicked as to leave the fertile and productive land of the orphans in their custody uncultivated.

Chapter 47

It thus seems to me that an absolutely implacable and unproclaimed war is being waged against intellectual undertakings and the scholarly nature, which destroys their vigor and strength, restricting them in every way, and confines and besieges them so that they cannot deal with their own affairs, which they are intent upon. This brings to mind people who ravage the lands of their enemies and destroy the grain and the other crops, which, if they were to remain intact, would bring immense benefit to their owners; they therefore inevitably force their enemies into utter desperation and dependence upon them.

I myself have experienced this situation and have understood it quite well, just as someone else may have, of course. I wanted to be extremely skilled in everything, to be truly competent in both occupations, not to be lacking in either of them, nor to be turned entirely upside down by being inclined more than necessary toward one or the other of the two. Previously, I believed that something of this sort was possible, so I distanced myself clearly from intellectual activities and concerned myself with certain public affairs, with which we are all familiar; I thus necessarily acquired

οἶμαι, οὐδ᾽ ἀποχωρήσων, οὐδ᾽ οὕτω καθάπαξ τῶν ἄρα καλῶν ἐκείνων καὶ γεννικῶν ἐρώτων καὶ τῆς πρότερον ἐν λόγοις καὶ παιδείᾳ σπουδῆς, ἧς τῷ ὄντι μάλιστ᾽, εἴπερ δὴ καὶ ἄλλος τις, ἥλων.

3   Νυνὶ δ᾽ ἀμέλει κινδυνεύω μαθεῖν, ὡς ἔοικε, πεπονθὼς ὃ μήποτ᾽ ὄφελον, ὡς πάντα μᾶλλον ἢ ἀμφότερα ταῦτα ἔξεστι σπουδάζειν ὀντιναοῦν, καὶ σφόδρα δὴ φιλονεικοῦντα, καὶ κατακτᾶσθαι κοινῇ. Τὰ γὰρ δὴ θήλεα καὶ ὁ νεογνής μοι παῖς οὗτος ἄρρην παντάπασί με κατέσχεν ἤδη καὶ πάντων ἀπέστησεν ἄρα καὶ ἀπήγαγε βίᾳ τῶν ἄλλων κατασκοπούμενον ἀεὶ καὶ μελετῶντα καὶ σφόδρα κατεργαζόμενον διὰ παντός, ὅ,τι ποτ᾽ ἂν αὐτοῖς εἴην χρήσιμος.

4   Ταῦτά με δὴ νυκτός τε καὶ μεθ᾽ ἡμέραν ἀεί πως γρηγορεῖν ἀναγκάζει τε καὶ καταπείθει, πάντ᾽, οἶμαι, τρόπον βίοτον σφίσι ποριζόμενον, ὅντινα ἔξεστιν, οὐ νῦν δὴ μόνον, ἀλλ᾽ ἄρ᾽ ἀσφαλῆ καὶ μεθύστερον, ἐμοῦ τελευτῶντος. Νόμος γὰρ οὗτος ἡμέτερος τῶν πλειόνων ἀνθρώπων κατέσχεν ἤδη πάλαι πρότερον, οὐ τὸ νῦν εἶναι μόνον ζητεῖν καὶ φροντίζειν, οὐδὲ τὸ καθ᾽ ἡμέραν αὐτὴν ἑκάστοθ᾽, ὅπως ἂν εἴη τοῖς γνησίοις καὶ φιλτάτοις καλῶς, ἀλλ᾽, ὡς ἔοικεν ἄρα, καὶ τοῦ μέλλοντος χρόνοις ὕστερον πορρωτάτω τὴν πρόνοιαν ἀποτείνειν, ὡς οἷόν τέ ἐστιν, ὀφείλομέν τε καὶ εἰσπραττόμεθα περὶ αὐτῶν καὶ παρασκευὴν εὐδαιμονίας σφίσιν ἔπειθ᾽ ἑξῆς ἀποχρῶσάν τε, οἶμαι, καὶ παμπλήρη τινὰ πρὸς τὸν βίον πραγματεύεσθαι.

5   Ταῖς γε μὴν παρθένοις αὐταῖς οὐκ ἄλλως ἢ θησαυρῶν πολυταλάντων ἔξεστι κήδη τινὰ καλλίω καὶ σεμνότερα πρίασθαι. Καὶ δὴ τοῦτ᾽ ἀεὶ πρόεισιν—οὐκ οἶδ᾽ ὅπως—μετὰ

property and the destiny of family life, but I thought that I would not relinquish or withdraw completely from those beautiful, noble passions or from my previous engagement with literature and education, which has truly captivated me more than anyone else.

I am now in peril of realizing, it seems, after having suffered what I wish I had not, that one can pursue anything more successfully than attaining these two in combination, no matter how hard one tries to do so. For the girls and this newborn boy of mine have already overwhelmed me completely, kept me away from everything, and carried me off perforce from the rest of my regular occupations, since I am constantly searching for, worrying about, and trying to find in any way possible what might be advantageous for my children. 3

These concerns, therefore, always compel me to be somehow on the alert all day and all night long, and force me, I think, to provide them somehow with a means of life that will not be only temporary but secure for the future, when I am gone. For this is our law, which has been followed by most people since ancient times, namely not to seek after and be concerned only about the present, in order to satisfy the daily needs of our beloved relatives, but it seems that we must extend our foresight even further into the future, insofar as this is possible; we are obliged to exact for their sake, I believe, sufficient means to secure them a comfortable and happy life hereafter. 4

For our daughters, in particular, there is no other way to find decent, respectable bridegrooms, unless we have treasures worth many talents to offer as dowry. As time goes on, this grows even worse—I do not know how—and we are 5

τοῦ χρόνου καὶ πλείω κατατιθέναι καὶ φέρειν ἀνάγκην
ἡμεῖς ἔχομεν ἢ καθ᾿ ὅσα ἀπημπολήμεθα ταῖς τῶν ἡμετέρων
αὐτοὶ παίδων μητράσι. Οἱ δὲ πολλοὶ καὶ φιλαυτοῦντες
ἡμῶν ἀπλήστως κἀνταῦθα καὶ κρείττω ἢ καθ᾿ ἑαυτοὺς
σπουδάζουσι κήδη καὶ χρημάτων πλειόνων ὠνήσιμα, ἀξιοῦντες τὸ μένον ἑαυτῶν καὶ τὴν διαδοχὴν ηὐξημένην καὶ
πόρρω δόξης ἀφικομένην καὶ ἀνύσασαν καταλιπεῖν.

48

Τοιγαροῦν, ὡς ἐνταῦθα ὄντα ἡμῖν τὰ πάντα πράγματα,
καταδαπανώμεθα τὸν ἄπαντα νοῦν καὶ ἀεὶ στρέφομεν
ἐν τούτοις, τῶν ἄλλων κατολιγωροῦντες ὡς ἀνονήτων
ἁπάντων καὶ μηδὲν ἤδη λοιπὸν προσπεριεργαζόμενοι. Καὶ
κατακτώμενοι μὲν δὴ καὶ κατορθοῦντες χαίρομεν εὖ μάλα
καὶ ἀεὶ πλεῖν ἔτι σπουδάζομεν, μετὰ τὴν ἐν πείρᾳ ἡδονὴν
ἐμοὶ δοκεῖν ἀμιλλώμενοι, ἀποτυγχάνοντες δὲ καὶ χαλεπῆς
πειρώμενοι τῆς τύχης, κακοὶ κακῶς ἀνιώμεθά τε σφόδρα
καὶ καταγχόμεθα πάντων ἀνεπίστροφοι.

2   Οὐ γὰρ δὴ μόνον, ὥς φασιν, οὐκ ἔξεστι τοῖς ἐν λύπαις
γεωμετρεῖν, ἀλλ᾿ οὐδὲ φιλοσοφεῖν ὅλως, οὐδ᾿ ἐπιχειρεῖν
λόγοις, ὧν οὐκ ἄλλως ἐστὶν ἐπικαίρως ἅπτεσθαι ἢ παρασκευῇ ψυχῆς ἀκμαζούσῃ καὶ διανοίας ἀσείστῳ φρονήματι,
ἀπηλλαγμένης συγχύσεως πάσης καὶ νόσου κακοσχόλου.
Οὕτω δὴ μετὰ πάσης ἀληθείας κομιδῇ δυσχερέστατον

forced to collect and offer even more money than we ourselves received upon marrying the mothers of our own children. On the other hand, many who are more self-centered and greedier than we are seek grooms of higher status than themselves who can be bought with even more money, because they deem it worthwhile to leave behind them offspring and successors of elevated social rank, who will reach and attain much greater fame.

Chapter 48

Therefore, as if all our affairs existed in this life alone, we devote and always turn all our attention toward these material concerns, utterly despising everything else as entirely useless and by no means bothering about such matters. Once we manage to acquire material goods, we are quite happy and are constantly eager for even more, striving after the experience of pleasure, I think; but if we fail and experience bad fortune, we are bitterly distressed and terribly anxious, and cannot deal with anything else.

For not only is it *impossible for those who are distressed to practice geometry,* as they say, but it is also impossible to deal with philosophy and education; and there is no other way to partake successfully in these fields than through the vigorous preparation of one's soul and the firm courage of one's thought, which has been cleansed from any sort of commotion or destructive mental trouble. In all honesty, therefore, it is very difficult for a person to remain steadfast and

διακαρτερῆσαι καὶ διασώσασθαι τὸν ἐν παιδείᾳ καὶ λόγοις
ἔρωτα παντάπασιν ἀμείωτόν τινα καὶ ἄτρεπτον, ταῖς κατὰ
τὸν βίον ταύταις ἐφάπαξ συμπλακέντα μικρολογίαις,
ἁπάσῃ βίᾳ κατεχούσαις τε καὶ μεθιστώσαις καὶ τὸν μάλιστα δὴ προτεθειμένον αὐτόν, μηδ᾽ ἂν εἴ τι γένοιτο,
μεθέσθαι τῶν ἀπὸ τῆς σοφίας ἀγαθῶν.

3   Καὶ τόν γε δὴ συνετὸν ὄντως καὶ σώφρονα ταύτης
ἐραστὴν καὶ πάντων μᾶλλον τὰ κατ᾽ αὐτὴν προελόμενον
καὶ τετιμηκότα τοῦτο δεῖ μάλιστα προϊδέσθαι καὶ φυλάξα-
σθαι, τῆς ἐν βιωτικοῖς αὐτοῖς σπουδάσμασι τερθρείας καὶ
περιπλανήσεως ὅλῃ σπουδῇ καὶ ῥώμῃ καθάπαξ ἀποσχέσθαι
καὶ μηδὲ κατὰ βραχὺ συμφύρεσθαι ταύτῃ πως συγχωρῆσαί
τε καὶ συνθέσθαι, εἴ γε δὴ πάντως ἀνῦσαί τι καὶ κα-
τορθῶσαι πρὸς τὴν ἔνστασιν δηλαδὴ τοῦ βίου ταύτην
ὀρθῶς αἱρεῖται, τἀντεῦθεν, ὡς ἔοικεν, ἅπαντ᾽ ἀλλαττόμε-
νον, ὁποῖά ποτ᾽ ἂν μέλλῃ ξυμβαίνειν, τῆς ἀπὸ ταύτης εὐγενείας καὶ δόξης καὶ μήθ᾽ ὅλως ἀποχωρεῖν ταύτης μήτ᾽
εἰς ἄρκυς ἐνταῦθ᾽ ἑκόντα εἶναι κακῶς τε καὶ ἀμαθῶς
ἐμπίπτοντα λαβυρινθώδεις τε καὶ δυσεκφύκτους, ἔπειτ᾽
οἴεσθαι ῥάδιον εἶναι καὶ ἀπαλλάττειν οὕτως εἰς ἅπερ εἶχε
πρότερον καὶ νόστου δή τινος μεμνῆσθαι φίλην ἐς πατρίδα
γαῖαν, μήθ᾽ ὥσπερ δυσμεταχειρίστῳ τινὶ καὶ πολυτρόπῳ
καὶ κακούργῳ καὶ βιαίῳ θηρίῳ συμπλεκόμενον, κατατι-
θασσεῦσαι λοιπὸν οὕτω δὴ δοκεῖν ῥᾷστα καὶ κημα-
γωγῆσαι, ὡς ἐξεῖναί οἱ τάχα καὶ πρὸς ἄλλοις ἔχειν καὶ δι-
αφέρειν, ἅττα δὴ πλείστης σπουδῆς καὶ ἀσχολίας ἁπάσης
δεῖται, ἀτεχνῶς ἄρα κατὰ τὸν Κυδίου λόγον, ὃν Πλάτων
αὐτὸς ἔφησε σοφώτατον *τὰ ἐρωτικά, κατέναντα λέοντος*

preserve completely undiminished and unaltered his love for education and learning, once he engages with these trivialities of life, which hold him perforce and distance him from his previous activities, even when he has every intention of participating in the blessings of wisdom, no matter what happens.

The truly prudent and wise lover of this wisdom, who 3 prefers and bestows the most honor on everything pertaining to it, should especially anticipate and keep watching out for this, namely how to detach himself with all his zeal and might from the minutiae and meanderings of the concerns of daily life itself once and for all, and to in no way allow or agree to get himself enmeshed in them even slightly. This he should do if he chooses rightly, at any rate, to accomplish and achieve something despite life's intrusions, from that moment on changing, it seems, everything from his previous life, whatever its course may have been, for the nobility and glory from this life, and not to distance himself from the latter at all, nor to fall willingly into the contorted and inescapable nets of daily life due to ignorance and wickedness, and then believe that it will be quite easy to free himself later on and return to his previous cares, and call to mind the day of his return to his beloved fatherland; nor believe that he will easily tame and muzzle the difficulties of life; for it is as if he will need to fight a beast that is hard to combat, devious, wicked, and violent; for this could scarcely happen or come to fulfillment in other occupations that require great devotion and full engagement. According to Cydias, whom Plato himself considered *greatly experienced in love affairs,* he will look like *a fawn encountering a lion and being*

νεβρὸν ἐλθόντα, μοῖραν αἱρεῖσθαι κρεῶν καὶ μὴ τοὺς ἀπ᾽ αὐτοῦ σπαραγμοὺς μήτε δεδιέναι μήθ᾽ ὑποχωρεῖν.

4   Ἀλλ᾽, ὅπερ ἔλεγον, ὅ γε σοφὸς ὄντως παιδείας ἐραστὴς ταῦτά τε δὴ προόψεται καὶ ἢ πάντα τρόπον, ὡς ἔξεστιν, εὐλαβήσεται καὶ ἀποφευξεῖται ἢ πρόνοιάν τινα ποιήσεται, καθάπερ οἱ πλέοντες ἀμέλει, μέλλοντες εἰς ρευματώδεις ἀνάγεσθαι θαλάσσας, ἐξ ὑπερτέρων ἀφιᾶσι πολλῷ, τὴν βίαν αὐτὴν τοῦ ρεύματος προϋποτεμνόμενοι καὶ τοῦτο δηλαδὴ μεταχειρίζοντες καὶ πολιτευόμενοι, ὡς ἂν τῷ περιόντι τῆς προλήψεως ταύτης καὶ προνοίας ὁ πλοῦς αὐτοῖς ἀσφαλὴς γίγνοιτο καὶ μὴ κινδυνεύσαιεν παρασυρῆναι τῇ σφοδρότητι τῆς ἐπιφορᾶς καὶ παραχθῆναι λοιπὸν ἄλλη ποι, καθ᾽ ἕτερα ἢ ἐσκοποῦντο, παραπλησίως ἐμοὶ δοκεῖν καὶ αὐτὸς πλείστη δὴ σοφίας παρασκευῇ καὶ τοῦ νοῦ πολλῷ κράτει προσαπτόμενος τῶν κατὰ τὸν βίοτον τῶνδε πραγμάτων, τεθαρρηκὼς πάνυ τοι τῇ περιουσίᾳ τῆς ἕξεως καὶ προκόψας οὕτως, ὡς ἄμεινον ἔχειν ἢ ὡς παντάπασιν ἐκλιπεῖν, κἂν εἴ τι ξυμβαίνῃ, μηδ᾽ ἐκπεσεῖν, ὧν μάλιστ᾽ ἠβούλετο. Οἱ δὲ πολλοὶ τῶν ἀνθρώπων ἀπροόπτως τε καὶ μηδενὶ ξὺν νῷ αὐτίκα αὐτόθεν μεταχωροῦντες ἐνταῦθα καὶ προστιθέμενοι, ἐοίκασιν ὥσπερ ὁ σίδηρος ἔτι ζέων εἰς ὕδωρ ἐμπίπτων παραχρῆμα σβέννυσθαί τε παντελῶς καὶ πρὸς μηδὲν ἀντέχειν.

seized as his portion of meat, without being terrified that the lion will devour it or beating a retreat.

As I said, however, the truly wise lover of education will 4 foresee these dangers and will either be cautious enough to flee from them in every possible way or will take some precaution, like sailors about to enter a sea with very strong currents who cast loose their ship well in advance in order to forestall the force of the current itself; and they employ this trick and behave according to custom so as to make their voyage safe by means of an excess of precaution and foresight, and to avoid the danger of being swept away by the vehemence of the currents and being diverted to some other destination than the one they had intended. I think this person deals in a similar fashion with these troubles of life, after having prepared himself well by means of wisdom and the great power of his mind. He has great confidence in the strength of his disposition and he has progressed to such an extent that he is in better shape than he might have been, had he entirely abandoned education; no matter what happens, he will not abandon what he wants the most. Most people leave one occupation and immediately take up another one, without foresight or giving it any thought; they resemble iron that is still hot and then, as soon as it is plunged into water, becomes completely cool; in the same way, most men cannot resist anything at all.

49

Καίτοι φασί τινες μήτ' ὀνίνασθαί τι, μένοντας ἀεὶ καὶ φιλοπονοῦντας ἐν τοῖς λόγοις, μηδέ τι πλέον πάντως προσκτᾶσθαι μήτ' αὖθις ζημίαν μηδεμίαν ἀποσχομένῳ ξυμβαίνειν, ἢν ἄρα τις ὁτιοῦν ὅλως ἐν αὐτοῖς γένηται. Καί τινος ἤκουσα χθὲς ἤδη καὶ πρότερον σφόδρα τοῦτ' αὐτὸ βουλομένου καὶ κατασκευάζοντος, σοφοῦ καὶ γενναίου καὶ μάλα ἐν τοῖς πρώτοις τῶν νῦν ἐν λόγοις ἀνδρῶν, οὐκ οἶδ' εἴτε συνηγοροῦντος, ὃν τρόπον εἶχεν, ἑαυτῷ—καὶ γὰρ τῶν τοῦτο καὶ αὐτὸς πεπονθότων ἦν—εἴθ' οὕτως ἴσως καὶ δοκοῦν αὐτῷ. Ἔφασκε γοῦν ὅτι, καθάπερ ἐπὶ τῶν σωμάτων, ἔστι ἄρα τι ποσὸν ἑκάστῳ τῶν ἀνθρώπων καὶ φύσεώς τις ὅρος ἀπαρεγχείρητος, εἰς ὃ δὴ περαίνειν ἀνάγκη.

2   [. . .] οὐδὲν ἀηδές, οὔτε ποτ' ἄρα φαίημεν ἴσως ἄν. Ἔνιοι δέ μοι δοκοῦσι καὶ δυσχεραίνειν, τῶν ἐν ὑπεροχαῖς μάλιστα καὶ βλάκες ἄνθρωποι, ἢν ἄλλου πύθοιντο περὶ τῶν ξυμβαινόντων ἀνάγκη τῇ φύσει καὶ ἀνθρώποις οὖσι, τὸν αὐτὸν ἐμοὶ δοκεῖν τρόπον, καθάπερ καὶ οἱ πολλοὶ τῶν ἀνθρώπων, ὀφθαλμοὺς ἢ χεῖρας ἢ πόδας παρακεκομμένοι τε καὶ λελωβημένοι, ἢν ἄρα τις μεμνῇτο καὶ προφέροι τὴν νόσον, βαρέως φέρουσι καὶ ὡς ἐχθρόν τινα τοῦτον καὶ σφόδρα ἐπίβουλον καὶ ἠδικημένοι ἀμύναιντ' ἄν, ὡς ἂν ἕκαστος οἷός τ' εἴη, καὶ ταῦτα πρὸ τῶν ἄλλων αὐτοὶ μάλιστα πᾶσι προδεικνῦντες, ἢν φεύγουσιν αἰσχύνην, δεινὸν νομίζοντες, ἤν τις ἐπαΐοι.

Chapter 49

Despite this, some people claim that there is no advantage for those who always remain faithful to and busy themselves with education, nor can they earn extra profit in any way; and again, they claim that no harm will come to someone who gives up education, even if he was wholly devoted to it. Just yesterday and the day before I actually heard a wise and noble man, one of the most prominent scholars of our age, strongly supporting this stance and arguing in favor of it; I do not know whether he was trying in this way to defend himself however he could—for he was himself a person who had suffered this fate—or whether perhaps this was merely his opinion. He was claiming that, as happens with bodies, so with each individual person there is a specific quantity and an inviolable physical limit to which we must restrict ourselves.

[. . .] not unpleasant, nor would we presumably ever claim 2 that. It seems to me, however, that some stupid individuals in prominent positions feel distress when they hear another person talking about what happens to all human beings by physical necessity. In this behavior they seem to me like many people who are crippled and handicapped with regard to their eyes, hands, or feet, and who, as soon as someone recalls and refers explicitly to their disability, become angry and, because they feel wronged, guard themselves, each as best as he can, against this man whom they consider an extremely dangerous enemy. They act like this even though they themselves, much more than anyone else, put the shame they are trying to avoid on display to everyone, because they think it dreadful if someone knows about it.

50

Ἀλλὰ ταῦτα μὴν ἔτ᾽ ἔξεστιν ἴσως λέγειν εἰς μήκιστον καὶ μάλιστα ξυνορᾶν ἐστι πλεῖστον ἢ ἔξεστι λέγειν, ὅστις δὴ προσέχει τὸν νοῦν, καὶ ἃ δὴ πείρᾳ λαμβάνομεν ἑκάστοτε ἐφ᾽ ἑκάστοις, οὐ μάλα δὴ ῥᾴδιον ἐρεῖν, ἀλλὰ νοοῦμεν οὐ πάντες μὲν ἴσως, οὐδὲ μὴν πάντα ῥᾷστα, λέγειν δὲ πάντ᾽ οὐχ οἷοί τέ ἐσμεν οὐκέτι, οὐδ᾽ ἃ λέγομεν, ἱκανῶς λέγομεν, ἀλλ᾽ ἧττον ἢ ὡς νοοῦμεν πολλῷ.

2 Καὶ μὴν ὑπὸ τῆς ἀληθοῦς ἔνιοι καὶ συνήθους πείρας ἐς τοσοῦτο δὴ κατεγνώκασι τῶν ὁρωμένων, ὡς μηδ᾽ ἔμβραχυ λοιπὸν ἀξιοῦν περὶ αὐτῶν ὁτιοῦν καὶ λέγειν, ἀλλ᾽ εἰς ἀφωνίαν δή τινα παντελῆ κατηντηκέναι, ἀρκούμενοι τῇ θεωρίᾳ μόνῃ, καίτοι γε μηδὲ ταύτῃ πάνυ τοι χαίροντες, μηδ᾽ ὥσπερ ἐντεῦθεν ἡνυκότες τι, ὅτι μηδ᾽ ἔστι τοῖς πολλοῖς ἐντεῦθέν τι πλέον, ἢ πρότερον εἴρηται. Τί γὰρ εἴ τις δὴ ξυννενόηκε μὲν κρεῖττον ἢ κατὰ τοὺς ἄλλους τἀνθρώπεια, περιπέπτωκε δ᾽ ὅμως αὐτοῖς, ἢ ἑκὼν πάντως ἢ ἄκων, τὸν αὐτὸν τρόπον κατὰ τοὺς ἄλλους; Οὐ γὰρ δῆθ᾽ ὅλως ἔξεστιν ἐκφυγεῖν τοὺς ἀρρήκτους τούτους δεσμούς, οὐδὲ καθάπαξ οὐκ ἀποδρᾶναι.

3 Εἴρηται δὴ τοῦτο πρότερον πολλάκις, ὦ φιλότης, εἴρηται, ὡς οὐχ ἃ βουλόμεθα δρῶμεν, οὐδ᾽ ἃ νοοῦμεν, ἅπαντα ἔξεστιν ἀνύτειν οὐκέτι· καὶ συλλογίζονται μὲν ἔνιοί τινες, καὶ ἐνίοτε κάλλιστα, ξυνέχονται δὲ ὅμως κοινῇ τοῖς ἄλλοις πᾶσι πράγμασι καὶ στροβοῦνται καὶ νοσοῦσι καὶ περιφέρονται καὶ περιπίπτουσιν, οὐ τοῖς ἄλλοις μόνον ἔξωθεν

Chapter 50

Whoever sets his mind to it can presumably talk about such issues at length, and indeed there is still much more to observe than can be said. It is not always easy to express verbally the conclusions we reach at every point due to our personal experiences on different occasions. We do not all perceive everything in the same way nor everything in the easiest way, we cannot mention everything, and we do not adequately discuss the topics we refer to, but we eventually convey much less than we perceive.

Indeed, as a result of this real and common experience, 2 some people go so far as to reject everything they observe, and deem it right not to say a single word about it; they reach a state of total speechlessness and are satisfied with mere observation, although they do not take much pleasure in it, nor do they get any benefit from it, since, as I said before, most people gain no profit from this. What is the real point, if a person understands human affairs better than others but still falls into the same difficulties as others do, either willingly or inadvertently? No one can completely avoid these unbreakable bonds, nor can one escape them once and for all.

This has indeed been said many times before, my friend: 3 we do not accomplish what we want, nor can we fulfill everything we have in mind. Some people have the very best thoughts occasionally, but like everyone else they are held fast by all of life's cares and are spun around, feel ill, are swung about, and come to grief. This is obvious not only to others who judge them from without, but to them them-

κρίνουσιν, ἀλλ᾽ ἀμέλει καὶ σφίσιν αὐτοῖς καὶ οἷς ξυνεώρα-
νται λογισμοῖς. Νομίζομεν δὲ κοινὴν ἀπολογίαν τὰ κοινὰ
πταίσματα καὶ οὐδεὶς λοιπόν, οἶμαι, δίκαιος ὁτιοῦν φρονεῖν, εἰ δ᾽ ἀμέλει φρονήσεις, αὐτίκα αἱρήσῃ, εἰ δὲ σεμνο-
λογήσεις, ἐγγελᾷ τἀναντία δρῶν, καὶ σοφὸς οὐχ ὃς οἶδέ
τε καὶ διδάσκει, ἀλλ᾽ ὃς οἶδε μέν, ἡττωμένῳ δὲ ξύνοιδεν
ἑαυτῷ.

4   Καὶ καταμεμφόμεθ᾽ ἀλλήλων ἅπαντες ἁπάντων ταῦθ᾽,
ἃ πράττομεν αὐτοί, φαῦλοι φαύλων καὶ συνετοὶ συνετῶν
καὶ συνετῶν φαῦλοι καὶ τοὔμπαλιν, ἔστι δ᾽ οὗ καὶ συγ-
γινώσκομεν καὶ συμφρονοῦμεν καὶ συλλαγχάνομεν οὐ
κοινὸν Ἑρμῆν, ἀλλὰ κοινὴν τύχην, καὶ τοῦτο τῆς παροιμίας,
καὶ οἷς ἐχόμεθ᾽ ἕκαστος, καὶ τοῖς ἄλλοις ἀξιοῦμεν συγχωρεῖν, καὶ πάντ᾽ εἰς ταὐτὸν ἄρα φέρει καὶ οὐκ ἔστι διελέσθαι
καὶ κατακεκύβευται μικρά τε καὶ μείζω καὶ ὁμοῦ πάντα
χρήματα, ὅς τε πελώριος ἀνὴρ ὅς τ᾽ ἐλάχιστος, καὶ ὥσπερ
ἐν πανθήρῳ τινὶ σαγήνῃ κοινῇ πάντες συνδεδέμεθά τε καὶ
καταγχόμεθα καὶ περιστρεφόμεθ᾽ ἄλλοτ᾽ ἄλλως ᾄττοντες
καὶ πάντ᾽ ἄφυκτα.

51

Τοιγαροῦν ἔνιοι βούλονται μὲν κρεῖττον ἢ ὡς πράττουσι, βούλονται δ᾽ ὅμως ὡς πράττουσι, καὶ ἀξιοῦσι μὲν
ἑαυτοὺς καλλιόνων ἢ ἔχουσι, φέρουσι δ᾽ ὅμως ἅττα ξυμ-

selves too by use of their intellect. We nonetheless consider the fact that these are common faults a common defense; I therefore believe that no one will be right to boast, and if you do boast, you will immediately be caught; if, on the other hand, you speak solemnly, you are laughed at for doing the opposite. It is not the person who knows certain things and teaches them to others who is wise, but the one who is knowledgeable but still realizes his own weaknesses.

We all accuse each other of the mistakes we ourselves 4 commit. Bad people accuse bad people, prudent people accuse prudent people, bad people accuse prudent people, and vice versa. Sometimes we show understanding and compassion, and we do not have a *shared Hermes* but a shared fortune, as the proverb again says. Then we deem it right to forgive in other people the shortcomings we too are locked in; therefore, everything comes to the same point, there is no chance for distinction, and everything alike, be it significant or insignificant, turns on its head, both for the mighty and the humblest man; it is as if all of us were joined together in some huge dragnet that catches everything, we are strangled by it and twist around within it, darting in different directions, but there is no way out.

Chapter 51

Some people, therefore, expect much better results from what they do, but are eventually satisfied with the outcome of their actions. They consider themselves worthy of greater rewards than what they have received, but because they

πίπτει σφίσιν ὑπ᾽ ἀνάγκης τινὸς ἢ δι᾽ ἑαυτοὺς ἢ φίλτατα ἤ
τινα εὔνοιαν ἀποπιμπλάντες ἐπιτηδείοις.

2   Οὐ γὰρ ἑαυτοῖς ἄρα ζῶμεν μόνον ἄνθρωποι, οὐδὲ
πειθόμεθα τῇ γνώμῃ, ἀλλὰ καὶ πρὸς τὴν τῶν πολλῶν
ἠρτήμεθα κρίσιν, οὐδ᾽ ὡς ὁ λόγος αἱρεῖ, νομίζομεν, ἀλλὰ
δυσωπούμεθα ἐνίοτε τοῖς ἔγγιστα, εἰ δὲ μή, τῆς ἁμαρτίας
αὐτοὺς ἀφορμὴν ποιούμεθα, οὐδ᾽ αἰσχυνόμεθα ἡμᾶς
αὐτούς, ἃ μὴ καλῶς ἔχει, ἀλλ᾽ οὐχ ἧττον καὶ τοὺς ἄλλους,
καὶ φίλους μάλιστα καὶ ἀμαθεῖς ἴσως καὶ μηδὲν ἐπαΐοντας
καὶ πολλοῦ τινος ἡμᾶς οὐκ ἀξιοῦντας, ἀλλ᾽ ὧν αὐτοῖς δοκεῖ καὶ ὧν σφίσιν ὄνησις ἡτισοῦν, καὶ οὐ τὴν αὐτῶν
ἀλογίαν, ἣν δὴ καθ᾽ ἡμῶν αὐτῶν, ἢν μὴ πειθοίμεθα σφίσιν,
ἐπιψηφίζονται, φεύγομεν, οὐδ᾽ ἀναδιδάσκομεν σφᾶς ἅττα
βέλτιστα, ἀλλ᾽ ἀνάγκην ἔχομεν ὡς ἀσφαλῆ καὶ πυθόχρη-
στα στέργειν ἃ κρίνουσι καὶ δουλείαν ἀντ᾽ εὐνοίας ἴσως
τῆς πρὸς ἡμᾶς ἀλλαττόμεθα.

3   Καὶ τοίνυν δὴ σπουδάζουσιν ἔνιοι σφόδρ᾽ εἰς ἃ δυσχεραίνουσι, καὶ συντείνονται πλεῖν ἢ πρὸς ἃ ἐρῶσι καὶ
γνώμης ὅλης σπουδάζουσιν ἕτεροι, καὶ οὐκ ἀποχωροῦσιν
ἐν μέσοις, οὐδ᾽ ἀποτρέπονται, ὧν μὴ καλῶς ἔχειν σφίσιν
ἀξιοῦσι ξυνεῖναι, αἰσχυνόμενοι μὴ δόξαιεν οὐ κρίνοντες
δρᾶν, ἀλλ᾽ ἡττώμενοι, οὐκ ἀποστέργοντες, ἀλλ᾽ ὑστερίζον-
τες, οὐκ ἀρρενωποί τινες, ἀλλὰ νοσοῦντες μᾶλλον, οὐ περὶ
ὧν ξυνορῶσιν ἰσχυροί, ἀλλ᾽ ἀλόγιστοι καὶ λειποτακτοῦντες

have no choice, they put up with what happens to them either for their own sake or for the sake of their relatives, or doing a favor for close friends.

For as human beings we do not live only for ourselves, nor 2 do we follow our own inclinations alone, but we depend on the opinion of the majority of our fellow men as well. We do not believe what our reason demands, but we sometimes respect those who are closest to us, and otherwise we consider ourselves responsible for our failure. We are not only ashamed of ourselves for our shortcomings, but no less of other people as well, and especially our friends, if they are ignorant and utterly unknowing and do not treat us as extremely valuable, but instead value us to the extent they consider appropriate or somehow profitable for them. We do not flee from the irrationality they hurl against us when we disbelieve them, nor do we attempt to change their minds by teaching them what is best, but we are forced to accept what they believe as if they were infallible Pythian oracles, and we become their slaves in order to gain their potential benevolence toward us.

Some people even engage ardently in activities they hate, 3 while others strive for them more than for what they love and pursue with all their will, and they do not abandon them in midcourse, nor do they turn away from activities in which they believe their engagement is not beneficial. This happens because they are ashamed to appear not to act according to their judgment, but to be defeated without loving the activities they undertake merely due to weakness; they are ashamed to appear not masculine but rather sickly, to appear not stable in what they believe but inconsiderate and

καὶ αὐθάδεις, οὐ φεύγοντες ὕβριν, ἀλλὰ βασκαίνοντες, οὐκ ἀπαξιοῦντες ταπεινὴν γνώμην, ἀλλ᾽ ἀπολίτευτοι δή τινες καὶ πρόωροι.

4   Τοιγαροῦν ἄλλοτ᾽ ἄλλας ἀείποτε μεταβολάς τε καὶ πολιτείας κατ᾽ ἔφεσιν καὶ νοῦν τρέπονται καὶ οὐδέποτε ταὐτὸν ἄρ᾽ ὁτιοῦν ᾕρηνται καὶ ξυντέθεινται σφίσιν αὐτοῖς ἐνεργεῖν εἰς ἅπαντα τὸν βίον, ἀλλ᾽ ὃ νῦν ἔδοξε (πῶς ἂν εἴποι τις;), γεννικῶς καὶ κεκύρωται, μετέδοξεν ἔπειτα καὶ μετέγνωσται, καὶ ὃ νῦν τοῦ παντὸς ἀξιοῦσι καὶ σπουδάζουσιν, ὡς οὐκ ἄλλο τίποτε προσῆκον μάλιστ᾽ ἀνδρὶ σπουδαίῳ καὶ μόνον τἀγαθὸν ἐν ἀνθρώποις τοῦτο λοιπὸν ὄν, μεθ᾽ ὕστερον οὐ πάνυ τοι κατωλιγώρηται παντάπασι καὶ περιπεφρόνηται καὶ δοκεῖ τὸ μένειν ἄλογον, ἀργία φαῦλον, φησιν, ἄκομψον.

5   Νῦν μὲν ἡσυχίας ἔρως ἄτρεπτος ἔχει, νῦν δὲ πραγμάτων ὅτι μάλιστα μετέβαλε· καὶ προΐστανται μέν, ὡς οἷόν τέ ἐστι, πρὸς τὴν ἀόριστον δηλαδὴ ταύτην περιπλάνησιν ἀταπείνωτον εὖ μάλα καὶ ἀνεπίστροφον φρόνημα, κηλοῦνται δ᾽ ὅμως καὶ τρέπονται πολιτικαῖς δή τισι συλαγωγίαις καὶ χάρισι καὶ τοῖς ἀπ᾽ αὐτῶν—οὐκ οἶδ᾽ οἷστισιν ἄρα—γλυκασμοῖς καὶ πολιτεύμασιν, ἀπὸ Δωρίου, φασίν, ἐπὶ Λύδιον, καὶ ποτὲ μὲν δὴ θύουσιν εὐκολίᾳ τινὶ καὶ καθάπαξ ἐρρᾳστωνευμένῳ βίῳ καὶ πάντων ἀπολύτῳ τε καὶ ἀπραγματεύτῳ, θύουσι δ᾽ ἐκ μεταστροφῆς ἄλλοτε τοὐναντίον φερεπόνῳ καὶ τολμηρᾷ γνώμῃ, κατορθοῦν καὶ πράττειν ἄττα δὴ καὶ φέρεσθαι καρπούς, οὓς ἂν οἷοί τ᾽ εἶεν, καὶ ,οὐδὲν ὅλως ἑστώς, οὐδ᾽ ὅρος εἷς ἀναμφίβολος, ἀλλ᾽ ἄνω καὶ κάτω

like audacious deserters, who do not avoid arrogance but are envious, who do not despise humble opinions but are simply unstatesmanlike and only partially developed.

For this reason they constantly change their minds and aspire to a different lifestyle every time; what they have opted for never remains the same, nor do they assent to pursue it throughout the whole course of their life. To the contrary, what they decide to do now (how could one put this?) and nobly affirm, they afterward change and regret; and what they now deem worthy of everything else and undertake, as if nothing else better befits an educated man and this were the only blessing left for human beings, they shortly afterward disregard completely and despise, and their persistence on a particular course seems irrational, their laziness *ugly and rude,* as he says. 4

Sometimes they have an invincible passion for solitary contemplation, and at other times for other matters, because their passion has changed completely. They resist this endless vacillation as much as possible through an unyielding and totally dedicated spirit; on the other hand, however, they are beguiled and diverted by the distractions and pleasures of public life, as well as by the attractions—I do not know which, exactly—stemming from it and the mode of conduct, and are then led to change direction *from the Dorian mode to the Lydian,* as they say. Sometimes they offer sacrifices contentedly with a way of life that is completely idle, utterly relaxed, and free from worldly anxieties, and then they change again and sacrifice instead with a patient, brave spirit in order to accomplish and do something and reap whatever benefits they can. Nothing remains stable and there is no strict boundary, but everything turns upside 5

μεταχωρεῖ τε καὶ τρέπεται ἀτεκμάρτοις τισὶ παντάπασι καὶ ἀορίστοις εὐμεταβόλου φύσεως καὶ λογισμῶν εὐρίποις καὶ κύβοις καὶ περικλίσεσιν εἰς πάνθ' ὁμοῦ καὶ τἀναντία πράγματα.

6   Καὶ πάντες μὲν ἐπαινοῦσιν, ἃ πράττουσι, κοινῇ, λέγουσι δ' ἐναντί' ἔνιοι ἢ πράττουσι, καὶ διδάσκουσι μὲν ὡς ἄριστα, δρῶσι δ' ὡς ἥκιστα, χρῶνται δ' οἷς ξυνορῶσι βελτίστοις οὔ, συγχωροῦσι δ' ἑαυτοῖς ὡς ἀκουσίως, καὶ τοὺς μὲν ἄλλους ἀξιοῦσι πείθειν, ἑαυτοὺς δ' οὔ, καὶ σωφρονίζουσιν, ἃ μὴ κατορθοῦν ἔχουσι, καὶ προδιδάσκουσιν ἄλλους, ὧν ἐλεγχόμενοι τὴν ἀτυχίαν αὐτοὶ ἀδυναμίαν ἀφορμὴν προβάλλονται, καὶ τῶν ἄλλων ἡγεμόνες ὄντες, ἔλαθον ἑαυτῶν ἀποιήτως ἔχοντες.

7   Οἱ δέ, καὶ τοῦτο πολλάκις, ἐπαινοῦσί τε καὶ δρῶσι τἀναντί' οἷς προσεῖχον πρότερον, καὶ οἱ μὲν ὀψὲ δὴ τῶν χρόνων, οἱ δὲ καὶ σφόδρα ἔγγιστα, οἱ μὲν ἑαυτοὺς αἰσχύνοντες, ὡς ἔοικεν, ὡς ἀμαθεῖς τοσαῦτα πάντως ἔτη πρότερον, ἃ κακῶς εἶχον, οἷς ἐχρῶντο, οἱ δὲ τοὺς ἄλλους, ἢν μὴ ξυνορῶεν καὶ κατελέγχοιεν τὸ τάχος μεταβαλλόντων ἀναίδην οὕτω.

down and changes, depending on every sort of boundless and indefinite current of variable nature and on the unstable dice game of our thoughts, into every direction and its opposite.

By common consent, everybody praises their own deeds, 6 but some say the opposite of what they do, and teach as excellently as possible but accomplish as little of this as they can. To the contrary, they do not engage in the course they consider best, but they forgive themselves on the grounds that they have acted unwillingly; and they want to persuade other people but not themselves. They advise them to undertake whatever they themselves cannot achieve, and they recommend to other people actions which, when accused of having failed to fulfill them, they put forward their incapacity as a pretext. Although they show the way to others, they forget that they cannot achieve these things themselves.

Often they even praise and pursue a course contrary to 7 what they were devoted to in the past. For some people this happens quite late in life, but for others quite swiftly. In the former case, people embarrass themselves, it seems, because they were completely unaware during all these past years that they behaved badly in what they were doing; in the latter case, they embarrass others, if they do not realize and criticize the speed with which they freely change their minds.

52

Καὶ μὴν τἀγαθὸν ἅπαντες ἑαυτοῖς, οἶμαι, ζητοῦντες καὶ βέλτιον ὡς ἔξεστι καὶ ῥᾷον καὶ ἄλλος ἄλλο τοῦτο νομίζων καὶ ἄλλοτ' ἄλλως ἴσως ἕκαστος, οἱ μὲν ἐν πράγμασι δή τισι τοῦτο ζητοῦσιν, ἤν που λάχωσιν, οἱ δ' ἐν ἀπραγμοσύνῃ μάλιστα καὶ ἠρεμίᾳ τινί, οἱ δ' ἐν ἄρα τελείᾳ φυγῇ καὶ πάντων, ὡς οἷόν τέ ἐστιν, οἱ δὲ οὐκ οἶδ' ὁτῳοῦν ἄλλῳ, καὶ πάντες ὅμως σχεδὸν εἰς ἕκαστ' ἀφ' ἑκάστων πολλάκις τοῦ βίου καὶ τῆς ζωῆς μεταχωροῦσι καὶ μετατίθενται, καὶ πολλοὶ μὲν καὶ τοῖς πράγμασιν αὐτοῖς εἰς προῦπτον, πολλοὶ δὲ ταῖς γνώμαις, τοῖς ἔργοις οὐκ ἔχοντες.

2   Καὶ μὴν πολὺς ὁ πλάνος ἐνταῦθα, οὐχ ἧττον διὰ τὰ ξυμπίπτοντα ἑκάστοτε ἢ τὸ τῆς ὕλης καὶ τῆς φύσεως ἀστάθμητόν τε καὶ ῥέον ἀεὶ καὶ οὐδενὶ πιστὸν οὐδ' ἀκλόνητον. Πολλοὶ γὰρ δὴ φεύγουσιν ὧντινων ἄρα καὶ προσχωροῦσιν ἑτέροις οὐχ ἧττον δι' ἀνάγκην ἡντιναοῦν, ἅττα δὴ ξυμπίπτει, ἢ κατὰ γνώμην ἀμέλει σφετέραν ἑαυτῶν. Καὶ πολλοὶ τοὔμπαλιν οὐ δι' ἑαυτούς, ἀλλ' ἀβουλήτως καὶ ὃν εἴρηται τρόπον, παραμένουσιν, οἷς ἄρα οὐχ ᾕρηνται, οὐδὲ αὐτοῖς ξυνδοκεῖ, καὶ ὧν μάλιστ' ἐρῶσιν, οὐχ ἑκόντες ὄντες ἀποτρέπονται.

3   Φεύγουσι δ' ἔνιοι μὲν τὰ πράγματα δι' ὀλιγωρίαν ἀληθῆ, σπάνιον τὸ χρῆμα, οἱ δὲ διὰ σφοδρὸν μάλιστα πόθον, ὡς ἂν αὐτῶν ἀτευκτοῦντες, οἱ δὲ δι' ἀργαλεότητα τὴν ἐν αὐτοῖς, ἀκύμονα ποθοῦντες βίον, οἱ δὲ δι' ἔρωτα θεωρίας

Chapter 52

All of us seek, I think, what is good for ourselves, in the best and easiest manner possible. Everyone has a different opinion about what this is and presumably changes his mind on different occasions; some people search for it in whatever business they happen to have, others especially in a quiet life and tranquility, yet others by abstaining completely from everything, to the extent this is possible, others still I know not how. Nearly everyone, however, frequently rejects one lifestyle only to take up another; many people in fact manifestly change even their actions, whereas others change only their opinions, because they cannot change how they behave.

As a result, great commotion arises in this area, due no 2 less to the incidents that occur each time than to the instability of matter and human nature, which is always in flux and is neither reliable in any regard nor unshakable. Many people abandon a particular course and embark upon another more because of some necessity relating to events that occur than in accord with their own judgment. Whereas many, on the other hand, remain faithful to things they do not want and do not like, not on their own volition, but unwillingly, as we said, whereas they reluctantly avoid what they truly love.

Some avoid public affairs out of true indifference, although this is rare indeed. Others avoid them due to excessive desire, because although they want them, they cannot achieve them; others due to their troubles, opting for the tranquil life; others because they love the contemplative

καὶ νοῦ καὶ κτῆσιν ἐπιστήμης καὶ δόξης, ἢ συνέτυχον ἄν,
δόξαν ἀλλαττόμενοι καὶ ἡδονὴν ἡδονῆς, οἱ δὲ δι' ἀνάσκη-
τον ἐν αὑτοῖς γνώμην, οἱ δὲ διὰ βασκανίαν, ἥν τε βασκαίνουσι τοὺς ὑπερέχοντας καὶ ἣν ὑπ' αὐτῶν πάσχουσι κακο-
δοξοῦντες, οἱ δὲ διὰ παντελῆ τύχης ἐρημίαν σεμνοὶ
φιλοσοφοῦσιν ἐφ' ἑαυτῶν καὶ πλάττονται ὥσπερ ἐν σκηνῇ
τινι τὴν ἀναλγησίαν, παραχωροῦντες ἃ μὴ δύνανται καὶ
φεύγοντες ὧν εἰσι πάνυ πόρρω καὶ κατολιγωροῦντες ὧν
οὐκ ἔχουσι, καὶ ἃ μή πως ἔξεστιν, οὐ βούλονται, μᾶλλον
δὲ βούλονται μέν, πλάττονται δ' οὔ, καὶ νοσοῦσιν, ἐφω-
πλίσθαι δέ φασι καὶ σφόδρα ἐρρῶσθαι καὶ γαλήνην μὲν
ἀείποτ' ἔχειν φασί, κῦμα δ' ὕπουλον διὰ παντὸς κυλίνδει
πόντον Αἰγίνης, ἡ παροιμία φησί, καὶ χειμὼν ἔσω λογισμῶν
τοῖς ἀνδράσι στροβεῖ τὰς ψυχάς, καὶ κρατύνονται μὲν
δῆθεν πρὸς ἅπαντα πράγματα, ἐλέγχονται δ', ἢν ἄρα
τύχωσι, κἄν πού τις αὔρα, καὶ βραχεῖα, σφίσι προσπνεύ-
σειεν, αὐτίκα αὐτόθεν μεταβέβληνται προδήλως καὶ προσ-
ετράπησαν καὶ πρύμναν ἐκρούσαντο καὶ πλησίστιοι, φασι,
φέρονται καὶ πρὸς τὴν τῆς τύχης ἔφοδον ταύτην Γοργόνα
Περσεὺς ἐχειρώσατο· καὶ ὁ τέως ἐκεῖνος ἀήττητος καὶ
πάντων παντάπασιν ἀνεπίστροφος κέχηνεν ἄελπτον πρὸς
δέλεαρ, φησὶν ἡ ποίησις, θύννος βολαῖος ὣς στροβούμενος,
καταγελώμενος οὐ τῆς νῦν μετὰ τῶν πολλῶν, ὡς ἄν τις
ἐρεῖ, συμπαθείας, τῆς δὲ πρότερον ἀηθείας ἐκείνης τε καὶ
ἀγερωχίας.

life, intellectual activity, and the possession of knowledge, and are ready to exchange the glory and pleasure they would have enjoyed in public life for the glory and pleasure of wisdom. Others still abstain from public life because they lack experience in such matters, others because of both the envy they feel for those who excel and that which they themselves suffer due to their misguided opinions. Finally, some shun public affairs because of their total lack of good fortune; they investigate the issue by themselves and majestically pretend, as on a stage, that nothing can disturb them, while they give up what they cannot have and avoid what is already far away, and despise what they do not have, and do not want what they cannot possibly have, or rather they want these things but pretend they do not. Although they suffer, they say that they are equipped for anything and are largely healthy; they claim that they are in a constant state of tranquility, but an insidious wave continuously *tosses the sea of Aegina,* as the proverb says, and a storm inside the minds of these men throws their souls into tumult. They purportedly have the power to confront all the difficulties of public life, but as soon as they happen to deal with such affairs, they are exposed. If a breeze blows on them, even a light one, they immediately and manifestly change attitude. They alter direction and back water, swelling the sails, as they say, and heading toward the onslaughts of fortune, as if *Perseus captivated the Gorgon;* the person who until very recently would not yield or ever change his mind in any way now gapes like a *violent tuna fish* that thrashes about at the unexpected sight of the bait, as the poem says. They therefore laugh at him, not because he is now suffering from the same things that many people suffer, as one could argue, but due to his previous odd and arrogant conduct.

53

Καὶ οἱ μὲν οὕτως, οἱ δὲ τοσοῦτον ἄρα τῆς κατὰ τὴν τύχην εὐπλοίας ἐξ ἀρχῆς ἡττήθησάν τε καὶ συνηρπάγησαν καὶ ὅλως ὑπόκουφοι δή τινες γεγόνασι καὶ μετέωροι, ὥστε καὶ παντάπασιν ἑαυτῶν ἐλάθοντο καὶ σφᾶς ἠγνοήκασι, νομίζουσί τε τὴν μὲν τύχην ἀμέλει τἀγαθόν, τὴν δὲ φύσιν ἔλαττον, ἢ τὸ μὲν ἴσως ἡγεῖσθαι, τὴν δὲ φύσιν σύμψηφον, ὡς ἄρ' ὅπου δὴ τὴν τύχην οὖσαν, ἐκεῖ λοιπὸν ἔπεσθαι καὶ ξυνεῖναι πάνθ' ὁμοῦ πράγματα καὶ πᾶσαν ἀρετὴν φύσεως καὶ εὐαρμοστίαν, καὶ τὸ πάντων μάλισθ' ὡς ἀληθῶς πλάνον καὶ πάντων ἀσταθμητότατον αὐτὴν μόνον εἶναι δοκοῦσιν τἀληθέστατον καὶ πάντων ἀσφαλέστατον καὶ σὺν αὐτῇ δὴ μόνοι τὰ πάντων ἔχειν, μόνοι τὰ πάντ' εἰδέναι, τά τ' ἐόντα τά τ' ἐσσόμενα πρό τ' ἐόντα, καὶ πρὸς πάνθ' ὁμοῦ πανδέξιοί τινες εἶναι δρᾶν καὶ κατορθοῦν εὔθηκτοι, ἐν Ἕλλησί, φασι, γράμματα διδάσκειν, ἐν Γαλάταις ὅπλα, ἐν Σκύθαις τόξα, ἐν Λυδοῖς ὀρχεῖσθαι καὶ κατ' οὐδὲν ὁτιοῦν, οὐδὲ τὸ φαυλότατον [. . .]

Chapter 53

So this is what happens with some people. Others, by contrast, have been defeated by the fair voyage of their fortune from the very beginning, they have been led astray and become completely fickle and absentminded, so that they entirely forget themselves and are ignorant of who they really are; they think that fortune is the blessing and that nature is of secondary importance, or otherwise that fortune presumably leads the way and nature merely consents to it. They believe that where fortune is situated, everything else follows and is assembled there, including the whole of virtue and the harmony of nature. Fortune, which is truly the most unstable and unpredictable thing there is, they regard as the only genuine, most stable thing of all, and they think that with fortune by their side they alone will be able to have everything, they alone will be able to know everything, *present, future, and past events.* They think that they are extremely dexterous in achieving everything and are keen on accomplishing all, for instance teaching letters to the Greeks, as they say, warfare to the Gauls, *archery to the Scythians,* dance to the Lydians, and that there is nothing, neither the most worthless [. . .]

54

[. . .] παραβαλλομένων, τῶν μὲν ὑψουμένων ὅσαι ὧραι καὶ καθ᾽ ἑκάστην τῆς ἀγαθῆς τύχης προϊόντων, τῶν δὲ τοὔμπαλιν ξυμπιπτόντων τε καὶ ὑπορρεόντων, τῶν μὲν πολυταλάντοις πλούτοις ὑβριζόντων τε καὶ ἐντρυφώντων, τῶν δὲ ὑπὸ ἐσχάτης πενίας ἀγχομένων τε καὶ προσταλαιπωρούντων, τῶν μὲν μετὰ τῆς εὐπραγίας ἅπαντα εὐπλοούντων καὶ κατορθούντων εὔδρομα ἐπιδιδόντα, τῶν δὲ μετὰ τοῦ ἐναντίου ξυντηκομένων τε καὶ ὑποσυλωμένων καὶ τὰ προσόντα, καὶ καθόλου τῶν μὲν καὶ λέγειν καὶ δρᾶν ὁτιοῦν ἰσχυόντων καὶ κατὰ τῶν ἄλλων, τῶν δὲ πάντα ἡττῆσθαι καὶ φέρειν ἀνάγκην ἐχόντων.

2   Ταῦτα μέντοι πάντα σφόδρα κλονεῖ καὶ διασείει τοὺς λογισμούς, καὶ ὅστις ἀνδρικώτατος, καὶ τὸ μὲν ἄρα προσέχειν τούτοις καθάπαξ καὶ προσηρτῆσθαι, νομίζοντας ἀσφαλῶς τε ἔχειν καὶ πάντα διαρκῶς, ἀληθῶς εὔηθες, τὸ δ᾽ αὖθις ἅπαντα μετρίως φέρειν καὶ παντάπασιν, οἶμαι, περιφρονεῖν, ὡς ἄρα γίγνοιτο, κομιδῇ δυσχερές. Ὡς δ᾽ ὅμως οἷόν τέ ἐστιν ἐπὶ τούτοις, ἀνθεκτέον πᾶσα ἀνάγκη τῶν βελτίστων λογισμῶν καὶ τὴν εἰρημένην ἤδη ταύτην ἀνωμαλίαν ἐντεῦθεν ἰατέον καὶ καχεξίαν καὶ μὴ παντάπασιν ὀλιγωρητέον πρὸς τὸ κοινὸν ἀφορῶντας, ὡς ἐφάμεθα, τόδε τοῦ βίου κατάντημα, ἔνθα δὴ τάχιστα ταῦτα πάντα, κατ᾽ ὀλίγον ἐμπομπεύσαντα ἡμῖν, ὑποχωρεῖ τε καὶ ὑπεξ-

Chapter 54

[. . .] when compared, some people are exalted at every moment and their good fortune increases daily, whereas others, by contrast, meet misfortune and come to grief. Some people pride themselves on and enjoy their excessive wealth, whereas others are choked by a most dreadful poverty and suffer miserably. Some people have only smooth, successful voyages and manage to handle capably the issues they administer, whereas others are worn away by adverse conditions and are even stripped of their possessions. In general, some people can say and do anything, even at the expense of other men, whereas others are forced to be defeated and bear everything.

All the examples above greatly agitate and trouble the mind of even the most steadfast person. When people turn their attention to such things and become involved with them once and for all, believing that they offer them security and that they will have them all forever, this is truly naïve. On the other hand, I also believe that it is enormously difficult for a person to endure these matters with equanimity and not care how they turn out. To the extent that this is possible, however, we must perforce cleave to the best reasoning and we must heal this deficiency and sickness we already discussed. We must not remain totally indifferent when we see, as we said, that this is a common evil in everyone's life, for every single thing first accompanies us for a while, but then quickly departs and secretly abandons us. We ought to keep in mind that this rationale is the only

ἴσταται, τοῦτο δὴ δοκοῦντας μόνον δεδόσθαι ἀλεξητήριον τῆς ἐπὶ τοῖς γιγνομένοις τῶν λογισμῶν νόσου τε καὶ τροπῆς.

55

Καὶ μήν, οἶμαι, νομίζουσιν ἕτερον ἔνιοι τρόπον, ὡς ἔτ᾽ ἔξεστιν ἀμέλει πρὸς ἅπασαν τύχην παραβαλλόμενον αὐτόν τινα ἑαυτὸν ἕκαστον ἐπανισοῦν καὶ μηδενὸς ἡττῆσθαι, μηδ᾽ ἄν εἴ τι γίγνηται, τῆς οἴκοθεν ὁρμῆς τε καὶ γνώμης πρὸς ἅπαντ᾽ ἐρρωμένως παρεσκευασμένον.

2 Ὅλως μὲν γάρ, ἥντινά τις ἐρεῖ τύχην ἅπασαν, ἀπατηλόν τέ ἐστι καὶ πλάνον καὶ παντάπασι καὶ ἀείποτε ψεύδεται καὶ οὐδὲν ἄρα μήποτε πρὸς οὐδένα ἀνθρώπων ἔχει πιστόν, ἄν τ᾽ ἀγαθή τις ἄν τε φαύλη, καὶ σώφρων ὡς ἀληθῶς ἐκεῖνος ἄνθρωπος, ὅστις μὴ πάντα ἐν πᾶσι ταύτῃ προσνένευκε, μηδ᾽ ἐπιπείθεται ἠμὲν καὶ χερείοσι δαίμονος ἠδὲ καὶ ἐσθλοῖς, ἀλλ᾽ οἶδε μὲν τοῦτο μάλιστ᾽ ἀσφαλῶς, ὡς ἔστιν ἐκ βελτιόνων ἀλλάξασθαι χείρω καὶ χρυσέων ὡς ἀληθῶς χάλκεα καὶ μεθ᾽ ὑγείαν νοσεῖν καὶ μετὰ πλοῦτον πένεσθαι καὶ μετ᾽ εὐδοξίαν ἄκρατον ὥσπερ ἀνδράποδον ἐπιτρίβεσθαι καὶ τὸν χθές τε καὶ πρώην καὶ νῦν ὑπερύψηλον ὅσον οὐκ ἤδη μελλήσειν κατατίθεσθαι τὸ δρᾶμα καὶ τὴν σκηνὴν ταύτην ἀλγεινότατα μὲν αὐτῷ, καταγελαστότατα δὲ τοῖς ἐχθροῖς καὶ βασκαίνουσιν, οἶδε δὲ ὡς ἔστιν αὖθις ἐκ κακίστων ἀλλάξασθαι κάλλιστα καὶ μετὰ χειμῶνα καὶ

remedy we have been given against the sickness and commotion of our intellect that comes about due to several events.

Chapter 55

But I believe that some people think that there is indeed another way in which everyone can maintain his composure and not yield to anything when encountering any misfortune, no matter what might happen, namely when he is prepared for any eventuality with the strength of his individual desire and judgment.

For what we generally call fate is deceptive and fickle, it deceives us in all respects and all situations, so that no one can ever trust it, be it good or bad. The truly wise man is the one who is not wholly inclined toward fate and puts no faith in either the good or the ill turns of fate, but is instead fully aware that matters can change from better to worse, from truly gold to bronze, that after health comes sickness, after wealth comes poverty, and that after enjoying supreme glory a person can be crushed like a slave. The truly wise man also knows that the person who only yesterday or the day before or even today is soaring exceedingly high is very soon destined to put aside the performance and this stage, although this will be extremely painful to him and result in great ridicule by his enemies and those who envy him. On the other hand, the wise man knows that one can pass again from great misfortune to great happiness, and after storms, 2

ζάλην πᾶσαν καὶ κλύδωνα πρύμναν τε κρούσασθαι καὶ ἐξ
οὐρίου δραμεῖν καὶ πάνθ᾽ ὡς ἀληθῶς τὰ κατ᾽ ἀνθρώπους,
ὡς ἅπαντες ξύνισμεν, ὥσπερ ἐν ἀτεκμάρτοις πεττείαις
μεταχωρεῖ καὶ μετακυβεύεται.

3   Ἀμείβει γὰρ ὁ μέν τις εὐπραγίαν εἰς τοὐναντίον, ὁ δὲ
θάτερον εἰς εὐπραγίαν καὶ τῷ μὲν εὐπραγοῦντι προσ-
δοκᾶν ἐστι τραπέσθαι καὶ χείρω τύχην, εἰ σωφρονεῖ—ἢ τί
γὰρ ἕτερον;—τῷ δὲ κακῶς πράττοντι πρόσεισιν ὅμως
ἔπειτα ἐλπίδες καὶ καλλίω μεταλαχεῖν τύχην, ἢν καὶ αὐτὸς
σωφρονῇ. Ὥσθ᾽ ὁ μέν, οἶμαι, πλουτεῖ νῦν, ὁ δὲ ταῖς ἐλπίσιν
ὕστερον κἄθ᾽ οὕτως ἐπανισωτέον, ὡς ἔοικεν, ἑαυτὸν πλέον
ἔχοντά, φασι, καὶ λειπόμενον λειπομένῳ παραπλησίως καὶ
πλέον ἔχοντι. Εἰ δ᾽ ὁ μὲν ὑβρίζει κακῶς τῇ τύχῃ φρονῶν,
ὁ δ᾽ ἀπογινώσκει τῶν ἀείποτ᾽ ἐν προσδοκίαις ὄντων, ἑκά-
τερος ἁμαρτάνει πάντως, τῶν γιγνομένων οὐ ξυνιέντες,
οὐκ οἶδα δ᾽ ὡς ἀληθῶς ὁπότερος μᾶλλον τῆς ἀνοίας μέμ-
φεσθαι δίκαιος. Ἁμαρτάνουσι δ᾽ ὅμως ἀμφοτέροις ἔλεος
ὀφείλεται καὶ συγγνώμη καὶ παιδευτέον, εἰ οἷόν τέ ἐστι,
τοὺς ἄνδρας καὶ ἀνορθωτέον ἀγνοοῦντας, οὐ συναμαρ-
τητέον νοῦν ἔχουσι. Καὶ μὴν ἀμφοτέρωθεν ἂν οὐκ ἀηδῶς
ἔχειν μοι δοκεῖ τὸ πρᾶγμα [. . .]

squalls, and waves, one can back water and voyage with a fair wind; and that indeed all human affairs, as we all understand, change and are turned on their head, exactly as with backgammon, a game of chance.

One person exchanges a state of well-being for the opposite, and at the same time someone else moves on to happiness. The prosperous person, if he is prudent, should expect that fortune can take a turn for the worse—or what else?—while to one whose affairs are faring poorly come hopes that his luck will improve in the future, if, of course, he too is prudent. As a consequence, the former, I believe, is rich now, the latter has hopes of becoming rich in the future, and accordingly, it seems, they must assess themselves equally; the one with many possessions, they say, must account himself nearly equal with the one who has nothing, and the poor man with the wealthy one. But if the rich person behaves arrogantly and is unpleasant because of his good fortune, whereas the poor person despairs of matters that are constantly in expectation, no doubt they both err, because they are unaware of what happens in real life, and I honestly do not know which of the two deserves more blame for stupidity. Although they are both wrong, one needs to forgive them and feel compassion for them, and if possible educate them and set the ignorant straight, since the wise should not share in their error. In any case, I think that this issue would not be at all unpleasant [. . .]

56

[. . .] δραμεῖν τε καὶ τῆς τοσαύτης εὐπραγίας αἰχμαλώτους ἀνδραποδίσασθαι σφᾶς καὶ κατατυραννῆσαι. Δοκοῦσι τέ μοι καθάπερ ἐν χειμῶνι λογισμῶν ἀείποτε ναυαγεῖν, ἐπ' ὀλίγου σκάφους μεγίστην εὐδαιμονίαν ἐμπορευόμενοι καὶ μηδέποτ' ἀνύποπτοι κινδύνου πλέοντες, ἀλλ' ἐν χρῷ πάντοτ' εἶναι καὶ βιοτεύειν νομίζοντες τοῦ δεινοῦ.

2 Τοιγαροῦν σφόδρα τε δεδίασι διὰ παντὸς καὶ ἴδῃς ἂν αὐτοὺς μνημονικωτάτους πλεῖν ἢ κατὰ τοὺς ἄλλους αὐτοῦ τοῦ θανάτου, ὃν ὡς ἔφεδρον ἐπίβουλον καὶ χαλεπὸν τύραννον καὶ συλητὴν ἀείποθ' ὑφορῶνται καὶ προφέρουσι, καὶ ὥσπερ οἵ τινας δυσοδίας καὶ χώρους ὑπόπτους τε καὶ δυσαντήτους, καὶ αὐτοὶ τὸν τῆς ζωῆς ἅπαντα χρόνον μεθ' ἁπάσης τῆς οὐσίας παριόντες, ἀνδραποδιστήν τιν' ἐνταῦθα τὸν θάνατον καὶ λωποδύτην ἑκάστοτ' ἐλλοχεῖν νομίζουσι καὶ μέγιστον ἀείποτε τὸν φόβον καὶ πλείστην ὅσην τὴν ἀνίαν εἰς ἅπασαν τὴν ζωὴν ἐκτραγῳδοῦσι καὶ καταστένουσιν, ἐλεεῖσθαι τοῦ πάθους, οὐ θαυμάζεσθαι τῆς τύχης ἄξιοι.

3 Μᾶλλον δ' ὅπερ ὁ λόγος ἐξ ἀρχῆς εἶχεν, ἐνταῦθα δὴ προσεκτέον εἶναί μοι τοῖς ἀνδράσι δοκεῖ καὶ τοσοῦτο συλλογιστέον, ὡς ἅπασα δυσπραγία τε καὶ τῶν δοκούντων ἀγαθῶν ἀτευξία πρὸς τοὺς τοσούτους ἐργώδεις καὶ πονηροὺς κομιδῇ φροντισμοὺς καὶ τὴν ἀγχόνην τῶν λογισμῶν τούτων, ὧν εἴρηται νῦν, οὓς αἱ μεγάλαι τύχαι τρέφουσι, μέγ' οὐδὲν ὄντως, οὐδὲ χεῖρον, ἀλλ' ἐπανισοῦται.

Chapter 56

[. . .] to rush and enslave those who are captivated by such enormous well-being, and subject them to tyrannical rule. They give me the impression that they always suffer shipwreck in a storm of thought by loading an extremely heavy cargo of happiness onto a small vessel, and they never sail without fearing the danger, but believe that their life is always on the brink of peril.

This is why they are much afraid of everything and you 2 might notice that they are more mindful than anyone else of death, which they always suspect and bring before themselves as a devious competitor, a cruel tyrant, and a despoiler. Like those who tread difficult paths and places that are suspect and bode ill, they spend their whole life carrying all their property with them, thinking that death is constantly lurking there in order to kidnap them or rob them. They continually lament and sigh over the great fear and extraordinary sadness they feel throughout their life, and they do not deserve admiration for their good luck but compassion for their misfortune.

Instead, as I stated already at the very beginning, at this 3 point I believe that I should examine these men and consider that no misfortune or deprivation of apparent blessings is truly significant or worse, but that it balances out evenly, compared to the troublesome, grievous reflections which, as we have just said, suffocate the person who has them and are nourished by great success in life.

4 Ὅλως μὲν γὰρ ἄπασαν ἡδονήν τε καὶ λύπην οἱ λογισμοὶ τίκτουσι, καὶ ὡς ἔχει τις ἀμέλει φρονήματος, ἀμφότερα, οἶμαι, πάσχει, καὶ δι᾽ ἑαυτὸν κακῶς τε πράττει καὶ μή, μᾶλλον δ᾽ ἔξεστιν ἴσως, ἔοικεν, ἀπονώτερον διάγειν τῶν λογισμῶν καὶ ἀνεπαχθέστερον ἐπὶ ταπεινῆς τύχης ἢ λοιπὸν ἐπ᾽ ἀμείνονος, καὶ τὸν μὲν ἀνιᾷ τὰ πράγματα μὴ παρόντα, τὸν δὲ παρόντα μὲν νῦν, ἀλλ᾽ ὅμως, ἀνάγκη πᾶσα, ὕστερον ἀφαιρησόμενα, σφόδρα ἀνιᾷ. Ἡ γὰρ μετὰ τὴν πεῖραν στέρησις ἀλγεινότερον, τὸ δὲ μέλλον ἐνταῦθ᾽ ὡς ἤδη παρὸν ἀσφαλέστατον.

57

Τοιγαροῦν δεῖξον ὡς κρεῖττον εἶ τοῖς λογισμοῖς—δύνη δέ—καὶ νενίκηκας τὸν ὑπ᾽ αὐτῶν ἀείποτ᾽ ἀγχόμενον. Δεῖξον ὡς ὁ μὲν ἔξωθεν εὖ ἔχει, σὺ δὲ γαλήνην ἔχεις ἐντὸς καὶ διάθεσιν ἵλεων, ὁ μὲν ἀλλοτρίοις αἴρεται καὶ θαρρεῖ τοῖς οὐχ ἑαυτοῦ, σὺ δὲ τῆς αὐτὸς αὐτοῦ παρασκευῆς ἔρρωσαι. Καὶ τοίνυν τῷ μὲν δῆλον ὡς οὐχ ἑαυτοῦ δεῖ, τινῶν δ᾽ ἄλλων ἔξωθεν, σοὶ δὲ σαυτοῦ καὶ νοῦ σώφρονος, ῥᾷον δὲ σαυτὸν ἔχειν ἢ βούλει πάντως ἤ τι τῶν ἔξω. Μὴ δὴ κάμῃς σεαυτόν, ὡς ἔξεστιν, εὖ ποιῶν, ἔξεστι δὲ οὐ πάνυ τοι

For every pleasure and every sorrow is a construction of 4
our thoughts, and I think that every person experiences
both of these emotions depending on his mood, and that he
fares badly or not because of himself. It is perhaps easier, it
seems, to lead a less painful life and one free from anxieties,
when one is of humble rather than higher status. The former individual is distressed by the lack of certain things,
whereas the latter is distressed even more by what he now
has but will inevitably lose later on. For it causes more grief
to be deprived of what you have already experienced, and in
the case of a wealthy man the future is as certain as if it were
already present.

Chapter 57

So simply show that you are better in the way you think—
you can—and you are victorious over the person who is always constrained by his thoughts. Demonstrate that he
prospers externally, whereas you have internal tranquility
and a quiet disposition; show that he is exalted by external
matters and does not derive courage from his own resources,
whereas you are strong enough due to your predisposition.
Obviously he cannot rely upon himself but needs external
substitutes, whereas you rely exclusively on yourself and
your prudent mind; and it is much easier to use your own
help, however you wish, than the help of something external. Do not weary yourself trying to prepare as much as possible; this can happen without too much difficulty; I have

δυσχερῶς. Εἴρηται, πολλάκις εἴρηται. Νικᾷ τῇ τύχῃ; Νίκα τοῖς λογισμοῖς. Ὑβρίζῃ; Μὴ ταπεινοῦ. Ἔμπληκτός ἐστιν; Ὑγίαινε σύ. Ἐπιδείκνυται τὴν εὐπραγίαν καὶ τετύφωται κατὰ σοῦ ὡς ἔχων τι πλέον; Μάλιστα μὲν μὴ πείθου, πλάττεται, ξύνοιδεν ἑαυτῷ μηδὲν ἀληθὲς ἀγαθὸν ἔχοντι, ἢν ὅλως νοῦν ἔχῃ.

2   Εἰ δὲ μή, δεῖξον, ἀλλ᾽ οὐδ᾽ ὡς αὐτὸς ἀλγεῖς, οὐδ᾽ ἧττον ἔχων φρονεῖς, ἀλλ᾽ εἰς ταὐτὸν ἀξίωμα γνώμης διάγεις περὶ αὐτοῦ καὶ ξυναισθήσεται μηδὲν λοιπὸν πλέον ἔχων, ὅτι μηδὲ τοῦ φρονήματος πλέον, ἐν ᾧ τὸ ἥδεσθαί τε καὶ μή, καὶ σφόδρα ὀδυνήσεται τὸ σὸν ἀνάλγητον. Ἐπιθήσεταί σοι λοιπὸν καὶ κακῶς δράσει, κράτος ἴσως ἔχων, ὡς ἂν ἀνιάσῃ καὶ δείξῃ τι πλέον ἔχων αὐτός; Ἀντεπίδειξον ὡς οὐκ ἐντρέπῃ, πρὸς δὲ τὸ μέλλον ὡς ἤδη παρὸν ὁρᾷς, ἐν ᾧ μάλιστα μὲν οὐκ ἀπροσδόκητον ταὐτὰ παθεῖν παρ᾽ ἄλλου καὶ αὐτόν, ἃ νομίζει προστρίβεσθαί σοι δεινά.

3   Εἰ δὲ μή, βραχὺς ὅμως ὁ χρόνος καὶ ἀμφοτέρους δεήσει πάντως κεῖσθαι τοῦ μηδενὸς ἐπίσης ἀξίους καὶ πλέον ὀντιναοῦν ἑτέρου μὴ φέροντα. Ἂν τοῦτο ἐπιδείξῃ καὶ οὐκ ἀνιάσῃ, σφόδρα αὐτὸς ἀνιάσεται καὶ πεπλήξεται μέσην αὐτὴν τὴν καρδίαν, ὅτι μηδὲν τῆς τύχης ἔχει σου πλέον. Κατακερτομήσει λοιπὸν καὶ καταμωκήσεται, φιλοσκώμμων τις ὢν καὶ φιλαίτιος, ὡς δῆθεν ἐντεῦθεν ἀπελέγξων ἑαυτὸν πλέον ἔχοντα καὶ σέ γε ἡττημένον; Ἂν μὲν ἐπὶ πολλοῖς μάρτυσι καὶ παρρησίᾳ δι᾽ ἐξουσίαν, οὐδ᾽ αὐτός, εἰ

said this, I have said this many times. Does someone have the best over you due to benevolent fortune? Defeat him with your thoughts. Does someone insult you? Do not lose spirit. Is he crazed? Retain your sanity. Does he show off his wealth and is he proud of having more possessions than you do? Do not believe him at all, he is dissimulating. He knows quite well, if he is sane, of course, that he has not a single genuine blessing.

If he does not realize that, you should show him that nei- 2 ther are you suffering nor do you feel inferior, but that you have the same reputation for judgment as he has, and he will thus understand that he has no more than you do, because nothing is more important than one's spirit, on which happiness and sadness depend; your own cheerfulness will cause him great sorrow. Will he then attack you and do you harm, presumably with force, in order to distress you and prove that he has more than you do? Show him in return that you are not afraid and that you look to the future as if it were already the present, in which future it is not unexpected that he may suffer from another person precisely the dreadful things he considers inflicting on you.

Even if he suffers nothing, time passes quickly; both of 3 you will inevitably be buried, and in the grave you will both be worth nothing and neither of you will take with him any more than the other. If you demonstrate this and are not upset, he will be very aggrieved and wounded in his heart, because his fortune is no better than yours. Might he then castigate and rebuke you, because he is fond of scoffing and censorious, in an attempt to prove that he himself is the one who has more and you are the inferior? If he does so in front of many witnesses and with the confidence he draws from

βούλει ταὐτὰ κακῶς δρᾶν, ἀπορήσεις τῶν ἀκροασομένων, οὐδ᾽ ἂν ὅπως ἔχοις, οὐδ᾽ ἂν ὅπως πράττοις, ἀλλ᾽ εὑρήσεις οὕστινας δὴ καί σοι παρέσονται καὶ προσκαθεδοῦνται καὶ μάλα τοι τὰς κατ᾽ αὐτοῦ προθύμως αἰτίας καὶ λοιδορίας ἀκούσονται, καὶ ἴσως καὶ κρείττους σοί γε καὶ ἀληθέστεροί τε καὶ συνετώτεροι, πάντως δ᾽ οὖν εὐνούστεροί γε καὶ ἡδύτερον ἀκροώμενοι.

4   Πρὸς σὲ μὲν γὰρ οὐδεὶς φθόνος, ἀλλὰ καὶ τυχὸν ἔλεος, τῷ δὲ οἱ πλείους βασκαίνουσι καὶ μεμψιμοιροῦσιν ἡδέως ἐπιτιμῶντες διὰ τὴν ὑπεροχὴν καὶ λοιδορούμενοι καὶ καταμεμφόμενοι. Εἰ δέ γ᾽ ἐφ᾽ ἑαυτοῦ μόνου, ἀλλὰ καὶ σοὶ ταὐτὸ τοῦτο μάλιστ᾽ ἔξεστιν ἐπὶ σαυτοῦ καὶ ἴσως ἐπ᾽ ἀμείνονος ἢ κατ᾽ ἐκεῖνον ἀκροατοῦ καὶ κριτοῦ καὶ ὡς ἂν τύχῃς αὐτὸς παρεσκευασμένος.

5   Ἐνταῦθα γέ τοι καὶ ὁ λόγος ἄριστός σοι θεωρὸς καὶ συνεξεταστὴς καὶ μάλιστ᾽ ἔστιν ἐν τούτοις προύργιαίτατον ἡ τῆς σοφίας παρασκευὴ καὶ λυσιτελέστατον, ἐπιστραφῆναι πρὸς ἑαυτὸν γεννικῶς καὶ πορίσασθαι πρὸς τὴν ἀνίαν ἀλέξημα κατοπτεῦσαί τε τἀλλότριον ἁμάρτημα καὶ καταστεῖλαι τὰ σφέτερα αὐτοῦ καὶ παιδαγωγεῖσθαι καὶ παρεξετάζειν ἅμα θ᾽ ἑαυτὸν καὶ τὴν τοῦ γείτονος ἀντίπαλον ἀμετρίαν, ὀρθὸν τὸν λόγον ἐπίσκοπον προβαλλόμενον ἐπ᾽ ἀμφότερα καὶ παραστάτην δεξιόν, μὴ κατολισθαίνειν, ὥσπερ ἄρ᾽ ἐκεῖνος ὁ βαρύστονος, οἶμαι, καὶ παλαμναῖος ἐμπίπτει διόλου καὶ δεινὰ πάσχει ἄνευ χειραγωγοῦ τινος προηγμένος καὶ ξυνίησι καὶ δεδαπάνηται

his alleged power, if you want to harm him in the same way, you will not be left without an audience either, no matter what your condition is, no matter how you are faring. You will find some people who will approach you and take a seat next to you, to eagerly hear the accusations and abuse you hurl against your enemy; perhaps those men will be better, more sincere, and more prudent with you, but at any rate they will certainly be quite well-disposed and very happy to hear you.

No envy will be directed against you; to the contrary, they 4 might feel sorry for you. But as for the person who accuses you, most people envy, blame, and attack him with pleasure because of his preeminence, and in addition they abuse and castigate him. If he insults you just by himself, you can do exactly the same by yourself, and you may perhaps find a better listener and judge than he can, depending on your preparation.

In this case indeed, education will become your best 5 spectator and fellow investigator, and especially in such instances, the acquisition of wisdom is very serviceable and beneficial: you will proceed bravely to self-introspection and provide yourself with protection against distress; at the same time, you will encounter the mistakes of your fellow men and restrain your own. You will be trained to compare yourself to the immoderation of the rivals who are near to you, employing the faculty of reason as an infallible arbiter in both cases, and as a kind comrade who will keep you from slipping, resembling that much-lamented, abominable man, I suppose, who falls completely and suffers terribly because he had no one to guide him when he initially set out. He

πλείστας ἐπιδραμεῖν λαβὰς παρέχων τῷ καλῶς ἐποπτεύ-
οντι καὶ ἡδομένῳ δυσμενεῖ, ἀσθενὴς ὄντως καὶ εὐεπι-
χείρητος τῷ καλῶς ἐσκευασμένῳ τε καὶ ὡπλισμένῳ τῇ ἐκ
τοῦ λόγου βοηθείᾳ καὶ νῷ σώφρονι.

58

Τοιγαροῦν ὁ μὲν οὐκ ἀηδῶς διάγει καὶ ξυλλογίζεται
μεθ᾽ ἵλεω γνώμης καὶ μετριάζει τῇ τῆς ψυχῆς εὐδίᾳ, ἐπ-
αναπαυόμενος τῷ λόγῳ καὶ ὥσπερ εὐαγώγοις τισὶ καὶ
εὐδρόσοις αὔραις ὑπ᾽ αὐτοῦ καταπνεόμενος, ὁ δ᾽ ἄρα ξυν-
τέτηκε καὶ κατάγχεται, οὐδὲν μήποθ᾽ ὁρῶν ἑαυτῷ πλέον,
καὶ φιλονεικεῖ μὲν ἀείποθ᾽ ὁτιοῦν, ἢν οἷός τ᾽ εἴη περιγενέσθαι, οὐκ ἔχει δ᾽ ὅστις γένοιτ᾽ ἄν, οὐδ᾽ ὅ,τι χρήσαιτο,
ὑπ᾽ ἀμαθίας ἐξηπορημένος. Κἂν μὲν ἴσως ἔπειτ᾽ ἀγαπῴη
καὶ μετριώτερον ἄρα καὶ ἠρέμα καταπαύων χρῷτο, ἡδὺς
ἂν οὕτως εἴη τοῦ λοιποῦ καὶ βελτίων, νοῦν τ᾽ ἔχων τινά,
οὐδὲν ἂν ἑαυτῷ παρέχοι πράγματα, τιμῶν ἡσυχίᾳ τἄμει-
νον.

2   Εἰ δέ τι περιεργάζεται καὶ φιλονεικῶν ἐπέξεισί τε καὶ
προσεπιδείκνυσι τὴν ὕβριν καταπολαύειν θ᾽ αἱρεῖται τοῦ
κράτους, ἔμπληκτος ἐπιτιθέμενος ἀείποτε καὶ μεμηνὼς
λόγοις τε καὶ οὐκ οἶδ᾽ οἷστισι πράγμασι, τύφῳ, περιβολαῖς,

understands how ill-fated he is, he is utterly destroyed, exhibiting a great number of weak points for attack to his enemy, who takes good notice of them and is content with them. This man is truly weak and easy prey for anyone who is firmly prepared and equipped with the assistance of reason and a prudent mind.

Chapter 58

The former person accordingly lives pleasantly, thinks with kindly judgment, and remains moderate as a result of the tranquility of his soul, since he relies on reason, which blows over him like fair and refreshing breezes, as it were. The latter person, on the other hand, is worn away and strangled as soon as he realizes that he is not at all superior to others. He is constantly striving to prevail in whatever he can, but because of his ignorance he is not even sure who he is or what he is doing. And if later on he might be satisfied with what he has and use it with more moderation and gentleness, putting an end to his extravagance, he could thus thereafter become better and agreeable, a reasonable man, could spare himself trouble, and could revere in quiet contemplation the better course in life.

Alternatively, he might waste his time in daily labors, assault others by quarreling and exhibiting his arrogance, and choose to enjoy his power fully, always attacking other people with vehemence and driven mad by words and actions of one sort or another: vanity, capricious and stupid prolixity, 2

ἐμπλήκτοις, ἀλογίστοις, πάντ᾽ ἀνίσοις ὁρμαῖς, ἀκαιρίᾳ
πομπικῇ, μέθαις, πᾶσι βλακεύμασι, κορδακισμοῖς, βδελ-
λυρίαις, φρυαγμοῖς, ἀναιδείᾳ πάσῃ καὶ ἀσωτίᾳ, συνελόντ᾽
εἰπεῖν, καταχρώμενος ἀμέτρως ἁπάσῃ τῇ τύχῃ, ὡς ἄν τι
πλέον ἐντεῦθεν ἀποφερόμενος· εἰ μὲν ἔπειθ᾽ ὅμως καὶ
οὕτω πάλιν ἐπάνεισι μετρίως τελευτῶν οἴκαδε καὶ ἐν ἑαυτοῦ γίγνεται καὶ καιρὸν ὀντιναοῦν λογισμῶν δίδωσι καὶ
ἀναφέρει, εὖ ἴσθι ὡς ἔτι πλέον τηνικαῦτα πάντ᾽ ἐλέγχει
ταῦτα καὶ οὐδὲν βέλτιον ἑαυτῷ ξυνορᾷ χρώμενος καὶ τοῖς
αὐτοῦ.

3   Εἰ δ᾽ οὐδὲν οὐδαμῶς ἑαυτοῦ γίγνεται καὶ κατ᾽ ὀλίγον
ἀποχωρεῖ, ἀλλ᾽ ἀεὶ τοῖς τοιούτοις ἀνεπίστροφος ἐμφιλοχω-
ρεῖ τε καὶ πρόεισι, τότ᾽ ἂν εἴη μᾶλλον ἀθλιώτερος ἑαυτοῦ
τε καὶ πάντων ἄνθρωπος, καὶ οὐκ οἶδ᾽ ὁπότερον ἂν φαίην
γελοιότερος εἴτε δυστυχέστερος, ἀηδίᾳ τοσαύτῃ καὶ νόσῳ
καὶ μοχθηρίᾳ ξυνοικῶν καὶ κατεχόμενος. Καὶ Διογένης
μὲν ὁ Κύων παριὼν Ἀθήνησιν οὕτω καὶ μειράκιόν τι τῶν
εὐγενῶν ἰδὼν ἐν καπηλείῳ, ἐπειδὴ καταιδεσάμενον ἐκεῖνον
προῆλθεν ἔσω κρυπτόμενον, "ἀλλὰ σύ γε," ἔφησεν, "οὐχ
ὁρᾷς ὡς ἔτι μᾶλλον ἔσω τοῦ δεινοῦ γίγνῃ καὶ τῆς αἰσχύνης,
ἣν δοκεῖς φεύγειν;"

utterly unfair violence, arrogant impropriety, drunkenness, all kinds of stupidity, indecent dancing, coarseness, insolence, every other sort of shamelessness and profligacy, to sum up, immoderately abusing all his good fortune as if he were going to derive some sort of profit from it. Nonetheless, if after such behavior, he returns home again ending his life in moderation, and comes to his senses, allowing time to reconsider his behavior and recover, you should know that he examines all these things even more in this case and realizes that he does not bring anything better to himself or his affairs.

If he does not come to his senses at all and gradually distance himself from his bad behavior, but on the contrary heedlessly abides by such behavior, so that it worsens, then he would in all instances be the most wretched man alive and the worst version of himself. I do not even know what to call him, the most ridiculous or the most unfortunate man, given that he shares his abode with and is possessed by such disgusting behavior, unsoundness, and malice. Likewise, when Diogenes the Cynic philosopher went to Athens and saw a noble youth in a tavern, who felt embarrassed by Diogenes and moved inside the tavern as a way of hiding himself, Diogenes said to him: "Can't you see that the deeper you flee inside, the more deeply involved you become in vice and shameful activities, which you think you are avoiding?"

59

Πρὸς δὲ τὸν ἔξεστιν ἴσως ἐρεῖν, οὕτως ὑβριστικώτερον καθόλου προηγμένον καὶ κακὸν κακῶς τε καὶ κάκιον ἀείποτ᾽ ἐμπομπεύοντα τῇ τύχῃ καὶ καταχρώμενον ἐπὶ τοῖς εὐγενέσιν ἀνδράσι καὶ ἐλλογίμοις, ὡς ἄρα ἔχοντά τι πλέον καὶ τῆς κατ᾽ αὐτῶν μάχης ἑκάστοτε προϊόντα καὶ σφᾶς ἡττημένους οὕτω παμπληθὲς τῆς ἑαυτοῦ περιουσίας καὶ μοχθηρίας· "Ἀλλὰ σύ γε, ὦ βέλτιστε, οὐκ αἰσθάνῃ ὡς χεῖρον ἀεὶ πράττεις καὶ προέρχῃ καὶ νικᾷς ἀεὶ σαυτὸν τοῖς κακίστοις, οὐ τοὺς σὺν λόγῳ σε κατοπτεύοντας καὶ κατεγγελῶντας, καὶ τῇ σῇ νόσῳ προστίθης, οὐ τῇ κατ᾽ αὐτῶν μάχῃ καὶ νίκῃ, μᾶλλον δὲ τοῖς μὲν καὶ εὐχερέστερον κατὰ σαυτοῦ δίδως νικᾶν καὶ ῥᾷον ἢ τέως ᾤοντο, σαυτὸν δ᾽ ἄγχεις μᾶλλον καὶ καταστρέφεις, ὥσπερ οἱ κατὰ τῶν κοντῶν ὠθούμενοι χοῖροι καὶ προσβιαζόμενοι μᾶλλον ἁπάσῃ ῥώμῃ τοῖς θηρευταῖς ἀπονώτερον τὸν κατ᾽ αὐτῶν ὄλεθρον ἀπεργάζονται, νομίζων τε κατ᾽ αὐτῶν ἀκολασταίνειν τε καὶ ἰσχύειν, σαυτὸν ἀθλίως ἀπόλλυς, εἰ καὶ μὴ νῦν γε δι᾽ ἀμαθίαν οὐ δοκεῖς, τοῖς αὐτὸς αὐτοῦ νοσήμασι καὶ κακοῖς ἐπεντρυφῶν.

2   "Οἱ δὲ ξυνορῶσι τό τε βέλτιον καὶ μὴ καὶ λόγῳ κρίνουσιν, ὃν συνέμπορον σφίσι, μᾶλλον δ᾽ ἄγρυπνον ἡγεμόνα καὶ διδάσκαλον ἔχουσιν, ὧν τε ἥδεσθαι χρὴ καὶ ὧν τοὐναντίον, παιδαγωγοῦντα περὶ τούτων αὐτῶν τῶν

Chapter 59

When a person who excels behaves so arrogantly, always bragging with increasing wickedness about his good fortune and abusing noble and educated men, because he believes that he is superior in some regard and can always advance against them in battle and defeat them with his abundant wealth and malice, we can perhaps say to him: "My dear friend, you do not understand that your behavior is growing worse and worse, that you increase in viciousness and that with your extremely bad behavior you are constantly defeating yourself and not those who use education to observe and mock you. You aggravate your disease, but you cannot defeat them in battle; rather, you are offering them the chance to defeat you more readily and more easily than they previously expected, while you are instead strangling and destroying yourself, behaving like boars who thrust themselves onto hunters' pikes as they rush against them with full force, bringing about their own destruction with less effort for the hunters. By assuming that you are behaving licentiously against them and that you control them, you are actually destroying yourself wretchedly, even if currently you do not seem to be doing so due to your ignorance, indulging yourself in your own sicknesses and woes.

"Your enemies, by contrast, can see what is better and 2 what is not, and can use their education, which they have as a traveling companion, or rather as a vigilant guide and teacher, to make distinctions between what should and should not please them; and it instructs them about these very matters, about how to perceive more precisely pleasant

ἡδέων τε καὶ λυπηρῶν ἀκριβέστερον ἐπαΐειν καὶ τεταγμένα
βαδίζειν κατὰ τὴν παροιμίαν."

60

Καίτοι γ' ἐνίων καὶ τοῦτ' ἔξεστιν ἀκούειν, ὡς ξὺν ὀλίγῳ
μάλιστα νῷ βιωτέον ἂν εἴη ἢ λόγον τε καὶ φρόνησιν προσ-
πορισαμένους πλείστην· μηδὲ γὰρ εἶναι πλέον ἐντεῦθεν
ἀλλ' ἢ πλέον τε ξυνιέναι καὶ πλέον ἀνιᾶσθαι, ἄμεινον δ'
εἶναι πολλῷ μήτ' ἐπαΐειν περὶ τῶν ὄντων πλεῖστον καὶ
βιοῦν ἀπονώτερον. Οὕτω δὴ πόρρω παντάπασιν ἀνοίας
τε καὶ ἀμαθίας σπουδάζουσι καὶ τοῦ παρόντος, ὅπως ἂν
ἥδοιντο μόνον, εἰσὶν ἐρασταί. Πρὸς οὓς οὐκ οἶδ' ὅ,τι ἂν
τις καὶ ἐρεῖ, μηδὲν οὕτως ἀμέλει ξυνιέντας, μηδὲ βουλο-
μένους.

2   Ὅμως δὴ πευσόμεθα τῶν ἀνδρῶν τοσοῦτο βραχύ, εἰ καὶ
πλέειν μέλλοντες βούλοιντ' ἂν πλέειν ἀξυνέτως παντάπασι
καὶ ἀπρομηθεύτως πρὸς ἅπασαν καὶ ἀνέμων ἐπιβουλὴν
καὶ χειμῶνος καὶ πειρατῶν ἐπήρειαν, ἵν' ἀφροντιστότερόν
τε καὶ ἀπονώτερον πλέοιεν, καὶ οὐ δέοι ἂν σφᾶς πράγματ'
ἔχειν ἑκάστοτε καὶ τρέπεσθαι πρὸς τὴν χρείαν καὶ πονεῖν
πλεῖστα, νῦν μὲν περιορῶντας τὸ πνεῦμα καὶ χρωμένους
ἄλλοτ' ἄλλως τοῖς καλῳδίοις τε καὶ ἱστίοις, νῦν δ' ὑφορω-
μένους ἐχθρῶν ἔφοδον καὶ χειμῶνος ἀκμὴν καὶ ἀνέμους
ἐξώστας τε καὶ δυσαντήτους καὶ τόπων καὶ λιμένων

and unpleasant issues, and to *move on in absolute order,* as the proverb states."

Chapter 60

It is possible, however, to hear some people say that we ought to spend our lives using our mind as little as possible rather than furnishing ourselves with reason and too much prudence. For no benefit comes from intellectual activity other than the fact that one perceives more and thus grows more distressed. They accordingly claim that it is far better not to know too much about how things are, and thus to pass one's life without too much pain. They are lovers to this extent of stupidity and ignorance in all matters, and they only strive to indulge themselves in the present moment. I do not know what one can say to them, since in this fashion they understand nothing, nor do they wish to do so.

Nonetheless, we will ask these men the following brief 2 question: if they were about to set sail, would they prefer to embark without any precautions or provisions against the adversity of winds, storms, or pirate attacks, simply in order to voyage with no cares or worries? Will they not need to engage themselves on every occasion with various issues, to turn toward what is needed, and make a huge effort, at certain times trying to control the wind by means of various ropes and sails, at other times watching out for a hostile attack or the height of a storm, violent and irresistible winds, dangerous regions and ports, which they sometimes need to

215

δυσχέρειαν, καὶ νῦν μὲν φεύγειν ταῦτα, νῦν δ᾽ ἐκεῖνα τολμᾶν τε καὶ εὐθαρσεῖν, καὶ τἄλλ᾽, ἅπερ οἱ τέχνῃ καὶ σὺν νῷ πλέοντες πλεῖσθ᾽ ὅσα φροντίζειν ἔχοντες ἀνάγκην ἀείποτε καὶ πονεῖν.

3 Πρὸς γοῦν ταῦτα τί δὴ φασίν, εἰ βούλοινθ᾽, ὅπερ ἔλεγον, ἀπηλλάχθαι πάντων ὁμοῦ καὶ μηδὲν ἐν νῷ κάμνειν καὶ δεδιέναι, πλέειν δ᾽ ὡς ἔτυχεν ἀνυπόπτως τε καὶ παντάπασιν ἀπεριμερίμνως; Τί δ᾽ εἰ καὶ στρατεύοντες βούλοιντο καθάπαξ ἄοπλοί τε καὶ ἀνεπαίσθητοι παντὸς δεινοῦ χωρεῖν ὁμόσε καὶ μηδὲν προορᾶν μήτε φυλοκρινεῖν ὡς τὸ μὲν τολμητέον, τὸ δ᾽ οὔ, καὶ τὸ μέν ἐστιν ἀνιαρὸν καὶ δέος ἔπειθ᾽ ἅπτεσθαι, τὸ δὲ εὔελπι καὶ ἀντιληπτέον ἐρρωμένως, ἀλλ᾽ οὐδενὶ σὺν λόγῳ, οὐδεμιᾷ μήποτε σὺν ἀσφαλείᾳ, πᾶσιν ἀλογιστότατά τε καὶ ἀλυπότατα ἐπιέναι διὰ τοῦτ᾽ αὐτὸ τὸ ἄφροντι καὶ ἀδεές, οὐκ οἶδα μέχρις ὅτου; Μαίνοιντο μέντ᾽ ἄν, εἰ οὕτω δρῷεν, εἰ οὕτω πλέοιεν, εἰ οὕτω στρατεύοιεν.

4 Τὸν δ᾽ αὐτόν, οἶμαι, τρόπον καὶ βιωτέον ἐστὶ καὶ μηδὲν μηδαμῶς τῶν τὰ τοιαῦτα λεγόντων οὔποτε ἀποδεκτέον. Πλέειν γάρ ἐστιν ὡς ἀληθῶς καὶ τὸ βιοῦν καὶ σωφρόνως ἐστίν, ἢν σὺν ὅτι πλείστῳ νῷ τε καὶ προμηθείᾳ, καὶ στρατεύειν τοῦτ᾽ ἐστὶ καὶ σωφρόνως αὖθίς ἐστιν, ἢν τὸν αὐτὸν τρόπον, ἅπαντα δηλαδὴ καταλογιζομένους καὶ κρίνοντας, κἂν δέοι τούτων ἔσθ᾽ ἅτινα ὑφορᾶσθαι καὶ ἀνιᾶσθαι, καὶ ἴσως τὰ πλείω, κἂν δέοι μή. Οὐδὲ γὰρ τοῦτ᾽ εὔλογον οὔθ᾽ ὅλως νοῦν ἔχον—πόθεν; πολλοῦ γε καὶ δεῖ—διὰ τὸ τὴν

avoid, at other times must venture into confidently? Will they not need to be concerned about everything else, the numerous significant matters that those who sail with skill and intelligence inevitably care about and take pains over?

What can they say in response to these points, if they truly want to be free, as I said, of every care, and wish to suffer no mental burdens or terror, but to voyage in a carefree manner with no concern whatsoever? What would they say if, while on campaign, they were to wish to advance close to the enemy unarmed, with no perception of the danger and no precautions, without distinguishing between what they should risk and what not, and without understanding that one situation is grievous and terrifying to deal with, whereas another is hopeful and we should take part in it vigorously? Would they want, on the contrary, to approach everything with no rational thought, with no security at any time, completely thoughtlessly and causing no pain, only in order to spare themselves cares and fears, and attain I do not know what goal? If they were to do this, if they sailed this way or waged war this way, they would certainly be insane.

I accordingly believe that we should live in the same manner and should by no means accept anything from those who make such pronouncements. Life is truly a voyage and is conducted prudently when it is accompanied by as much thoughtfulness and advance planning as possible. Life is also a military campaign, which again is conducted prudently if it is conducted in the same manner, namely when we calculate and evaluate all possibilities, whether some of these, perhaps the majority, must be viewed with caution and cause distress, or not. It is certainly neither sensible nor wholly reasonable—how could it be? Far from it!—for a person to

πεῖραν τέως καὶ ξυναίσθησιν φεύγειν τῶν ἀνιαρῶν ἐσχάτην
πάντων παντάπασιν ἀμαθίαν ἑαυτοῦ κατεύχεσθαι, καὶ ὡς
ἂν μηδὲν ἀνιῷτο, πρὸς μηδὲν ἐπαΐειν, καὶ ὡς ἂν μηδενὸς
ἅπτοιτο δυσχερῶς, μηδενὸς ἅπτεσθαι ξὺν νῷ.

5   Καὶ ὀρχεῖσθαι μὲν οὐκ ἔστιν ὅτι μὴ σὺν τέχνῃ καὶ λύ-
ραν, οἶμαι, κρούειν οὐχ ὡς ἔτυχεν οὔτ᾽ αὐλοὺς οὔτε κιθά-
ραν οὔτ᾽ ἄλλην μουσικὴν ποίησιν, μὴ προορῶντ᾽ εἰ σὺν
ἁρμονίᾳ ἢ μή, εἰ δὲ μή, γελῷτο ἄν, ὡς ἔοικε, καὶ συρίττοιτο
καὶ κακὸς κακῶς ἐμοὶ δοκεῖν ἐπιτρίβοιτο, βιοῦν δέ ἐστιν
ἄμεινον παντάπασιν ὡς ἀληθῶς ἐξορχούμενον ἀναρμόστως
τε καὶ ἀξυνέτως τῶν τε βελτίστων καὶ τῶν ἐναντίων, ἵνα
μηδένα πόνον, μηδ᾽ ἄλγημ᾽ ἔχῃ;

6   Καὶ τὸ μέν γε σῶμα τρέφειν οὐχ ἁπλῶς οὕτως, οὐδὲ
πᾶσιν οἷόν τέ ἐστιν, οὐδ᾽ ἀλογίστως, καὶ μάλιστ᾽ ἂν εἴ τις
τύχῃ νοσερὸν ἔχων καὶ εὐόλισθον, ἀλλ᾽ ἐξετάζοντα πάνυ
τοι πλεῖστον καὶ μετὰ πάσης ἐπιμελείας τὸν νοῦν προσ-
έχοντα καὶ καταλογιζόμενον, ὧν τε ἐδεστέον καὶ ποτέον
ἐστὶν ὧν τε μὴ καὶ ὡς τὰ μὲν ἡδυντέον ἐστί, τῶν δέ—κἂν
εἰ πάνυ πλείστων—ἀνιατέον, ὅμως ἀπεχόμενον, εἰ μέλλει
καλῶς σχήσειν, εἰ δὲ μή, κλαιήσει μετ᾽ ὀλίγον καὶ κακὸς
κακῶς ὀλεῖται ἀφροντιστῶν τε καὶ μηδὲν ἐπαΐων περὶ τῶν
εὖ τε καὶ φαύλων καὶ πάντων ἀλογίστως ἐφαπτόμενος· τῇ
δέ γ᾽ ἔπειτα σαυτοῦ ψυχῇ, ὃ κρεῖττον μὲν ἔχεις, εἴ γε
ξυνίῃς, ἐπιμελείας δὲ πλείονος καὶ ἀσφαλείας δεόμενον, εἴ
γε μέλλει σοι καλῶς ἔχειν, ὅτι δῆτ᾽ εὔτροπόν ἐστιν ἀεὶ καὶ
πολύνοσον καὶ πλείστας ἄρα καὶ παρὰ πλείστων ἔχει καὶ

aspire to ultimate ignorance for himself in all respects merely so as to avoid experiencing and perceiving grief, and it is likewise absurd not to learn anything so as not to be distressed in any way, or not to engage in any rational activity simply in order to encounter no difficulties.

No one can dance if he is unacquainted with the art of 5 dancing, and I think that no one can play the lyre casually, or the flute, the cithara, or any other musical instrument if he does not give thought to the question of whether he performs with harmony or not. If he does not, he will be laughed at, it seems, he will be hissed at, and, I think, he will be abused in a thoroughly nasty manner. But is it truly better to lead our lives in all respects as if we were dancing with no rhythm and with no distinction between what is best and its opposite, merely in order to avoid pain and anxiety?

A man cannot nourish his body thus foolishly, or with ev- 6 ery food, or thoughtlessly, especially if he has one that is sickly or unstable. To the contrary, he should take fully into account, reckon, and examine carefully and with due caution what he can and cannot eat and drink from this category and that, since he is allowed to enjoy certain foods but must refrain from others—indeed most of them—and must avoid them even though this makes him unhappy, if he wants to preserve his health; otherwise, he will soon shed tears and die a miserable death, because he does not care or know anything about good and bad food, and eats everything indiscriminately. With regard to your soul then, which, if you are in a position to understand, is your finest possession and requires great attention and security if you plan to be in good condition, given that it varies constantly, is susceptible to disease, and must confront numerous, extremely

λίαν ἐργώδεις μεταχειρίσαι λαβάς τε καὶ ἐπιβουλὰς καὶ
περὶ πλείονος ὄντως ἡ τούτου ζημία· ταύτῃ δὲ λοιπὸν
βέλτιόν ἐστιν ἀνυπόπτως παντάπασι καὶ ἀδεῶς καὶ ἀνέτως
βιοῦν, οἷς ἂν ἐντύχοι χρωμένῃ, καὶ μήτε νοῦν ἔχειν κυβερνήτην μήτε λόγον ἐξεταστὴν καὶ ἐπόπτην, ἅ τε κάλλιστα
καὶ ἃ πᾶν τοὐναντίον ἅ τε ἥδεσθαι καὶ ἃ λυπεῖσθαι χρή,
πάντ᾽ ἀκριβῶς τε καὶ ἀσφαλέστατα ξυνιέναι καὶ κατοπτεύ-
ειν, ἀλλ᾽ ἀλογώτατά τε εἶναι καὶ ἀπροόπτως καθάπαξ,
ὅθεν τι μελλήσει κακῶς ἕξειν καὶ ἀνιάσεσθαι, καὶ μήτε
λογίζεσθαι μηδὲν οὐκ ἔχειν, οὐκ οἶδ᾽ ὁπόσον τινὰ τοῦτον
χρόνον καὶ ὅπως, μήτε λυπεῖσθαι;

61

Τοιγαροῦν ἐντεῦθεν, ὡς δὴ σὺ λοιπὸν ἐμοὶ δοκεῖν καὶ
τυφλὸς ἡδέως ἂν εἴης καὶ τώ γε ὀφθαλμὼ ἀμφοτέρω με-
μυκώς τε καὶ παρακεκομμένος, ἵνα μηδὲν ὁρῴης τῶν
ἀηδῶν, καὶ ἕλοιο ἂν μήθ᾽ ὁρᾶν ὅλως μήτ᾽ ἀνιαρὸν μηκέτ᾽
οὐδοτιοῦν; Ἀλλ᾽ οὐκ ἔγωγε, οἶμαι, ὦ βέλτιστε, οὐδ᾽ ὅστις
ὅλως νοῦν ἔχει, ἀλλὰ πάνθ᾽ ὁρῴην ἄν, καὶ εἰ μέλλω πάντα
ἀνιᾶσθαι, πάντα ἀνιῴμην, ὅμως δ᾽ οὖν ὁρῴην. Καὶ δὴ τοίνυν κἀνταῦθα ταὐτὸ τοῦτο δῶρον ὑπὸ Θεοῦ τὸν νοῦν τε
καὶ λόγον λαβὼν πλεῖν ἢ κατὰ τὰ ἄλλα ζῷα, πλείστῳ δὴ
τούτῳ χρώμην καὶ ἐπασκοίην εἰς ὅσον ἂν ἐξείη, μάλιστα

troublesome attacks and plots launched by many enemies, what would matter more than its loss? Is it better for your soul to live with no suspicion or fear whatsoever, comfortably, dealing readily with whatever it encounters, without rationality as a captain, or education as an examiner and supervisor of what is best and what is the complete opposite, with what it should be pleased and with what it should be aggrieved? Should the soul know and understand all this precisely and with utmost security, but behave absurdly and without foreseeing whence the evil will come and cause it grief, simply in order to have nothing to think or feel sad about? I do not know how long this can be so or exactly how it can occur.

Chapter 61

In light of the above, therefore, I think that you would be pleased to become blind by shutting both your eyes and cutting them out simply to avoid unpleasant sights; but would you prefer to see nothing whatsoever that is disturbing? I think, my friend, that neither I myself nor any other sensible man would do so; but I would prefer to see everything, and if I am going to be distressed by everything, let me be distressed by everything, but still be able to see it. To return to this case, since God has given me this very gift, namely mind and reason, to a greater degree than other animals, I should use them to the greatest extent and exercise them as much as possible in order to bring the purpose of this gift to

καταρτίζων εἰς τέλος τοῦ δώρου τοὔργον, καὶ εἰ μέλλω
πλέον ἀνιᾶσθαι, σὺν ἀεὶ πλείονι νῷ τοῦτ᾿ ἂν εἴη μᾶλλον ἢ
τοὐναντίον καὶ ἀνιῴμην καί κεν τὸ βουλοίμην καί κεν πολὺ
κέρδιον εἴη.

2   Ἢ σὺ μὲν θοἰμάτιον μέλλων ἀφαιρήσεσθαι, πλεῖστ᾿ ἂν
ἄχθοιο καὶ δεινὰ πάσχειν ἡγοῖο, μᾶλλον δὲ σὺ μὲν ἄρα,
εἴπερ, ἐφ᾿ οἷς ἔχεις, ἐξείη σοι προστιθέναι πλείω καὶ περι-
ουσιάζειν, ἑτοιμότατα ἂν ἕλοιο, καὶ εἰ μέλλεις ἐπ᾿ αὐτοῖς
πλείους καὶ τὰς φροντίδας ἔχειν καὶ ἴσως δέος ἔτι καὶ
ὑποψίαν πλεῖν ἢ πρότερον, ἐμοὶ δὲ τολμᾷς λέγειν μηδὲν
εἶναι πρᾶγμα, εἰ μὴ προστιθείην ὅσ᾿ ἂν οἷός τ᾿ εἴην, ἐφ᾿ οἷς
τῆς Προνοίας ἔτυχον λογικοῖς δώροις, καὶ προσεπαύξοιμι,
κἂν εἰ μέλλω σαφέστερον κρίνειν καὶ καθορᾶν τἀνιαρὸν
καὶ θάτερον, μᾶλλον δὲ μηδεμίαν εἶναι ζημίαν μήθ᾿ οἷον
ὑπολογίσασθαι καὶ δυσχερᾶναι χρῆναι, ἢν ὅτι πλεῖστον
ἐμαυτὸν ὀλιγώσας τε καὶ καθείρξας, ᾧπερ ἔχω καλλίονι
καὶ περιόπτῳ μάλιστα κτήματι καὶ κόσμῳ, νῷ, καὶ τοῦτο
δὴ παντάπασιν ἀπ᾿ ἐμαυτοῦ διώξας καὶ ποιησάμενος,
ἔπειτα βιῴην ἀλογίστως καθάπαξ, ἀκρίτως, ἀνεπαισθήτως,
πάντων ἀσυνέτως, ἐμαυτοῦ, τῶν ἔξω, καὶ μηδὲν ὁτιοῦν
μήτε συνιεὶς μήτ᾿ ἀνιώμενος, καὶ τοῦτ᾿ εἶναι μάλιστα εὐδαιμονίαν ἄκρατον, τὸ ἀνόητον ἐρεῖν ἔμβραχυ καὶ ἀμαθὲς
καὶ ἀνάλγητον;

3   Ἀλλ᾿ οὐκ ἄν σοι πείθεσθαι δίκαιος εἴην νοῦν ὅλως ἔχων
καὶ σωφρονῶν. Οὕτω γὰρ ἂν οὐ μόνον τῶν ἀνθρώπων
ὅσοι πλεῖστον μετέχουσιν ἀγνοίας καὶ ἀμαθίας νικῷεν εὐ-
δαιμονίᾳ τοὺς νουνεχεῖς καὶ σώφρονας, ἀλλὰ καὶ τούτων
αὐτῶν καὶ τῶν ἄλλων ἔτι μᾶλλον τἄλογα τῶν ζῴων, καὶ

its fullest fruition. Even if I am going to be more distressed, this would make greater use of my intellect on every occasion and not the other way around, so let me feel distressed; *I would prefer this and it* would be *much better for me.*

If you were about to be deprived of your clothes, would 2
you not be extremely annoyed and think that you were suffering dreadfully? Indeed, if you were in a position to add more wealth to what you currently possess and to have abundant property, would you not choose this eagerly, even if under these conditions you were going to have more cares and perhaps more fears and suspicions than before? How do you then dare to say to me that there is no problem if I fail to add as much as I can to the rational gifts awarded me by Providence and increase them, regardless of whether I am going to judge matters more clearly and distinguish unpleasant from pleasant situations? Indeed, how dare you say that this will not harm me and that I should not contemplate this and be aggrieved, if I greatly diminish myself and restrict my mind, my most beautiful, glorious possession and adornment, and repel and banish it from myself, and then lead a life that is entirely irrational, lacking judgment, oblivious, imprudent in everything that has to do with my own affairs and the affairs of other people, ignorant of what happens around me but free of distress? Do you dare to say, in brief, that stupidity, ignorance, and lack of feeling are to a large extent pure happiness?

If I am sound in mind and a prudent person, I would not 3
act fairly if I believed you. For in that way not only people who have a large share of ignorance and stupidity would exceed wise and sensible men in happiness, but also irrational animals would still be more blessed than stupid people and

βοῦς καὶ ἵππος καὶ ὄϊς καὶ ὗς, τὴν τελεωτάτην εὐδαιμονίαν ἀποφέροιντο καὶ τἀγαθὸν πλῆρες ἔχοιεν αὐτὰ μᾶλλον πλεῖν ἢ κατὰ πάντας ἀνθρώπους, ὡς οὐκ ἔστι παράλληλα θεῖναι, οὕτω παντάπασιν ἀλογίστως καὶ ἀνεπαισθήτως τῶν ἀνιαρῶν βιοῦντα, καὶ τὸ δοκοῦν οὕτω κάλλιστον εὐεργέτημα καὶ τῆς Προνοίας μέγιστον ἀνθρώποις δῶρον, τὸ λογικὸν θεῖον πνεῦμα, καὶ ᾧ μέγιστον ἄνθρωπος κατὰ τῶν ἄλλων ζῴων φρονεῖ, ἐν δευτέρῳ καὶ τοῦ μηδενὸς ἂν ἄξιον εἴη, μᾶλλον δὲ καὶ μεγίστης ἀφορμὴ δυστυχίας, ὅσα γε ἐκ τῶν νυνὶ λόγων, καὶ συμφορῶν τῶν ἀπευκταιοτάτων ἀρχή, καὶ τὰ μέγιστα δοκοῦντες ἔχειν καὶ ξυλλογίζεσθαι, τὰ μέγιστα ἴσως ἀγνοοῦμεν καὶ γέλωτα προσοφλισκάνομεν οὕτω πονηρῶς ἔχοντες, ὥσπερ οἱ μεθύοντες τοὺς ἄλλους κλονεῖσθαι νομίζουσι, τοῦτ᾽ αὐτοὶ πάσχοντες καὶ τοὺς ἄλλους περιφέρεσθαι καὶ κακῶς ἔχειν, αὐτοὶ νοσοῦντες, μᾶλλον δὲ ὥσπερ ἔνιοι τῶν μαινομένων δοκοῦσιν εὐδαιμόνως μάλιστα πάντων ἀνθρώπων εἶναι καὶ βασιλεύουσιν ἐν τῇ νόσῳ καὶ προστάττουσι καὶ πλουτοῦσι καὶ ἥδιστα βιοῦσιν ἐν σφίσιν αὐτοῖς οἱ πάντων ἀθλιώτατοι.

anyone in general; the ox, horse, sheep, and pig would obtain the most perfect bliss and would be so much more completely blessed than all men, that their blessings cannot possibly be compared to human blessings, given that they live in complete irrationality and perceive no sorrow at all. The seemingly most beautiful benefaction and the most important gift Providence gives human beings, namely the divine spirit of reason, thanks to which man boasts that he is superior to other animals, would become of secondary importance and worthless, or rather it would become the cause of great misfortune and the beginning of quite undesirable calamities, according to your current argument. Although we think that we comprehend and reason out what is most important, perhaps we fail to perceive what is most important and deserves mockery because we are in such a worthless condition; just as drunks think that other people are agitated, when it is they themselves who suffer this. They believe as well that others spin in circles and are in a terrible shape, although this is their own problem. Or rather, they are like raving madmen who believe that they are the most blessed people on earth, and under the influence of their insanity think that they are rulers and command and abound in wealth and lead a most pleasant life by themselves, when they are actually the most miserable people there are.

62

Δέδοικα μὲν οὖν μὴ πᾶν εἴη τοὐναντίον ἐνταῦθα καὶ μαινοίμεθ᾽ ἂν κατ᾽ αὐτούς, εἰ οὕτω λέγομέν τε καὶ κρίνομεν ἥδιστα βιοῦν καὶ πλέον ἢ κατὰ τοὺς ἄλλους, ὁπότε πλεῖστον δυστυχοῦμεν καὶ κακῶς μάλιστ᾽ ἔχομεν. Καὶ γάρ, εἰ μὴ τοῦτ᾽ ἂν εἴη, οὐκ οἶδ᾽ ὅ,τι ποτ᾽ ἂν μᾶλλον εἴη τὸ μαίνεσθαι, ἄμεινον ἡγεῖσθαι τἄλογα τῶν ζῴων βιοῦν ἢ καθ᾽ ἡμᾶς. Καὶ εἰ μὲν ἄλλος—οὐκ οἶδ᾽ ὅστις—βούλοιτ᾽ ὄϊς τε μᾶλλον εἶναι καὶ ὗς ἢ καὶ ὁστισοῦν ἄνθρωπος καὶ τῶν ἀνιαρῶν οὕτως ἀλογίστως καθάπαξ καὶ ἀνεπαισθήτως τρυφᾶν, αἱρείσθω τε τοῦτο καὶ τρυφάτω καὶ ἀγνοείτω καὶ καθ᾽ ἑαυτοῦ ταῦτα δὴ τὰ βέλτιστα εὐχέσθω. Ἀλλ᾽ ἔγωγ᾽ οὐκ ἄν ποθ᾽ ἑλοίμην, μηδ᾽ οὕτω μανείην, ὡς ταῦτα δόξαι καὶ καταπροδοῦναι ῥᾷσθ᾽ οὕτω καθάπαξ ἡδονῆς ἀλογίστου καὶ ἀλύπου βίου τὸν λόγον, τὸ κάλλιστον τῆς φύσεως, ὧν ἔχω, ὥσπερ ἐν τῷ Καρὶ κινδυνεῦσαι μέλλων, ἀλλ᾽ οὐκ ἐν αὐτοῖς τοῖς φιλτάτοις τε καὶ βελτίστοις καὶ ὄντως ἀναγκαιοτάτοις τῶν ἄλλων ἁπάντων.

2   Ἀλλ᾽ εἰ μὲν ἄρα ξυνέμιξεν ὁ Θεὸς ἀμφότερα ταῦτα, τόν τε σοφώτατον βίον καὶ ἥδιστον, ὥσπερ, οἶμαι, τοῖς πλείοσι τῶν παλαιῶν τε καὶ νέων σοφῶν δοκεῖ, τοῦτ᾽ ἂν ὡς ἀληθῶς εἴη τὸ κάλλιστον καὶ ἀγαπῴην ἂν σφόδρα τῇ ξυντυχίᾳ ταύτῃ, ἐξόν τε ἅμα λόγῳ τε καὶ σοφίᾳ συνεῖναι καὶ τοῖς κατὰ τὸν βίοτον εὐπραγεῖν καὶ ἀλύπως τε καὶ ἡδέως ἔχειν, τοῦτό μοι δοκεῖ πάντων κατ᾽ ἀνθρώπους εὐκταιότατον.

Chapter 62

I am afraid that in this case exactly the opposite might occur and we would be as insane as they are, if we express such opinions and assume that we live far more pleasantly than others, when we are in fact utterly miserable and suffer wretchedly. For I really do not know what else could be considered madness if not this, namely the belief that irrational animals lead better lives than we do. If someone else—I do not know who—prefers to be a sheep or a pig rather than a human being, and to live luxuriously without taking into account the misfortunes of life, and in a totally senseless fashion, let him choose this, let him luxuriate in a state of ignorance and wish those magnificent things for himself. As for me, I would never make such a choice, I would never become so insane as to hold these views and for the sake of irrational pleasure and a painless life betray so easily once and for all reason, the most beautiful gift I received from nature, as if I were about *to place my risk on the Carian mercenary* and not on one of the most beloved, beautiful, and truly necessary things there are.

If God combined both of these blessings, the life of supreme wisdom and pleasure, as I think most ancient and contemporary sages believe, that would truly be the best thing of all, and I would be quite satisfied if something of that sort were to happen to me. If we could associate with education and wisdom and at the same time live a prosperous, happy life with no sorrows, I believe that this would be the best we could wish for anyone.

2

3   Εἰ δ’ οὐκ ἔστιν οὕτως, ἀλλ’ ἔστι μὲν οὗ ξυμβαίνει ταῦτα
καὶ ξυγγίνεται τυχὸν οὕτως, ἔστι γε μὴν ἔνθα ποτ’ οὗ καὶ
οὐκ ἀνάγκη τις ἀμφότερα συνέλκει δεσμοῖς ἀρρήκτοις
ἐργῶδές τέ ἐστι σφόδρα καὶ παγχάλεπον τἀγαθὸν τέλειον,
τὴν εὐγένειαν ἔγωγε βουλοίμην μᾶλλον τῆς φύσεως, τὸ
τοῦ λόγου δῶρον, καὶ ἀσκοίην οἷός τ’ ὤν, εἰς ὅσον ἂν
ἐξείη, κράτιστον ἑαυτοῦ καὶ τελεώτατον καὶ καθαρώτα-
τον, καὶ εἰ μέλλει μοι πράγματ’ ἔνια παρασχεῖν καὶ μὴ
παντάπασιν ἐρρωστωνευμένον βίοτον ξυλλογίζεσθαι· εὖ
γὰρ τοῦτ’ οἶδ’ ὡς οὐ παντάπασιν ἀνιαρώτατον.

63

Τοῦτ’ οὖν αὐτὸς ἐμαυτῷ προτίθημι, τοῦτ’ ἀξιῶ καὶ σοί
γε, ὦ φιλότης, τοῦτο βούλομαι ξυνδοκεῖν ἢ παντελῶς ἀσυνέτως, ἀφροντίστως, ἀνεπαισθήτως, ὥσπερ τἄλογα τῶν
ζῴων βιοῦν, πάντων ἀνιαρῶν ἀπηλλαγμένος διὰ τὸ μὴ
φρονεῖν, μηδ’ ἐπαΐειν ὁτουοῦν τῶν ἐν φύσει καὶ κατ’
ἀνθρώπους. Οὕτως ἐγὼ περὶ τούτων φρονῶ καὶ τούτοις
ἄρα τοῖς λογισμοῖς τῶν ἐν κόσμῳ δὴ πάντων ἄλλων ἄμεινον τίθεμαι λόγον.

2   Ῥώμῃ μὲν γὰρ προὔχειν ἔστι παραπλησίως καὶ ζῴοις
ἄλλοις, ἔστι καὶ κρεῖττον κάλλει, καὶ τὸν αὐτόν, οἶμαι, ἔχει
τρόπον μεγέθει, καὶ μάλισθ’ οὕτω πάντων οὐκ ἔστιν ἐφ’

But if this is impossible, and these things sometimes oc- 3
cur jointly and happen to combine, but at other times not,
and they are not necessarily linked by unbreakable bonds, so
that it is extremely laborious and difficult for a person to acquire this blessing in its entirety, I would still prefer the nobility of nature, namely the gift of reason. I would like to be
able to exercise it to the highest degree possible, until it becomes extremely powerful, perfect, and far purer than it already is, regardless of any anxieties it might cause me in the
future, so that I might not consider my life wholly idle. For I
know quite well that even such a life is not entirely troublesome.

Chapter 63

This is the task I set myself, this is my claim, and I want
this to seem good to you, too, my dear friend, and that you
not choose to live entirely devoid of reason, without caring
about anything, without perceiving anything, like the irrational animals, removed from all distress, since you will be
unable to think or to understand anything that happens in
nature and among human beings. This is my opinion regarding these issues, and it is on the basis of this rationale that I
judge reason superior to everything else in the world.

For other animals can be nearly equal or superior to men 2
in physical strength, they can surpass them in beauty, and
the same goes, I think, for size as well as all other qualities

ὅτῳ οὔ, ἡ δ᾽ ὄντως τοῦ λόγου χάρις μόνον ἐξαίρετον
ἀνθρώποις ἀγαθὸν καὶ πάντων κάλλιστον, ἐπιστάτης καὶ
διδάσκαλος ἀληθοῦς εὐδαιμονίας καὶ χρήσεως ὀρθῆς ἐν
ἅπαντί τε καθάπαξ τῷ κόσμῳ καὶ ἐν αὐτῷ ὁτῳοῦν μάλιστα, προορωμένη τε καὶ καταρρυθμίζουσα πάνθ᾽ ἕκαστα
ἀτεχνῶς κατὰ τὸν Αἰσχύλου λόγον, μόνη *ἐν τῇ πρύμνῃ*
καθημένη τῆς πόλεως, πάντα κυβερνῶσα καὶ πάντων
ἄρχουσα εὖ γ᾽, ὡς ἂν χρήσιμα ποιεῖν, ἥντινα δὴ βούλεταί
τις πόλιν καλεῖν, εἴτε τὸν βίον ἅπαντα καὶ τὴν τοῦ κόσμου
καθάπερ ἑνὸς ἀληθῶς ὄντος ἅπαντος θεωρίαν, εἴτ᾽ αὐτὸν
ὁντιναοῦν ἄνθρωπον ἕκαστον, ἐν ᾧ καθάπερ εὐγενὴς
προστάτης καὶ τῆς φύσεως βασιλεὺς ἡγεμονικῶς ὁ λόγος
τε καὶ νοῦς προκάθηται καὶ προορᾷ τὰ βελτίω καὶ θεσπίζει,
κατασυλλογιζόμενος καὶ νομοθετῶν ἐμμέτρως ἅπασαν
πρᾶξιν, ἅπασαν κίνησιν καὶ καθιστάνων τελείαν εὐνομίαν
τε καὶ ἰσότητα καὶ δικαιοσύνην καὶ πολιτείαν ἡρμοσμένην
ἐν τοῖς αὐτοῦ τινος μέρεσιν ἑκάστου, οὐχ *ὑπερβάθμιον*
τείνειν πόδα, οὐδ᾽ *ἔξω σκοποῦ βάλλειν* κατὰ τὴν παροιμίαν,
ἀλλ᾽ ἐν ὅροις ἀσφαλέσιν ἅπασι καὶ νενομισμένοις, *ἔνθ᾽*
ἀριπρεπέες δμῶες ἀνέρες τ᾽ ἠδὲ δμωίδες ἐφράσαντ᾽ ἠδ᾽
ἔταξαν, ὡς ἄρ᾽ ἤνδανε βασιλῆι κατὰ φρένα καὶ κατὰ θυμόν,
μάλιστα δὲ τέρπετο λεύσσων· οἶμαι δὴ συλλογισμοί τινες
τοῦ νοῦ δοῦλοι καὶ διάνοιαι καὶ δόξαι καὶ προτάσεις συν-
υπηρέτιδες ἅπαντ᾽ ἐν μέτρῳ καθιστάνουσαι καὶ συμπλη-
ροῦσαι καὶ κατεργαζόμεναι κάλλιστα καὶ ὡς ἂν ὁ βασίλειος
ἀμέλει νοῦς, ἐποχούμενος αὐταῖς καὶ κατοπτεύων ἔπειθ᾽
ὕστερον, ἕκαστα μέλλοι προσίεσθαί τε καὶ τοῖς καλῶς
εὑρημένοις καὶ τεταγμένοις ἥδεσθαι. Καὶ τοίνυν οὐδὲν

without exception. The genuine grace of rationality, however, is human beings' only exceptional advantage and the best there is. It is the supervisor and teacher of true bliss and proper behavior throughout the world and indeed in every human being individually, foreseeing and regulating every situation; as Aeschylus aptly says, it is seated alone *on the stern of the city* and directs all things, governing them all efficiently, so that they are made serviceable. By "city" one could refer to anything one likes, be it the entirety of life and the world as a whole taken as a true unity, or each person individually, in whom rationality and the mind preside authoritatively as noble guardians and kings of nature, anticipating and foretelling what is best for him, considering matters thoroughly and establishing appropriate laws for every deed and action, until they establish a perfect legal order, equality, justice, and in the separate sections of each person a balanced constitution, where no one can *step over the threshold,* as the proverb says, nor *shoot wide of the mark.* To the contrary, the person stays within quite secure, traditional limits, where distinguished male and female slaves have planned and arranged a place for him to stay, so that the king's heart and *soul were pleased,* and he *looked upon this with delight.* I think that the various mindsets, thoughts, opinions, and auxiliary assumptions are the servants of the mind, since they arrange everything in moderation, complementing and elaborating it very beautifully, so that this kingly mind that rides upon and supervises them will later be able to approach everything and take pleasure in the fine arrangement and order. In this case, therefore, there is

ἐντεῦθεν οὔτ' ἄλογον οὔτ' ἀόριστον οὔτ' εὔτροπον ὁπωσοῦν οὔτε κινούμενον παντὶ τρόπῳ, ἀλλ' ἀσφαλέστατά τε ἔχει καὶ παντάπασι πέπηγεν, ὅσα δὴ ξυνεώραται, μᾶλλον δὲ ξυνεργάζεται καὶ κατατεχνιτεύει διάνοια, προστατοῦντος τοῦ νοῦ, καὶ οὐκ ἄλογοι κινήσεις, οὐδ' ὁρμαὶ φύσεως κατισχύουσαι στασιώδεις ἀεὶ περιτρέπουσιν ἄλλοτ' ἄλλη τὰ δίκαια καὶ κατασύρουσι.

3   Καὶ τὰ μὲν Δαιδάλου τοῦ μηχανοποιοῦ φησιν ὁ θαυμάσιος Πλάτων ἔργα τε καὶ τεράστια βελτίω μάλιστ' εἶναι τὰ δεδεμένα τῶν μὴ τοιούτων, καὶ ὅσα τις ἐν δεσμοῖς ἐώνητο, ἀσφαλῶς τε καὶ καλῶς ἐώνητ' ἂν καί οἱ παρέμενον οἵ ἐώνητο, ἂν δ' ἄρα τις ἀγνοήσας μὴ τοιαῦτα μᾶλλον, ἀλλ' ἄδετα πρίαιτο, φεύγοντα παραχρῆμα οἴχεσθαι καὶ ζημιοῦν ἀμέλει τὸν πριάμενον. Οὐ μὴν ἀλλὰ κἀνταῦθα πᾶσαν δὴ πρᾶξιν καὶ γνώμην καὶ κρίσιν, λόγῳ τε δεδεμένην καὶ ἠρτημένην αἰτίας ἀναγκαίας καὶ ἡρμοσμένην, οὕτω καλλίστην τε εἶναι ξυμβαίνει καὶ ἀσφαλεστάτην καὶ κάλλιστα δὴ λοιπὸν καὶ ἀσφαλέστατα καὶ πεπράχθαι καὶ ἐρρῶσθαί τε καὶ εἰρῆσθαι, ὃ δὴ μόνης ἐπιστήμης ἔργον ἀληθῶς εἶναί φησιν οὑτοσὶ Πλάτων.

4   Ἂν δ' ἄρα δόξα τις ἄδετος αἰτίας μόνη καὶ κρίσις ἄλογος ὥρμηται καὶ δρᾷ, οὐκ ἀσφαλές, οὐδ' ἔμμονον εἰς τέλος, ἂν δ' ἄρ' ἐνίοτε καὶ μέχρι τινὸς ἔδοξεν εὐστοχῆσαι καὶ κατωρθωκέναι, τελευτῶσα δ' ὅμως νοσοῦσ' ἐμπίπτει καὶ καταστρέφει καὶ περιτρέπεται.

5   Οὕτως ἐστὶν ἀκλόνητον λόγος μόνον καὶ ἀληθὴς εὐγένειά τε καὶ πλοῦτος, ὃ μόνος καρποῦσθαι τῶν ἄλλων ζῴων ἁπάντων γέρας ἄνθρωπος ἔχει, δι' οὗ τά τε οἰκεῖα

nothing irrational, vague, variable, or much changing, but everything is very firm and deeply rooted, at least what human reason oversees or rather what it constructs and artificially produces under the mind's leadership. In this case, nature cannot be taken over by irrational changes or prevailing and impetuous impulses, which constantly divert justice now here, now there and eventually overturn it.

The admirable Plato says that among the prodigious con- 3
structions of the inventor Daedalus, the firmly *fettered* ones were much better than the unfettered. If someone bought the fettered statues, that would be a nice, safe purchase, since the product *would remain* the same as when he bought it; but if someone out of ignorance bought not the fettered statues but the unfettered ones, they would run away immediately and abandon the buyer, causing him loss. In our case, every action, opinion, or judgment that is tied to reason, attached to the necessary causes, and fixed on them happens to be quite beautiful and steadfast, and it has been produced, maintains its strength, and has been pronounced quite beautifully and steadfastly. Plato says that this can in fact be the product of knowledge alone.

If a single opinion, however, is not dependent on a spe- 4
cific cause, but an irrational judgment rushes forward and creates something, it is not durable and cannot be expected to last. Even if it sometimes seems to hit the mark and succeeds to some extent, eventually it grows sick, and as it dies, it falls down, is overturned, and comes to an end.

Therefore, only reason is unshakable, it represents true 5
nobility and wealth, which man alone of all animals can enjoy as a prize of honor. By means of reason man has arranged

αὐτοῦ πάντ' εὖ κατεστήσατο καὶ συνεσκεύασε καὶ τέχναις καὶ μεθόδοις καὶ ἁρμονίαις πάσαις κατακεκόσμηται τά τε τῶν ἄλλων ζῴων ἁπάντων δεσποτικῶς νομοθετεῖ, ὥσπερ ἐξ ἀκροπόλεώς τινος καὶ μυρίων ὅσων ὁπλοφόρων τε καὶ δορυφόρων—τῶν τοῦ λογισμοῦ δυνάμεων—ἐπιτάττων καὶ τοῖς μὲν συμβαίνων καὶ καταλλασσόμενος ὑπηρετικῶς χρῆσθαι, πρὸς δ' ἔνι' ἄττα τῶν ἀτιθάσσων καὶ ἀείποτ' ἐπιβούλων πόλεμον ἄσπονδόν τε καὶ ἀκήρυκτον παντάπασιν ἀνῃρημένος.

64

Τοιγαροῦν ἀμείνους γ' ἂν εἴημεν ὡς ἀληθῶς τοῦ δώρου τούτου τοσούτου καὶ τῆς ἀγαθῆς εὐμοιρίας ξυνιέντες καὶ κατασπαζόμενοι καὶ τιμῶντες ἢ προφέροντες εἰς ὅσον οἷόν τέ ἐστι καὶ τὸν ἐν ἡμῖν ζωτικὸν ὄντως ἐνεσπαρμένον καὶ λογικὸν σπινθῆρα ὥσπερ ἐν σποδιᾷ τινι τῷ σώματι κεκρυμμένον ἀναχωννῦντες αὐτοὶ μάλιστ' ἐπίτηδες καὶ προδεικνῦντες καὶ ταῖς ἀεὶ γιγνομέναις ἐπιμελείαις καὶ παρατρίψεσιν εἰς πυρσὸν ἀνάπτοντες, ἀλλὰ μὴ μᾶλλον ὑπ' ἀμελείας τινὸς καὶ ἀμαθίας καὶ ὑγροῦ καὶ διακεχυμένου καὶ ἀκολάστου βίου καὶ τρυφῆς κατασβεννῦντες, καὶ τὸ πλουτεῖν οὕτω δὴ κλῆρόν τινα τοῦτον μεγαλοπρεπῆ τε καὶ πολυέραστον λαβόντες, αὐτοὶ δὴ λοιπὸν οἴκοθεν προσεισενέγκωμεν δι' ἐπιμελείας καὶ χρήσεως ἀγαθῆς καὶ προσεπαυξήσωμεν.

all his affairs well, has organized everything with the assistance of the crafts and other means, and has adorned them with every sort of agreement, while he governs all other animals very strictly, as if from an acropolis and in command of countless soldiers and spearmen—namely his mental powers. With some of these animals he comes to terms and requires in exchange that they serve him, and with other animals which are reckless and always plot against him, he has undertaken an implacable, undeclared war.

Chapter 64

At any rate, we would be in a better position indeed if we were conscious of the immensity of this gift and of its happy possession, and if we embraced and honored it; or rather if we advertised it as much as possible and ourselves unearthed the truly vital spark of reason begotten in us, which is hidden in our bodies like embers in the ashes, and if we deliberately showed it around and kindled it into a huge torch with systematic care and attention; we should not extinguish this spark due to negligence, ignorance, a luxurious, relaxed, lascivious lifestyle, or extravagance. From now on, we should contribute to this wealth, which we received as a magnificent, much-desired legacy, from our own resources with diligence and wise management, and we should increase it.

2   Τὸ μὲν γὰρ ἐλάβομεν καὶ χάρις, τὸ δ᾽ ἡμέτερόν ἐστιν,
ἐφ᾽ οἷς ἐλάβομεν, καὶ τὸ μὲν καὶ πολλοῖς ἄλλοις κοινόν, τὸ
δὲ τοῦ κατορθοῦντος εἰς ἰδιάζουσαν εὐδοξίαν, καὶ τὸ μὲν
τυχεῖν οὐχ ἡμῶν, ἡ δ᾽ ἀγαθὴ χρῆσις ἐπαινεῖται, καὶ τὸ μὲν
εὐμοιρεῖν τὰ κάλλιστ᾽ οὐ μέγα, μᾶλλον δὲ μέγα μέν, ἀλλ᾽
οὐ τοῦ λαβόντος, τὸ δ᾽ ἐπαΐειν τε καὶ περιέπειν ποιεῖ τοῦ
λαβόντος, καὶ τὸ μὲν λαβεῖν εὕρημα, τὸ δὲ χρῆσθαι καλῶς
ὄφλομεν καὶ θαυμαστὸς οὐχ ὁ τἀγαθοῦ τυχών, ἀλλ᾽ ὁ συν-
τηρήσας. Τὸ μὲν γὰρ τιμᾶται μόνον, τὸ δὲ θαυμάζεται,
μᾶλλον δὲ ὁ μὲν λαβών τε καὶ ἀπολέσας ᾔσχυνεν ἑαυτὸν
καὶ τὸν δόντα, ὁ δὲ σπουδάζων τὸ δῶρον συνηγόρησεν
ἑαυτῷ τε καὶ τῷ δόντι καὶ τιμῶν ἑαυτὸν ἐκεῖνον τιμᾷ καὶ
σοφὸν δείκνυσιν ὡς τοῖς ἀξίοις νέμοντα.

3   Καὶ μὴν τὸ μὲν λαβεῖν τε καὶ συντηρῆσαι κάλλιστον, τὸ
δέ γε καὶ ἐπαυξῆσαι βέλτιον, βέλτιον δὲ ὄν, τὸ αὐτὸ καὶ
ῥᾷστόν ἐστι. Πλουτῆσαι μὲν γάρ φασιν ἐργῶδες πάνυ,
πλουτήσαντα δ᾽ ἐφάπαξ τὴν οὐσίαν ἐπαύξειν οὐκέτι. Καὶ
τίς οὕτως ἄθλιος, ὅστις, ἐξὸν οὕτως, οὐχ ἕλοιτ᾽ ἂν πλέον
ἑκάστοτε προστιθέναι καὶ πλουτεῖν ἀεὶ πλοῦτον ἀληθῆ
τινα καὶ οὐκ ἀλλότριον, οὐδ᾽ ἀλλοτρίων, οὐδ᾽ ἔξωθεν ἄρα
ἐπίδημον, ἀλλ᾽ ἡμέτερον ὄντως αὐτῶν καὶ ξυμπεφυκότα

CHAPTER 64

For what has been bequeathed to us came as a gift, 2 whereas what we added as our legacy is exclusively our own. Many people receive an inheritance, but increase of it furnishes good repute only to the person who succeeds in this respect. The former is not up to us, but its good management will be the object of praise. It is insignificant if someone acquires the best blessings due to fortune, or rather it is significant but not up to the recipient. Knowing and treating blessings with respect, however, renders them true possessions of the recipient; and the receipt of an inheritance is a bit of good fortune, but its proper management is an obligation. We should not admire the person who received something good by chance, but the one who managed to preserve it. For the former, that is possessing something, is honorable in itself, whereas the latter, that is preserving it, is admirable. To put it better, the person who receives something but loses it embarrasses both himself and the donor, but the person who takes care of his gift advocates for both himself and his donor, and by honoring himself he honors the donor as well and shows that the latter is prudent because he distributes his gifts to worthy recipients.

When someone receives something and preserves it, 3 therefore, this is a most beautiful thing, but it is even better if he increases it, in fact it is not just better but easier as well. For they say that it is very hard to become rich, but that once you are rich it is easy to increase your holdings. And who can be so miserable as to have this capability but still not choose to constantly add even more and possess genuine, not merely external wealth, wealth that does not belong to others, nor did it merely pass time in our home being from a distant country, but that is truly ours, part of our own

237

καὶ βελτίω πολλῷ καὶ τοῦ βελτίονος τῆς ψυχῆς μέρους, οὐδὲ μυρίαις ὅσαις ἐπιβουλαῖς τε καὶ λόχοις ὑποτεμνόμενον καὶ ἡττώμενον καὶ ἀείποτ' ἐγρηγορέναι καὶ δεδιέναι καὶ καταστυγνάζειν καταναγκάζοντα, ἀλλὰ πολυαρκέστατόν τε, οἶμαι, καὶ πάντων ἀσύλητον πραγμάτων, δι' ὃν ἡμεῖς τε ἠσθήμεθα κεκτημένοι, πλέον ἔχοντες τῶν ἄλλων ἀληθῶς, καὶ αὐτοί γε ξυντέθεινται καὶ ξυνεωράκασιν ἧττον ἔχοντες, ἢν σωφρονῶσιν, εἰ δὲ μή, πολλῷ γ' ἧττον τῇ ἀληθεῖ' ἔχουσιν.

4   Ἔτι καὶ τοῖς καλῶς καθορῶσι καὶ βοῦς γάρ, οἶμαι, καὶ ὄϊς οὐδὲν ἐπαΐει πλέον ἔχοντος ἀνθρώπου, τῇ δ' ἀληθεῖ' οὕτως ἔχει καὶ σφόδρ' ἥττηται. Καὶ δὴ καὶ οὗτοί γε τότε μάλιστ' ἂν εἶεν, μὴ ξυνιέντες, ἀθλιώτεροι καὶ πενέστεροι. Ὧι γὰρ οὐκ ἔχουσι, τὸ τοσοῦτ' ἠγνοήκασι καὶ παρὰ τοσοῦτον ἀμαθίᾳ πένονται, παρ' ὅσον οὐδ' ἤσθηνται, ὥσπερ ἄρα καὶ τῶν μελαγχολώντων ἐκείνοις ἡ νόσος ἐστὶ βαρυτέρα καὶ μάλιστ' ἐργώδης χρῆσθαι, ὁπόσοι μηδὲ νοσεῖν ὅλως, καθάπερ ὁρῶμεν ἐνίους, οἴονται καὶ δυσχεραίνουσι πάντως πρὸς τοὺς ἰᾶσθαι πειρωμένους καὶ κηδομένους ὡς σφᾶς ἀδικοῦντας καὶ διαβάλλοντας καὶ μηδὲν αὐτῶν βελτίους.

5   Οὕτω δὴ παντάπασι τῆς νόσου κάτοχοι καὶ περιγεγένηται σφῶν, ὥστ' οὐδ' ἴσασιν ἡντιναοῦν ἀπαλλαγήν, οὐδὲ ζητοῦσιν, οὐδὲ πιστεύουσιν ἄλλο τίποτ' ἀγαθὸν μήποτ' εἶναι, μηδ' ἄν τις πάσῃ σπουδῇ προδιδάσκῃ. Καὶ τυφλῷ δὴ γεννηθέντι τε καὶ βιοῦντι τίς ἂν ἀμέλει ξυναίσθησις

nature? This wealth is much more precious, and it belongs to the more precious part of our soul; they cannot take it away from us no matter how many tricks and plots they employ, it cannot be defeated by anything, and it does not force us to be constantly on the alert, to be concerned, or to feel threatened, but I think that it very much supplies our wants and under no circumstances can it be violated. On account of this wealth we feel happy, because when we possess it, we indeed have more than others, and they in turn realize and see clearly that they have less, assuming they are prudent, of course; otherwise they are truly in a much worse position.

In any case, for those who perceive correctly, I think, nei- 4 ther the ox nor the sheep understands more than its owner, but they are far inferior to him, and this is simply the truth. So these people would then be even more miserable and poor, if they do not realize these things. For they do not perceive what a significant thing they do not possess, and they suffer to such a degree from their ignorance, since they lack perception. The same happens to those who suffer from mental disturbance; the illness is far more serious and far more difficult to treat in the case of patients who do not believe they are ill, as we frequently see happening with some persons. These patients are even upset by those who take care of and try to treat them, because they assume that they are assaulting and insulting them without being better than them in any way at all.

They are so oppressed and overtaken by the grip of their 5 illness that they do not know or seek any means of escape, nor do they believe that any other good will ever come to them, no matter how earnestly someone tries to advise them beforehand. Can the person who is born blind and

φωτὸς γένοιτο ἢ τίς ἄρα ποτὲ μάθησις παρ᾿ ὁτουοῦν, ὅσης ἡμεῖς ἀπολαύομεν ἐπ᾿ αὐτοῦ τε καὶ δι᾿ αὐτὸ τρυφῆς;

65

Καὶ τοίνυν καὶ τοῖς ἀνδράσιν ἐνταῦθ᾿ οὐκ ἔστιν ὁτιοῦν μάθημα, οὐδὲ διδάσκαλος. Οὕτω δὴ πόρρω πάνυ πένονται καὶ ἀγνοοῦσιν, ὥστ᾿ οὐδ᾿ εὖ παθεῖν ἔχουσιν, οὐδ᾿ οἷοί τ᾿ ἐσμὲν τοὺς τοιούτους εὐεργετεῖν. Καὶ πένης μὲν ἄρ᾿ ὃς ξύνοιδέ τε καὶ προσίεται δῶρα, χάριν ἔχων ἅπασαν διδόντι, σοφός τέ ἐστι καὶ ἴσως ἄν ποτε γένοιτο πλούσιος.

2   Οὗτοι δ᾿ ἐοίκασιν οὕτω παντάπασι σκαιοί τινες εἶναι καὶ ἀγροῖκοι καὶ δυστυχεῖς καὶ οὐκ οἶδ᾿ ὅπως ἀμαθεῖς καθάπαξ ἑαυτῶν, ὥστ᾿ οὐδὲ παθεῖν εὖ οἴδασι, καὶ μάταιος εἴη πόνος, εἰ πειρῷτό τις εὐεργετεῖν, ἀτεχνῶς ὥσπερ ἂν εἴ τις χοίροις χρυσόν τε καὶ ἄργυρον διδῷ κατὰ τὴν παροιμίαν, μήτ᾿ εἰδόσι μήτε βουλομένοις μήτ᾿ ἔχουσι χρῆσθαι· ἀλλ᾿ ὅμως ταῦτ᾿ ἐστὶ καὶ ἄργυρος καὶ χρυσὸς καὶ τίμιον.

3   Κἀνταῦθ᾿ οἱ μὲν οὔτ᾿ ᾔσθηνται οὔτ᾿ ἔχουσιν ὅπως αἰσθήσονται καὶ νοήσουσι τὸ βέλτιον καὶ χρήσονται, ἀλλ᾿ ὅμως τόδε ἐστὶν ὄντως, ἔγωγ᾿ ἂν φαίην, ἀληθῶς πλοῦτος φύσεως ἀνθρώποις, ἡ σοφία, καὶ πολυέραστος, δι᾿ οὗ φίλους τε ἔξεστιν εὖ ποιεῖν καὶ σεμνύνειν—τὰ μάλιστα τοῦ

remains blind all his life experience the sense of light, or can someone explain to him how much joy we derive from it and on account of it?

Chapter 65

In the case of such men too, there is no lesson or teacher. They are so needy and ignorant that they cannot possibly receive any benefit, nor can we show any kindness to such men. Even a poor man who accepts gifts and is aware of the benefaction conferred upon him, if he shows great gratitude toward his benefactor, is both wise and might become rich at some point.

These people, to the contrary, seem to be utterly stupid, 2 boorish, and unfortunate, and somehow they are so ignorant of their individual conditions as not to realize that they have been treated well, and it would be labor in vain if one tried to help them. To put it simply, it is as if someone were to offer gold and silver to swine, as the proverb says, which do not know what to do with them, nor do they want them, nor can they use them. But those metals are still silver and gold and very valuable indeed.

In our case, these men do not understand, nor do they 3 know how to understand and apprehend what is better, and use it. I would nonetheless still claim that wisdom is a truly genuine, beloved wealth that nature bestows on human beings. By means of this wealth, one can benefit his friends and exalt them—a major feature of wealth—as well as cause

πλουτεῖν ἴδια—καὶ ἀνιᾶν ἐχθροὺς καὶ κακῶς δρᾶν, ὃ δῆτ᾽ ἄλλῳ καὶ πρότερον εἴρηται, καὶ οὐκ ἔστιν ὅπως ἄν ποτε μάλιστ᾽ ἐχθροὺς ἀνιάσαις ἢ καλός, φασι, γενόμενος, οἶμαι δ᾽ ἔγωγε καὶ σοφὸς προσθεῖναι, καθ᾽ οὗ σοι μήτ᾽ ἐπιβουλεύειν μήτε δρᾶν ὁτιοῦν κακὸν ἔχουσι καὶ δάκνονται νύκτα τε πᾶσαν καὶ μεθ᾽ ἡμέραν, τῷ καλλίστῳ σε κτήματι ξυνόντα καθορῶντες καὶ φθόνου καὶ μάχης πάσης κρείττονι καὶ δι᾽ οὗ μετὰ ῥᾳστώνης ἁπάσης καὶ καθαρωτάτης βιοῦντ᾽ αἰσθάνονται, κἂν μὲν ἄρα καὶ τοῖς ἔξωθεν εὖ χρῇ καὶ τοῖς ἐνταῦθα τούτοις εὐπραγῇς κατὰ τὸν βίον, κἀνταῦθα μάλιστ᾽ ἐπανθοῦντα τούτῳ τε καὶ κεκοσμημένον, εἰ δὲ μή, μηδ᾽ οὕτω παντάπασι πενόμενον, μηδ᾽ ἀτυχοῦντα τῶν βελτίστων, ἀλλὰ τῷ μεγίστῳ καὶ καλλίστῳ τῷδε μέρει πλουτοῦντα.

4   Ὄλβιος γὰρ ἀεί, ὃν Μοῖσαι φιλέοντι, φησὶν ἡ Σαπφώ. Ἀληθὴς ὁ λόγος καὶ οὔποτ᾽ ἐλέγχεται, καὶ ἃ δὴ νῦν ἤδη πρότερον εἴρηται, καὶ αὖθις μένει, τρυφᾶν τε ἐν ἑαυτοῦ διὰ τῆς ἐν σοφίᾳ ταύτης παρασκευῆς καὶ φίλους τε εὖ ποιεῖν καὶ τοὐναντίον ἐχθροὺς καὶ πᾶσιν, οἷς οἱ πλουτοῦντες, ὡς ἔφημεν, χρῆσθαι καὶ μηδενὸς ἐνδεῖν ὁτουοῦν, ἀλλ᾽ ὅτου δήποθ᾽ ἑκάστοτε δεῖ, δι᾽ αὐτοῦ δρᾶν καὶ καταλλάττειν καὶ ἀπολαμβάνειν τε καὶ ἀποδιδόναι ὁτινοσοῦν ἑκάστου πράγματος σοφίας ἀμοιβὰς καὶ λόγου χάριτας, καὶ ὅ,τι ποτ᾽ ἄρα παθών, οὐκ ἂν ἴσως μήποτ᾽ ἀπορήσαις ἀντιδοῦναι, καὶ ὅτου ποτ᾽ ἐρῴης ἂν καὶ τύχῃς, ἔξεστιν ὑποστῆναι καὶ συναλλάξαι λόγου δόματα.

5   Καὶ τοῦτ᾽ ἔξεστι μὲν ἐπ᾽ ἀνθρώπων, ὡς οὐδείς ποθ᾽

grief to and harm his enemies. This is what someone else claimed in the past: they say that there is no better way to grieve your enemies than by being kind and, I would add, by being wise as well, because in this way they cannot plot against you or harm you in any manner; they gnash their teeth all day and night, seeing that you are absorbed in the best possession there is, which is much stronger than any envy or strife, and they realize that this possession allows you to live in absolute tranquility. If you happen to be well-off outwardly too, and you flourish in the course of your life in this respect as well, this is the occasion on which they will best understand that you are flourishing and embellished. Otherwise, that is, even if your living conditions are not good enough, they still know that you are not completely impoverished or deprived of what is best, but that you are rich in such a magnificent, beautiful domain.

For Sappho says that *he whom the Muses love is* always 4 *blessed.* This is certainly true and has never been questioned. Everything previously said applies on this occasion as well: a certain person, however poor he may be, can with the means he receives from wisdom live luxuriously on his own, benefit his friends, damage his enemies, and enjoy all the advantages of the wealthy without lacking anything, as noted. Whatever you might need on any occasion, you can accomplish this via the gift of wisdom or use it as an item of exchange, you can enjoy the rewards of wisdom and the graces of reasoning and offer them as compensation for anything, and if anything were to happen to you, you would not face any difficulty in paying it back; and whatever you might love and partake in can be substituted, offering instead the gifts of reason.

This could happen also to human beings, of course, be- 5

οὕτως ἄθλιος, οὐδ᾽ ἀμαθής, ὃς οὐκ ἂν πρίαιτο μάλα πρόθυ-
μος λόγους ἀγαθοὺς καὶ δόξαν ἐντεῦθεν εὐμεγέθη, πάντ᾽
ἂν ἀποδούς, ὅσα ἂν οἷός τ᾽ εἴη. Ἔξεστι δὲ μάλιστ᾽ ἐπὶ τῶν
θείων χρῆσθαι καὶ τοῦ φιλανθρώπου καὶ κοινοῦ Δεσπότου
πάντων αὐτοῦ καὶ τῶν αὐτοῦ φίλων τε καὶ δούλων, ἔνθα
δὴ φίλα μάλισθ᾽, ἃ μόνα δύναιτ᾽ ἄν τις δῶρα, φίλαι δ᾽ αἱ
τοῦ λόγου παρ᾽ ἡμῶν φοραί, ὡς οὐκ οἶδ᾽ εἴ τι τῶν ἄλλων,
μᾶλλον δὲ πλεῖν ἢ κατὰ τὰ ἄλλα πάντα.

6   Καὶ δεῆσαν ὁτουοῦν σοι τῶν Θεοῦ φίλων καὶ παρ᾽ αὐτοῦ δυναμένων ἐν δυσχερείᾳ τινὶ παραστάτου, ἐν κινδύνοις,
ἐν νόσοις, ἐν χαλεποῖς ἅπασιν ἀλεξίκακον εὑρεῖν τὴν ἐνο-
χλοῦσαν ἐπήρειαν, ῥᾷον εὔξασθαι πάνυ τοι κατ᾽ εὐφημη-
τηρίου λόγου καὶ χαριστηρίου τυχόν τι συνεισενεγκεῖν,
καὶ μέντοι καὶ τυχόνθ᾽ ὅτου δέοι ἄν, ἔπειτ᾽ εἰσενεγκεῖν, καὶ
τοῦτο πολλάκις, ἄλλοτ᾽ ἄλλῳ καὶ ἐπ᾽ ἄλλῃ τῇ χρείᾳ. Οὐ
γὰρ μήποτ᾽ ἀπορήσαις, ὥσπερ οἱ ταῦτα δὴ τὰ μήτ᾽ αὐτάρκη
καὶ ὀλιγάριθμα πλουτοῦντες ἐκλείπουσι, τῶν ἐνόντων
σοι παμπλείστων καὶ ἀεὶ μεστῶν θησαυρισμάτων καὶ τῆς
ἀμειώτου παρασκευῆς, ἣν βούλει.

7   Καὶ οἶδά ποτ᾽ ἔγωγε καὶ αὐτὸς καὶ οὕτως εὐξάμενος καὶ
τυχών τε καὶ ἀποδούς, μάλιστα μὲν ἱκανῶς ἔχων καὶ ἄλλως
ἀποδοῦναι καὶ ποιήσασθαι τὴν εὐχήν, καθ᾽ ὧν καὶ τοῖς
ἄλλοις νομίζεται, ὡς δ᾽ οἶμαι, βέλτιον, ὧν εἶχον, τόδε μάλιστα κρίνων, τοῦτο καὶ προελόμενος, ψυχῆς ἁγνὸν δῶρον
καὶ νοῦ, οὐχ ὕλης, καὶ πολυαρκές, οὐ τάχιστ᾽ ὀλλύμενον,
καὶ μένον ἀεί, μὴ συλώμενον.

cause no one can be so miserable and ignorant as not to be eager to buy fine rhetorical speeches and the weighty fame that comes with them, offering whatever he can in exchange. But it is also possible to use these speeches especially for divine purposes, in our relation with the merciful common Master of us all, as well as with his own friends and servants. In this area, the gifts of reason are particularly beloved, since these are the only gifts one can offer, and the tributes of reason on our own part are welcome like nothing else I can think of, in fact more welcome than anything else.

If you need someone among the friends of God who can 6 for his part protect you in a troublesome situation, for example when you are in danger, sickness, or in any other difficulty, you can easily rid yourself of the affliction that troubles you by promising to contribute somehow a laudatory thanksgiving oration. And once you get what you need, you can make the same contribution many times, asking for the help of another saint on another occasion of need. You will never be in want of the plentiful, always abundant treasures found inside yourself, or of the undiminished resources, should you need them, as may happen to those who are wealthy in things that are not self-sufficient and countable.

I personally know this, because I made such a promise, 7 and after achieving my goal I offered an oration as a token of gratitude. Of course, I could have made a sufficient expression of my gratitude in another way and have fulfilled my promise, something many people do, I believe. I nonetheless chose this, that is, to compose an oration, which I considered my finest possession, a pure gift of my soul and mind, not something of material value but something durable, that does not perish quickly, that lasts forever and cannot be stolen.

Abbreviations

Cohn-Wendland = Leopold Cohn and Paul Wendland, eds., *Philonis Alexandrini opera quae supersunt*, 7 vols. (Berlin, 1896–1915; repr., Berlin, 1962)

CPG = Ernst L. Leutsch and Friedrich G. Schneidewin, eds., *Corpus paroemiographorum Graecorum*, 2 vols. (Göttingen, 1839, 1851; repr., Hildesheim, 1958)

Cramer = John A. Cramer, ed., *Anecdota Graeca e codd. manuscriptis bibliothecae regiae Parisiensis*, vol. 1 (Oxford, 1839; repr., Hildesheim, 1967)

Demetrakos = Demetrios Demetrakos, ed., *Μέγα λεξικὸν ὅλης τῆς Ἑλληνικῆς γλώσσης*, 9 vols. (Athens, 1933–1951)

Dindorf = Wilhelm Dindorf, ed., *Aristides*, 3 vols. (Leipzig, 1829; repr., Hildesheim, 1964)

Hense = Otto Hense, ed., *Ioannis Stobaei anthologium*, vol. 1 (Berlin, 1884)

Karathanasis = Demetrios K. Karathanasis, *Sprichwörter und sprichwörtliche Redensarten des Altertums in den rhetorischen Schriften des Michael Psellos, des Eustathios und des Michael Choniates sowie in anderen rhetorischen Quellen des XII. Jahrhunderts* (Munich, 1936)

Lampe = Geoffrey W. H. Lampe, ed., *A Patristic Greek Lexicon* (Oxford, 1961)

LbA = Michael Grünbart and Alexander Riehle, eds., *Lexikon der byzantinischen Autoren* (forthcoming)

LbG = Erich Trapp et al., eds., *Lexikon zur byzantinischen Gräzität: Besonders des 9.–12. Jahrhunderts* (Vienna, 1994)

Lenz-Behr = Friedrich W. Lenz and Charles A. Behr, eds., *P. Aelii Aristidis: Opera quae exstant omnia,* 4 vols. (Leiden, 1976–1980)

LSJ = Henry G. Liddell, Robert Scott, and Henry S. Jones, eds., *A Greek-English Lexicon,* 9th ed. (Oxford, 1940); with a revised supplement (Oxford, 1996)

OCD = Simon H. Hornblower and Antony Spawforth, eds., *Oxford Classical Dictionary,* 4th ed. (Oxford, 2012)

ODB = Alexander Kazhdan et al., eds., *Oxford Dictionary of Byzantium,* 3 vols. (New York, 1991)

PG = Jacques-Paul Migne, ed., *Patrologiae cursus completus: Series Graeca* (Paris, 1857–1866)

Pistelli = Hermenegildus Pistelli, ed., *Iamblichi protrepticus ad fidem codicis Florentini* (Leipzig, 1888)

PLP = Erich Trapp, ed., *Prosopographisches Lexikon der Palaiologenzeit,* 12 vols. (Vienna, 1976–1996)

Polemis 2002 = edition by Ioannis Polemis, Θεόδωρος Μετοχίτης. Ἠθικὸς ἢ περὶ παιδείας, Κείμενα βυζαντινῆς λογοτεχνίας 1 (Athens, 1995; rev. ed. 2002)

Polemis-Kaltsogianni 2019 = latest edition by Ioannis Polemis and Eleni Kaltsogianni, eds., *Theodorus Metochites Orationes,* Bibliotheca scriptorum Graecorum et Romanorum Teubneriana (Berlin and Boston, 2019), 347–429

Sophocles = Evangelinos A. Sophocles, ed., *Greek Lexicon of the Roman and Byzantine Periods* (New York, 1900)

Strömberg = Reinhold Strömberg, *Greek Proverbs: A Collection of Proverbs and Proverbial Phrases Which Are Not Listed by the Ancient and Byzantine Paroemiographers* (Göteborg, 1954)

TrGF = *Tragicorum Graecorum Fragmenta,* 5 vols. (Göttingen, 1971–2004): vol. 1, *Didascaliae tragicae, catalogi tragicorum minorum,* ed. Bruno Snell (1971); vol. 2, *Fragmenta adespota, testimonia, etc.,* ed. Richard Kannicht and Bruno Snell (1981); vol. 3, *Aeschylus,* ed. Stefan Radt (1985); vol. 4, *Sophocles,* ed. Stefan Radt, 2nd ed. (1999); vol. 5, *Euripides,* ed. Richard Kannicht, 2nd ed. in 2 parts (2004)

Note on the Text

On Morals was first edited in 1995 by Ioannis Polemis, who published a revised version in 2002. The two Polemis editions are accompanied by an extensive introduction, modern Greek translation of the work, and useful notes. Prior to Polemis, in 1975, Ihor Ševčenko ("Theodore Metochites, the Chora") provided transcriptions of short passages, and in 1982 ("Théodore Métochite, *Logos* 10"), he transcribed a longer section of the Greek text (fols. 217v–219r at pp. 148–49) with French translation (at pp. 142–47). While this Dumbarton Oaks Medieval Library volume was in preparation for the press, a third edition appeared, in Ioannis Polemis and Eleni Kaltsogianni, *Theodori Metochitae Orationes,* 347–429. The minor changes I have made to the Polemis-Kaltsogianni edition are listed below in the Notes to the Text, preceded by a brief note explaining the editorial principles employed.

On Morals survives in a single manuscript, Vindobonensis phil. gr. 95 (fols. 189r–233v), dated to the fourteenth century, which contains Metochites's rhetorical works arranged in chronological order; see Herbert Hunger, *Katalog der griechischen Handschriften der Österreichischen Nationalbibliothek,* vol. 1, *Codices historici, codices philosophici et philologici* (Vienna, 1961), 202–4; for a fuller bibliography, see Polemis and Kalt-

sogianni, *Theodori Metochitae Orationes,* vii–viii. Part of the manuscript was written by the imperial notary Michael Klostomalles (*PLP,* no. 11867), who was active in Constantinople in the first half of the fourteenth century. For identification of the hand, see Erich Lamberz, "Das Geschenk des Kaisers Manuel II an das Kloster Saint-Denis und der 'Metochitesschreiber' Michael Klostomalles," in Λιθόστρωτον: *Studien zur byzantinischen Kunst und Geschichte, Festschrift für Marcell Restle,* ed. Birgitt Borkopp and Thomas Steppan (Stuttgart, 2000), 155–65, especially 158–59; and Brigitte Mondrain, "Les écritures dans les manuscrits byzantins du XIVe siècle: Quelques problématiques," *Rivista di Studi Bizantini e Neoellenici* 44 (2007): 157–96, at 185–86. Klostomalles was also evidently at Metochites's disposal for a long period for the manuscript of the *Sententious Remarks* (Parisinus gr. 2003), probably copying under Metochites's direct supervision (see Förstel, "Metochites and His Books," especially 258–59). Förstel also notes that Nikephoros Gregoras annotated Vindobonensis phil. gr. 95.

The text of *On Morals* presents four major gaps, as indicated by Polemis in his 2002 edition (159*–60*): 1) two folios are missing between the end of fol. 203v and the beginning of fol. 204r; 2) another lacuna is in evidence between the end of fol. 220v and the beginning of fol. 221r; 3) two folios are presumably missing between the end of fol. 223v and the beginning of fol. 224r; 4) finally, there is a gap of about four folios between the end of fol. 224v and the beginning of fol. 225r. Ihor Ševčenko (*La vie intellectuelle,* 178) was the first to identify these lacunae, hypothesizing that there is another gap after fol. 219, which on codicological and other grounds

has not been accepted by Polemis. More than one correcting hand worked on the manuscript.

Ibereticus 388 (fols. 54r–60v) preserves an adaptation of *On Morals,* produced by the sixteenth-century scholar and monk Theophanes Eleavoulkos (Meletiadis, Ἡ ἐκπαίδευση στὴν Κωνσταντινούπολη, 43–56). According to Polemis's 2002 edition (164*), Eleavoulkos's version has no editorial significance, as it is merely an apograph of Vindobonensis phil. gr. 95.

Notes to the Text

SIGLA

[. . .] = lacuna
<. . .> = editorial insertion
V = Vienna, Österreichische Nationalbibliothek, cod. Vindobonensis
phil. gr. 95 (fourteenth century)

The Greek text comes from the 2002 edition by Polemis, who kindly permitted his text to be reproduced for the needs of the present volume. A new edition by Ioannis Polemis and Eleni Kaltsogianni appeared in 2019. I gained access to this when my translation was at an advanced state of preparation, and I was therefore unable to take full advantage of it. A thorough cross-examination of the 2002 and 2019 editions has led me to conclude that the two versions of the text differ in no significant respect other than punctuation, accentuation, chapter numbering, and minor changes to a very few readings. I have adopted some of those readings that help improve interpretation of the text; these are indicated below with references to the Polemis-Kaltsogianni chapter numbering.

In dividing the text into chapters, I followed Polemis's 2002 division for the most part, except where there is an extensive gap in the manuscript, in which case I choose to begin a new chapter. The subdivisions into subsections/paragraphs with corresponding section numbers are my own. My interventions in the 2002 Greek text involve mainly tacit corrections of typographical errors mostly in accentuation, slight changes to capitalization and punctuation, the use of italics to indicate quotations, and the adoption of alternative variants or conjectures I take to be more apt to the meaning of the passage. In general, I have retained orthographic peculiarities in

line with Polemis's edition, since they are probably to be traced to the author himself (see Note on the Text).

2.2   πρὸς τὴν νῦν *Polemis-Kaltsogianni 2019 (2.10, p. 348)*: πρὸ τὴν νῦν *Polemis 2002 (2.1, p. 6)*

3.2   μὲν αὐτοί <αὑτούς>: *I have added Polemis-Kaltsogianni 2019's (4.18, p. 349) conjecture,* αὑτούς *after* αὐτοί; *compare also Polemis 2002 (3.2, p. 10)*.

6.1   ἥν μοι ἔξεστιν *Polemis-Kaltsogianni 2019 (9.8, p. 352)*: ἥ μοι ἔξεστιν *Polemis 2002 (6.17, p. 22)*

6.2   ὄντως ἀγαθοῦ *Polemis-Kaltsogianni 2019 (10.4, p. 353)*: ὄντος ἀγαθοῦ *Polemis 2002 (6.16, p. 24)*

10.1   καὶ ὅ,τι τις: καὶ ὅ,τι τίς *Polemis-Kaltsogianni 2019 (16.2, p. 358)*: καὶ ὅ,τι τὶς *Polemis 2002 (10.2, p. 44)*

12.3   τοὐναντίον ἅπαν τἀνδρὶ *Polemis-Kaltsogianni 2019 (19.15, p. 361)*: τοὐναντίον ἅπαντ᾽ ἀνδρὶ *Polemis 2002 (12.9–10, p. 54)*

18.4   ἀλλ᾽ ἅπασιν εἴαται *Polemis-Kaltsogianni 2019 (32.18, p. 371)*: ἀλλ᾽ ἃ πᾶσιν εἴαται *Polemis 2002 (18.7, p. 86)*

20.5   λυσιτελεστάτην [. . .]: *There is a gap in the manuscript; two folios appear to be missing.*

21.3   θηρωμέναις *Polemis-Kaltsogianni 2019 (39.7, p. 375)*: θηρωμένοις *Polemis 2002 (21.4, p. 104)*

23.1   Καίτοι πόσαι ταὐτὰ: *I adopt the alternative suggestion by Polemis-Kaltsogianni 2019 (41.4, p. 377),* ταὐτὰ *rather than the* ταῦτα *of their accepted reading.*

38.2   δοκοῖεν αὐτοὶ κακῇ μόνοι: *I follow the alternative suggestion by Polemis-Kaltsogianni 2019 (61.27–28, p. 394),* μόνοι *rather than the* μόνη *of their accepted reading.*

49.2   [. . .] οὐδὲν: *There is a gap here of uncertain length in the manuscript.*

50.2   ἐκφυγεῖν τοὺς ἀρρήκτους: *I print* ἀρρήκτους *following the conjecture by Polemis-Kaltsogianni 2019 (77.15–16, p. 407) instead of* ἀρρήτους V; *see also 10.2,* ὥσπερ ἀρρήκτοις τισὶν ὑπὸ τούτων δεσμοῖς ἐχόμεθα, *and 62.3,* δεσμοῖς ἀρρήκτοις

53   φαυλότατον [. . .]: *There is a gap here in the manuscript; two folios are likely missing.*

55.3   τὸ πρᾶγμα [. . .]: *There is a gap here in the manuscript of about four folios.*

Notes to the Translation

title   The sole manuscript preserving the text retains a marginal annotation referring to the title that reads λόγος ι′ (oration 10).

1.1   *a few things about education*: Here λόγοι is a synonym of παιδεία (education), used in the same way elsewhere in Metochites, for instance in his Poem 3.66–67 (Polemis, *Carmina,* 76). The author introduces the generic persona of an unknown young man, who conveniently remains anonymous throughout so as to appeal to a broader readership, in line with the conventional trope in moralizing works; see also Introduction, "Structure and Summary."

    leisure activity: Metochites uses ῥᾳστώνη with reference to the leisure time that allows for intellectual endeavors; Poem 1.1147 (Polemis, *Carmina,* 45). The term is a counterpart to the Latin *otium* (free time) as a contrast to *negotium,* the busy and stressful schedule of daily business.

1.2   *However, whenever this consideration . . . occupied with a task*: The author wishes to engage his reader's goodwill by raising constructed difficulties that supposedly hampered him in his task of composition. This may function here as a traditional *captatio benevolentiae,* begging the indulgence of his readers.

    completely base and inappropriate for free men: That is, servile.

    Yet it is they that damn . . . longs for virtue: The language in the concluding sentence is particularly strong, especially the author's cursing of the destructive impact of daily anxieties on one's intellect.

2.1   *practice advances every activity*: Hesiod, *Works and Days* 412.

2.2 *So, this is how I came . . . imagined or expected*: See Plutarch's pro-
grammatic statement in the introduction to his *Lives of Ae-
milius and Timoleon* (1.1), where he too claims that his *Parallel
Lives* project will facilitate the ethical development of both his
readers and himself.

3.3 *People who adore . . . have been prepared*: See Metochites, *Sententious Remarks* 6.2.6 (Hult, *Theodore Metochites on Ancient Authors*,
p. 68, lines 27–29).

5.1 *this multitude of people . . . their nature*: Comparing men with animals is traditional in works of a protreptic nature.

5.2 *They have obscured . . . sunk into darkness*: The notion of intellectual darkness goes back to Plato's *Republic* 527d–e.

they cannot even open . . . herms in the streets: See Thucydides, *History of the Peloponnesian War* 6.27.1; Plato, *Symposium* 215b. Herms
were four-cornered pillars with a head, most commonly that of
the god Hermes, and male genitals. Used as road and boundary
markers, they were situated in public places, for example at the
entrance of the Acropolis, in the Agora, in front of temples,
and outside private houses, and were thought to protect from
harm or evil.

without a helmsman: Κυβερνήτου δίχα; see Metochites, *Byzantios*
119 (Polemis and Kaltsogianni, *Orationes*, p. 537, line 17).

6.1 *I shall send the ship down upright*: The same expression is found
elsewhere in Metochites, for example in *Sententious Remarks* 79
(Wahlgren, *Sententious Notes*, p. 184, lines 24–25), most probably
inspired by Aelius Aristides, *The Rhodian Oration* (Dindorf, vol.
1, p. 802, line 4).

6.2 *substantial hypostases*: A term referring to the individual proper-
ties of the Father, Son, and Holy Spirit as different "persons,"
as contrasted with the substance, essence, or nature of the divinity. See *ODB*, vol. 2, p. 966.

6.3 *Logos of the immortal God*: A reference to Jesus Christ.

his indistinguishable seal: Gregory of Nazianzus, *On the Father*, PG,
vol. 37, col. 400A.30–31; Athanasius, *On the Annunciation*, PG,
vol. 28, col. 924.43–44.

7.2 *let sleeping dogs lie*: The literal translation of this proverb is

"do not shake the *anagyros*" *(anagyris foetida)*, the stinking bean-trefoil, a malodorous plant, in order to prevent an unpleasant smell. See Gregory of Cyprus, *Proverbs* 1.22 (*CPG*, vol. 2, p. 95, lines 5–6); Apostolius, *Proverbs* 9.99 (*CPG*, vol. 2, p. 483, lines 8–11); Mantissa, *Proverbs* 1.94 (*CPG*, vol. 2, p. 758, lines 13–15); LSJ, under ἀνάγυρος; see also Demetrakos, under ἀνάγυρος.

as the Carpathian hare: The inhabitants of the island of Carpathos did not have any hares and sent for some, considering them a rare animal; the hares afterward multiplied so fast that they ate up the Carpathians' grain. Hence the proverb "as the Carpathian hare," which criticizes those who create self-inflicted troubles—people seeking to do themselves good, but eventually doing themselves a mischief. See Mantissa, *Proverbs* 1.91 (*CPG*, vol. 2, p. 758, lines 1–4).

the goat carries the knife: Another proverb about those who ask for trouble. See Gregory of Cyprus, *Proverbs* 1.13 (*CPG*, vol. 2, p. 94, line 12); Diogenianus, *Proverbs* 1.52 (*CPG*, vol. 1, p. 188, line 19 through p. 189, line 2). At an annual sacrifice the Corinthians wished to offer a goat to Hera. The sacrificial knife was carried and hidden by some people involved in the sacrifice, but the goat that was about to be sacrificed stirred the ground with its feet and eventually unearthed the knife. So the goat in a way provoked its own death.

stir up the fire with your hands: That is, you should not irritate an already angry man; see Apostolius, *Proverbs* 11.5a (*CPG*, vol. 2, p. 516, line 15 through p. 517, line 9).

7.3   *Or how could one not condemn you harshly for acting thus*: Short rhetorical questions are a main feature of the genre of the diatribe.

You were not caught . . . Icarus's wings: See Zenobius, *Proverbs* 4.92 (*CPG*, vol. 1, p. 112, lines 7–31). See also *Scholia in Aelium Aristidem* (Dindorf, vol. 3, p. 692, lines 19–25).

8.1   *the Pythagorean Golden Words*: *Golden Words* (Χρυσῆ Ἔπη), a collection of ethical precepts comprising seventy-one hexameters, is ascribed to Pythagoras but is more likely one of the Pythagorean pseudepigrapha from the Hellenistic period; see *OCD*, under Pythagoras.

not to walk on busy roads: Philo, *Every Good Man is Free* 2 (Cohn-Wendland, vol. 6, p. 1, lines 7–11).

to move on in absolute order: Aelius Aristides, *Against Plato, In Defence of the Four (Statesmen)* (Dindorf, vol. 2, p. 159, lines 20–21; most recently edited by Lenz-Behr, vol. 1, pt. 2, p. 296, lines 2–3). Also see below in *On Morals,* chapter 59.2.

8.4   *light wings*: This image is found in Aristophanes's *Birds* 1453 and became a traditional image, as in, for example, Nonnus, *Dionysiaca* 18.1.

beggars of the stage and the dramatic plays: Metochites is fond of employing theatrical terminology; see his *Byzantios* 106 (Polemis and Kaltsogianni, *Orationes,* p. 527, lines 18–19), 119 (Polemis and Kaltsogianni, *Orationes,* p. 537, line 20).

9.1   *significant testimony . . . power of goodness*: Plato, *Theaetetus* 176a–b, preserved also in Philo, *On Flight and Discovery* 63 (Cohn-Wendland, vol. 3, p. 123, lines 22–26).

9.2   *to draw the water out of the sea with a jar*: See *CPG,* vol. 1, appendix 4.58, p. 446, lines 7–8.

10.2   *nothing is permanent or stable*: Metochites devotes a whole essay of the *Sententious Remarks* 87 (Müller and Kiessling, *Miscellanea philosophica,* pp. 570–74) to the instability of human affairs.

10.3   *whereas on the other hand . . . he longs to do so*: Metochites usually complains about the intellectual stagnation of his day, arguing that the brilliance of the classical past has condemned Byzantine scholars to sterility and uncreative imitation. See especially the preface to his *Sententious Remarks* (Hult, *Theodore Metochites on Ancient Authors,* pp. 20–26).

11.1   *fame is exalted to heaven*: Οὐρανόμηκες κλέος; see Aristophanes, *Clouds* 357, 459.

11.2   *servant in old age*: For γηροτρόφος, see Plato, *Republic* 331a; Plutarch, *On Tranquility of the Soul* 477b, *On Brotherly Love* 480c, 481b.

11.3   *even when someone dies . . . the body no longer exists*: The quotation comes from Euripides's fragmentary tragedy the *Temenidai* (fragment 734; Kannicht, *TrGF,* vol. 5, p. 728).

nothing sound or stable . . . upside down: See Plato, *Phaedo* 90c.

12.2   *courage*: Lampe, under λῆμμα 5.

13.1   *swift-footed horses*: The image of the swift-footed horses comes from *Iliad* 8.88, 16.833, 23.294.

13.2   *way of life*: LSJ, under ἔνστασις A 2.

        on the mountains: See Homer, *Iliad* 4.452.

14.2   *Not only do these . . . in any way*: This is the Stoic belief of the morally "indifferents," which holds that externalities such as wealth and social status do not account for individual virtue and happiness.

14.3   *perfect virtue*: The expression comes from Aristotle, *Nicomachean Ethics* 1100a4.

15.2   *this issue*: That is, the connection between virtue and reason.

15.3   *education and the blessings . . . human possession does*: See Pseudo-Plutarch, *On the Education of Children* 5e.

16.1   *matters mentioned previously*: That is, wealth, luxury, fame, and the like.

16.3   *the arrows that . . . bite deeply*: The source is unknown.

17.1   *Dionysius*: Dionysius the Younger or Dionysius II (ca. 397 BCE– 343 BCE) ruled the city of Syracuse in Sicily from 367 BCE to 357 BCE, and then again from 346 BCE to 344 BCE.

        Dionysius caused Plato grief . . . concerned with your issues: Plutarch, *Life of Dion* 20.2–4: "Dionysius sought to disprove his enmity to Plato by giving banquets in his honor and making generous provisions for his journey, and went so far as to say something like this to him: 'I suppose, Plato, you will bring many dire accusations against me to the ears of your fellow philosophers.' To this Plato answered with a smile: 'Heaven forbid that there should be such a dearth of topics for discussion in the Academy that anyone mention you.'" English translation by Bernadotte Perrin, *The Parallel Lives by Plutarch*, vol. 6 (Cambridge, Mass., and London, 1918), 41 (slightly altered).

        he controls himself . . . philosophical spirit: The notion of self-management is common in the ethical literature of the post-Hellenistic period. It occurs most frequently in later Stoic moralists such as Seneca and Epictetus, but also in Middle Platonism, especially in Plutarch.

17.2   *free of anxieties*: Ἀπεριφροντίστως is a *hapax legomenon*.

      using both feet energetically: The proverb refers to people who are very eager to materialize their goals. See *Scholia in Aelium Aristidem* (Dindorf, vol. 3, p. 104, lines 2–12).

17.3   *Spending time in . . . great relief*: Plutarch, *On the Tranquility of the Soul* 469a. Metochites is very fond of this image.

18.1   *genuine friends consider it . . . life in check*: Aristotle, *Nicomachean Ethics* 1171b21–25.

      Yet could anyone find . . . through their books: See Metochites, Poem 4.61–62 (Polemis, *Carmina*, 87).

18.2   *Plato says that young . . . route in advance*: Plato, *Republic* 328d–e; with *Sententious Remarks*, 112 (Müller and Kiessling, *Miscellanea philosophica*, p. 747, line 11 through p. 748, line 1).

18.4   *like a free offer . . . means of our senses*: See Metochites, *Byzantios* 67 (Polemis and Kaltsogianni, *Orationes*, p. 488, lines 26–28).

      As the ancient saying . . . even if they are dead: An anecdote attributed to the Stoic philosopher Zeno found in Diogenes Laertius, *Lives of Eminent Philosophers* 7.2.

18.5   *oxen with rolling gait*: Homer, *Iliad* 9.466; for other Homeric descriptions of feasts, see *Iliad* 1.315–16, 18.524, 21.448, 23.166; *Odyssey* 1.92, 4.320, 9.46, 11.289, 12.136.

19.1   *Diogenes the Cynic*: Also known as Diogenes of Sinope, ca. 412/403–ca. 324/321 BCE. He pursued a life in accordance with nature rather than law/convention, proclaimed self-sufficiency and physical toughness as a requirement of virtue, and contended that wisdom was a matter of action rather than thought. He also embraced the tradition of the wise man who promises converts happiness or salvation. Diogenes Laertius, *Lives of Eminent Philosophers* 6.54, reports that Plato called Diogenes "a Socrates gone mad."

      used to wander around . . . to find an honest man: Diogenes Laertius, *Lives of Eminent Philosophers* 6.41; "honest" is not in the text but it is a popular, accepted translation.

      to happen by necessity: That is, when one is obliged to suffer in order to acquire things.

20.1   *the celebrated Socrates . . . to think and live*: Xenophon, *Memorabilia* 1.6.14.

20.3   *so that every individual . . . adorn himself however he could*: The au-
        thor refers to the ability of the competent orator to assume a
        socially acceptable persona before his audience, even if this de-
        viates from reality.

20.4   *beginning is half done*: Diogenianus, *Proverbs* 1.83 (*CPG*, vol. 2, p. 13,
        line 9).

20.5   *whether*: The second εἴτε must have been lost in the lacuna that
        follows.

        the complete simplicity . . . comes through magnanimity: The impli-
        cation is that, in contrast to rhetorical prose, philosophical
        works traditionally lack rhetorical sophistication.

        beneficial [. . .]: A gap in the manuscript; two folios appear to be
        missing. See Note on the Text.

21.1   *Every day we encounter people . . . I cannot identify*: Metochites, *Sen-
        tentious Remarks* 112 (Müller and Kiessling, *Miscellanea philoso-
        phica,* p. 749, lines 4–10). The reference to embassies might
        echo Metochites's *Presbeutikos* (*On the Embassy,* edited by Po-
        lemis and Kaltsogianni), where he discusses the negotiations
        between Serbia and Byzantium over Byzantine influence on
        Slavic royalty.

21.2   *a fair for all townsfolk*: *Panegyreis* are normally fairs connected
        with the feast days of saints; see *ODB,* under "Feast," vol. 2,
        pp. 781–82.

21.3   *I have already discussed this very fair*: Metochites does not refer to
        the notion of the fair anywhere else in the *On Morals*. This is
        thus presumably a cross-reference to his *Second Kingship Ora-
        tion,* chapter 7 (Polemis and Kaltsogianni, *Orationes,* p. 272, line
        16).

22.1   *qualifications*: See Demetrakos, under ἑστία 10 (vol. 4, p. 2987).

22.2   *They have scarcely failed to mention any of their achievements*: This
        section is close to Metochites's Essay 93 of the *Sententious
        Remarks;* see especially Agapitos, Hult, and Smith, *Theodoros
        Metochites on Philosophic Irony,* p. 34, lines 5–8.

        Solon . . . conquered the city: See Plutarch, *Life of Solon* 8–9.

        Pericles, the man whose name . . . with a hundred triremes: Thucydi-
        des, *History of the Peloponnesian War* 2.56; Plutarch, *Life of Peri-
        cles* 19.2.

Chabrias: Athenian general (ca. 420–357/6 BCE) who fought for Athens and for the kings of Cyprus and Egypt against Persia.

with a hundred ships urged the Egyptians to oppose the Persian king: Plutarch, *Life of Agesilaus* 37; Diodorus Siculus, 15.29.2, 15.92.3.

Iphicrates . . . conquered Sestos with three ships: Plutarch, *Life of Agesilaus* 24.

a trireme from Samos . . . and destroyed its walls: Plutarch, *Life of Lysander* 15.1.

and shortly thereafter became quartermaster of Agesilaus's army: Plutarch, *Life of Lysander* 23.11.

and soon after that was killed in Haliartos: In the Battle of Haliartos (in central Boeotia) in 395 BCE, the Thebans defeated a Spartan force attempting to seize the town and killed the Spartan leader, Lysander. This battle led to the Corinthian War, which ended in 387 BCE.

as a peltast or a Lacedaemonian heavily armed soldier: Plutarch, *Life of Lysander* 28.10. A peltast was a soldier equipped with a light shield.

22.3   *Agesilaus himself . . . Greek feat of the time*: Xenophon, *Hellenica* 3.4.5–29.

23.4   *Theopompus*: Theopompus was a Greek historian and rhetorician (ca. 380–ca. 315 BCE) who composed the *Hellenics,* the *History of Philip,* and several panegyrics and hortatory addresses, including a *Letter to Alexander.* Only fragments of his works survive.

24.2   *Alexander had died at Susa*: Alexander actually died in Babylon in 323 BCE.

Demades: Athenian statesman (ca. 380–319 BCE) prominent in the two decades following the Greek defeat at the Battle of Chaeronea (338 BCE).

the whole world would have smelled his corpse long ago: Plutarch, *Life of Phocion* 22.5.

24.3   *What Thucydides said . . . rest in peace*: Thucydides, *History of the Peloponnesian War* 1.70.9.

the Romans did not allow other people to relax: See Plutarch, *Life of Themistocles* 3.4.

They therefore truly reigned . . . and their fame: This aligns with what Metochites said about the reputation of the Romans in *On Morals,* chapter 24.2.

25.1   *As Plato says . . . cut off from it*: Plato, *Phaedo* 83d–e.

25.3   *sybaritic banquets*: Sybaris was a Greek colony in South Italy, founded in 720 BCE by Achaean and Troezenian settlers. Due to its agricultural and trading wealth, the city's luxury, feasts, and sensuality became proverbial in ancient literature.

        dress . . . artificially: LSJ, under μαγγανεύω A II.

25.4   *Choose the best . . . make it pleasant*: The quotation from Pythagoras survives in Plutarch's *Precepts of Healthcare* 123c, *On Tranquility of the Soul* 466f, and *On Exile* 602c, and in Stobaios's *Anthology* 3.1.29 (Hense, vol. 1, p. 14, lines 1–2).

26.2   *close their ears*: LSJ, under ἐπιτίθημι B II.

26.3   *beautiful combination of colors*: A reference to the rainbow.

27.2   *after a brief struggle, you can never have great fame*: A fragment from a lost tragedy of Sophocles (fragment 938; Radt, *TrGF,* vol. 4, p. 588).

28.2   *Gorgonian monster*: This expression comes from the myth of the Gorgon, a legendary creature that supposedly turned to stone those who looked at her. In Greek mythology, there were three Gorgons, the sisters Stheno, Euryale, and Medusa, with snakes for hair. Medusa was killed by Perseus, and the winged horse Pegasus is said to have sprung from her blood. Thereafter, "gorgon" became a standard term for a frightening or repulsive woman or spectacle generally.

        Pray that we not be ill . . . be left to us: The quotation is from Crantor (ca. 335–275 BCE), a philosopher of the early Academy and the first commentator on Plato. Metochites must have taken it from *Consolation to Apollonius* 102d (attributed to Plutarch).

28.3   *If injustice is necessary, it is best to act unjustly*: Euripides, *Phoenissae* 527–28; the passage was very popular in the literature of the Imperial period and is cited for instance by Plutarch, *Precepts of Healthcare* 125d.

29.1   *is brought to us as a secondary purpose of our journey*: LSJ, under πάρεργος A II; see also Metochites, *Sententious Remarks* 71.12.8

(Hult, *Theodore Metochites on Ancient Authors,* p. 242, lines 1–2). The proverb is attributed to Pythagoras and survives in the *Protrepticus* of the Neoplatonist Iamblichus (Pistelli, p. 106, lines 21–23).

evil with something that is . . . not evil: Aeschylus, fragment 349 (Radt, *TrGF,* vol. 3, p. 415); Herodotus, *The Histories* 3.53; see Thucydides, *History of the Peloponnesian War* 5.65.

remain firm: LSJ, under ἔχω C III.

30.3   *On the other hand . . . in the best possible manner*: Metochites accepts the Aristotelian bipartition as outlined in general terms, which supports the division of the soul into a rational and a nonrational part; see, for example, *Nicomachean Ethics* 1102a26–1103a3.

30.4   *the best part*: That is, the rational faculty.

pack animal . . . the best part considered useful: The image comes from the well-known allegory in Plato, *Phaedrus* 246a–254e.

32.1   *unswerving*: Ἀνέκδημος seems to be a *hapax legomenon.*

as in a solo pipe performance: That is, in absolute isolation.

opens: Demetrakos, under διαίρω 1 and especially 6 (vol. 4, p. 1871).

countless: Demetrakos, under ἀμύθητος (vol. 1, p. 343).

32.2   *until it reaches bliss*: The Greek phrase βάλλ' ἐς μακαρίαν is used to indicate a wish for something good; see Diogenianus 2.4 (*CPG,* vol. 2, p. 18, line 9); see also Apostolius, *Proverbs* 4.72 (*CPG,* vol. 2, p. 324, lines 9–10) with a negative sense; also in Plato, *Hippias Maior* 293a. Metochites uses the expression in its literal sense.

33.1   *from the . . . beginning*: Ἀφ' ἑστίας is used for those who undertake something from the beginning. See Apostolius, *Proverbs* 4.61 (*CPG,* vol. 2, p. 321, line 5 through p. 322, line 2).

caught in my own snare: LSJ, under περιπίπτω A II 3.

34.1   *Phidias*: The famous Greek sculptor, painter, and architect of the fifth century BCE, especially notable for his colossal statues of Athena Parthenos at Athens and Zeus at Olympia.

Polygnotus: A Greek painter of the fifth century BCE, from Thasos, responsible for the supervision of the design of the *Stoa*

Poikile (Painted Porch) in Athens. His most important works were his representation of the sack of Troy on the wall of the *Stoa Poikile* and his frescoes in a building at Delphi erected by the people of Cnidus. In antiquity, Polygnotus was known for his innovative artistic techniques, especially for introducing a novel kind of large-scale painting (Pliny, *Natural History* 7.205; Plato, *Ion* 532e).

Eulalios: A mosaicist and icon painter who flourished during the reign of Manuel I Komnenos (1143–1180); he is said to have painted the images of the Pantokrator and the Myrrophoroi in the church of the Holy Apostles in Constantinople; see *ODB*, vol. 2, p. 745.

Zeuxippus: According to Plato (*Protagoras* 318b), Zeuxippus of Heraclea (fifth century BCE) was a teacher of painting active in Athens.

Lysippus: A bronze sculptor from Sicyon (ca. 372–306 BCE) and head of the school at Argos and Sicyon in the time of Philip of Macedon. Especially active during the reign of Alexander the Great, Lysippus was famous for the detailed proportions of his sculpture and its lifelike naturalism. In the history of art, he is noted as a precursor of Hellenism.

35.1   *For Plato and anyone else . . . management of men*: Plato, *Republic* 473d.

      Yet no matter how exhaustively . . . this choice of his: See Aelius Aristides, *Against Plato, In Defence of the Four (Statesmen)* (Dindorf, vol. 2, p. 182, lines 10–14; most recently edited by Lenz-Behr, vol. 1, pt. 2, p. 315, lines 21–24).

36.2   *I also believe that even . . . circumstances that might occur*: The allegory of the helmsman as a representation of the politician comes from Plato, *Republic* 489a, 489c; see also Plato, *Politicus* 297e–299c; *Laws* 709b–c, 961e–963b.

36.4   *This happens not because good . . . as some people thought*: This is a reference to the Stoics, who defined the good as "what is complete according to nature" (Cicero, *On Ends* 3.33).

38.2   *To put it in a few words . . . a construction of men*: See Plato, *Gorgias* 492c.

without meaning: LSJ, under ἄλλως A II 3.

39.2   *As I have already said*: See chapter 8.4.

40.1   *held in repute*: LSJ, under δοκέω A II 5.

40.2   *slave in the mines . . . Sicilian proverb*: See Apostolius, *Proverbs* 6.68 (*CPG*, vol. 2, p. 382, lines 1–6).

       bastard child at Kynosarges at Athens: Metochites, *Sententious Remarks* 12.2.3 (Hult, *Theodore Metochites on Ancient Authors*, p. 116, lines 1–3); Apostolius, *Proverbs* 6.66 (*CPG*, vol. 2, p. 381, lines 1–3). Kynosarges was a public gymnasium outside the walls of Athens that functioned as a cult center for Heracles. It was the traditional gathering point for the *nothoi*, or offspring of mixed Athenian or non-Athenian parentage, such as Themistocles (Plutarch, *Life of Themistocles* 1.1–3).

41.3   *had they tended to*: See LSJ, under βουκολέω A 2. Such a proverb does not seem to be listed in *CPG*.

41.4   *the wealth of their household*: The expression is found in Plutarch, *On the Sign of Socrates* 583f.

41.5   *Just as Diogenes . . . to gilded arrows*: From an unknown source.

42.1   *achievement*: Δοκίμησις is a *hapax legomenon*.

42.2   *But as for what they are unable . . . to accomplish this*: Thucydides, *History of the Peloponnesian War* 2.35.2.

44.1   *share in our luck*: See LSJ, under Ἑρμῆς II 2: κοινὸς Ἑρμῆς means "shares in your luck!" See Diogenianus 5.38 (*CPG*, vol. 1, p. 259, lines 1–2); Plutarch, *On the Fact That the Philosopher Ought Most of All to Converse with Leaders* 777d; also in *Sententious Remarks* 8.3.3 (Hult, *Theodore Metochites on Ancient Authors*, p. 86, lines 14–15). The proverb is attested for the first time in Aristotle, *Rhetoric* 1401a21–22.

44.2   *our community*: Metochites refers to his contemporary scholars.

45.3   *shamelessly*: Demetrakos, under ἀνέδην 5 (vol. 1, p. 492); for ἀναίδην as incorrect for ἀνέδην, see Sophocles, under ἀναίδην.

45.4   *To the contrary . . . different anxieties each time*: The author refers back to familiar notions he expressed in his proem, chapter 1.

       as the proverb says: I was unable to identify this proverb. Some proverbs might derive from the vernacular tradition and were presumably never written down.

46.1   *at full speed*: See LSJ, under φέρω B I 2.

46.2   *What cultured product . . . myriad disgusting things*: This is a verbal echo of the final sentence of chapter 1.

46.3   *for such men*: That is, scholars.

47.2   *I myself have experienced . . . of course*: This might be a reference to Philo of Alexandria, *On Dreams* 1.105–7 (Cohn-Wendland, vol. 3, p. 227, line 11 through p. 228, line 5).

47.3   *For the girls and this newborn . . . advantageous for my children*: See Metochites, Poem 2.379–92 (Polemis, *Carmina*, 65).

48.2   *impossible for those who are distressed to practice geometry*: A proverb found in a slightly different form in Karathanasis, no. 111, p. 64, and Strömberg, 59. The same idea features in *Scholia in Aristotle's Nicomachean Ethics* 1152b34 (Cramer, p. 219, lines 13–15).

48.3   *to his beloved fatherland*: Φίλην ἐς πατρίδα γαῖαν is a Homeric echo; see *Iliad* 5.687.
        muzzle: See *LbG*, under κημαγωγέω. This is a *hapax legomenon*.
        According to Cydias . . . beating a retreat: See Plato, *Charmides* 155d. Cydias was a love poet popular in Athens, mentioned in Plato but also in Plutarch's *On the Face in the Moon* 931e.

48.4   *excess*: See LSJ, under περίειμι A III 2.

49.2   *[. . .] not unpleasant*: There is a gap of uncertain length in the manuscript.

50.4   *shared Hermes*: See above, chapter 44.1.

51.4   *their persistence on . . . as he says*: With reference to Euripides and a well-known fragment from *Likymnios* (fragment 473; Kannicht, *TrGF*, vol. 5, p. 520). The two adjectives referring to the feminine noun ἀργία (laziness) are neuter (φαῦλον, ἄκομψον). This is a matter of stylistic preference; see Homer, *Iliad* 2.204: "οὐκ ἀγαθὸν πολυκοιρανίη."

51.5   *from the Dorian mode to the Lydian*: This seems to be an expression dear to Metochites; see, for example, *Sententious Remarks* 116 (Müller and Kiessling, *Miscellanea philosophica*, p. 795, lines 14–15). The expression is proverbial; see Apostolius, *Proverbs* 3.61 (*CPG*, vol. 2, p. 302, lines 1–2), although the proverb contrasts the Dorian to the Phrygian rather than the Lydian mode. The variation makes sense, since both the Phrygian and the

Lydian modes were considered relaxed and cheerful, as opposed to the Dorian, which was tense and solemn.

52.3   *tosses the sea of Aegina*: The same proverb appears once more in Metochites's *Sententious Remarks* 60.3.2 (Hult, *Theodore Metochites on the Human Condition*, p. 214, line 22).

Perseus captivated the Gorgon: This proverb is used of someone who achieves something extremely brave. See Apostolius, *Proverbs* 5.58 (*CPG*, vol. 2, p. 349, line 5 through p. 350, line 26).

the person who until very . . . as the poem says: This is a fragment of a lost tragedy (fragment 391; Snell and Kannicht, *TrGF*, vol. 2, p. 118) preserved in Plutarch's *Life of Lucullus* 1.5 and *On God's Slowness to Punish* 554f. This is another indication of Metochites's close acquaintance with Plutarch's corpus.

53.1   *they think that fortune is . . . nature merely consents to it*: A similar idea is expressed in Philo, *Embassy to Gaius* 1 (Cohn-Wendland, vol. 6, p. 155, lines 4–9).

present, future, and past events: Homer, *Iliad* 1.70; also quoted, for example, by Plutarch in *On the E at Delphi* 387b.

archery to the Scythians: Plutarch, *Symposium of the Seven Sages* 163f.

most wicked [. . .]: There is a gap in the manuscript. Two folios are likely missing.

54.2   *we must perforce cleave . . . we already discussed*: See above, chapters 43.1 and 46.3.

55.2   *For what we generally call fate . . . be it good or bad*: The notion of the instability of fortune and the stability of virtue is common in the genres of the diatribe and the protreptic.

The truly wise man is the one who . . . the ill turns of fate: See Metochites, Poem 2.428–29 (Polemis, *Carmina,* 67). The language is Homeric; compare *Iliad* 1.576 and *Odyssey* 18.403–4.

but is instead fully aware . . . from truly gold to bronze: See *Iliad* 6.236.

that after health comes sickness . . . crushed like a slave: This is the Stoic premeditation of future calamities, a philosophical technique that sensitizes a person to possible calamities so as to help him withstand them when they come.

The truly wise man also knows . . . the performance and this stage: Epictetus, *Manual* 17. The imagery originates with Plato.

exactly as with backgammon: The simile of life as a game of backgammon is a conventional *topos* in classical literature, for example, Stobaios, *Anthology* 4.56.39 (often attributed to Socrates).

55.3   *unpleasant* [. . .]: A gap of about four folios.

58.2   *if after such behavior, he returns home again*: That is, to his old manners.

        recover: LSJ, under ἀναφέρω A II 7 b.

58.3   *Likewise, when Diogenes the Cynic . . . saw a noble youth*: The incident is recorded by Plutarch in his *On Progress in Virtue* 82c–d. According to *Lives of the Ten Orators* 847f (attributed to Plutarch), and Diogenes Laertius, *Lives of Eminent Philosophers* 6.2.34, the young man referred to was the orator Demosthenes.

59.1   *that you increase in viciousness*: LSJ, under προέρχομαι A 4.

59.2   *to move on in absolute order, as the proverb states*: Aelius Aristides, *Against Plato, In Defence of the Four (Statesmen)* (Dindorf, vol. 2, p. 159, lines 20–21; most recently edited by Lenz-Behr, vol. 1, pt. 2, p. 296, lines 2–3). The proverb also appears above, in chapter 8.1.

60.4   *Life is also a military campaign*: On the metaphor of life as military service, see Epictetus, *Discourses* 3.24.31–35, also 1.9.24 and 1.16.20.

60.6   *foolishly*: LSJ, under ἁπλῶς A II 5.

61.1   *I would prefer this and it would be much better for me*: Homer, *Iliad* 3.41, *Odyssey* 11.358, 20.316.

62.1   *to place my risk on the Carian mercenary*: "On the Carian mercenary" means "on a worthless corpse." The meaning of the proverb is to decline to fight your own battles and have someone expendable do it for you. Apostolius, *Proverbs* 7.25 (*CPG*, vol. 2, p. 401, lines 11–12); see Plato, *Laches* 187b.

63.2   *it is seated alone on the stern of the city*: Aeschylus, *Seven Against Thebes* 2; also in 760.

        step over the threshold: Apostolius, *Proverbs* 17.62 (*CPG*, vol. 2, p. 702, lines 1–7).

shoot wide of the mark: See Xenophon, *Cyropaedia* 1.6.29; Homer, *Odyssey* 11.344.

the king's heart and soul were pleased: The language is Homeric; see *Iliad* 1.24.

looked upon this with delight: Homer, *Iliad*, 19.18–19, *Odyssey* 8.171.

63.3   *fettered*: Plato, *Meno* 97d.

would remain: Plato, *Meno* 97d. In this passage, Socrates purportedly embraces the old legend according to which Daedalus, a half mythical person considered the first sculptor, contrived a wonderful mechanism by means of which his statues could move their eyes and walk about. See Plato, *Euthyphro* 11c. Metochites uses the same story in *Sententious Remarks* 2.2.3 (Hult, *Theodore Metochites on Ancient Authors*, p. 28, lines 24–29).

Plato says that this can in fact be the product of knowledge alone: Plato, *Meno* 97d–98a.

65.1   *In the case of such men too*: The reference is to people who do not realize their psychic weakness and lack of culture.

there is no lesson or teacher: That is, no one can teach them anything.

65.2   *to offer gold and silver to swine, as the proverb says*: The proverb occurs somewhat differently in Matthew 7:6: "Do not waste what is holy on people who are unholy; do not cast your pearls before swine! They will trample the pearls, then turn and attack you."

65.3   *This is what someone else claimed in the past*: Diogenes in Plutarch, *On Listening to Poetry* 21f and *On How to Profit from Your Enemies* 88b.

If you happen to be well-off outwardly too: This is a peculiar expression; I take ἔξωθεν (outwardly) to refer to the impression one gives about one's material state, as opposed to the inner state described above. See above, chapter 57.1–2, where ἔξωθεν refers to a number of factors the agent cannot determine, as opposed to one's inner state, which is under the agent's control. The distinction is of Stoic origin; see Epictetus, *Discourses* 1.22.10.

embellished: That is, honored.

65.4   *he whom the Muses love is always blessed*: The quotation is not attested anywhere in Sappho's surviving corpus, but it is found in Hesiod's *Theogony* 96–97: "ὁ δ' ὄλβιος, ὅντινα Μοῦσαι / φίλωνται."

65.5   *This could happen also to human beings . . . offering whatever he can in exchange*: The purchase of rhetorical speeches or their production at the behest of elite individuals seems to have been common practice in Byzantium, a manifestation of social status and wealth.

        his own friends: The author refers to the saints; see Psalms 138:17.

Concordance of Chapter Numbers

Dumbarton Oaks	Polemis-Kaltsogianni 2019
1	1
2	2–3
3	4–5
4	6
5	7–8
6	9–11
7	12
8	13
9	14–15
10	16
11.1–3	17
11.4–12.1	18
12.2–3	19
13.1	20
13.2–3	21
13.4	22
14.1	23
14.2–3	24
15.1–2	25
15.3	26

Dumbarton Oaks	Polemis-Kaltsogianni 2019
16	27
17.1–4	28
17.5	29
17.6	30
18.1–2	31
18.3–5	32
19.1	33
19.1–2	34
20.1	35
20.2–4	36
20.5–21.1	37
21.1–2	38
21.3	39
22	40
23.1–2	41
23.3	42
23.4	43
24.1–2	44
24.3	45
25.1–3	46
25.4	47
26	48
27	49
28	50
29	51
30	52
31	53
32.1	54

Dumbarton Oaks	Polemis-Kaltsogianni 2019
32.2	55
33	56
34	57
35	58
36	59
37	60
38	61
39	62
40	63
41	64
42	65
43	66
44	67
45.1–4	68
45.4	69
46	70
47.1–2	71
47.3–5	72
48.1–2	73
48.2–4	74
49.1	75
49.2	76
50	77
51.1–2	78
51.3–7	79
52	80
53	81
54	82

Dumbarton Oaks	Polemis-Kaltsogianni 2019
55.1–3	83
55.3–56.2	84
56.3–4	85
57.1–3	86
57.4–5	87
58.1–3	88
58.3–59.2	89
60.1–2	90
60.3–61.1	91
61.1–2	92
61.3	93
62.1	94
62.2–63.1	95
63.1–2	96
63.2–5	97
64.1–3	98
64.4–5	99
65.1–4	100
65.5–7	101

Bibliography

EDITIONS AND TRANSLATIONS OF *ON MORALS*

Polemis, Ioannis. Θεόδωρος Μετοχίτης· Ἠθικὸς ἢ περὶ παιδείας. Athens, 1995. Rev. ed. Κείμενα Βυζαντινῆς Λογοτεχνίας 1. Athens, 2002.

Polemis, Ioannis, and Eleni Kaltsogianni, eds. *Theodori Metochitae Orationes*. Bibliotheca scriptorum Graecorum et Romanorum Teubneriana. Berlin and Boston, 2019. *On Morals* is on pages 347–429.

EDITIONS OF WORKS BY METOCHITES

Agapitos, Panagiotis, Karin Hult, and Ole L. Smith. *Theodoros Metochites on Philosophic Irony and Greek History: Miscellanea 8 and 93*. Nicosia and Göteborg, 1996.

Bydén, Börje. *Theodore Metochites' Stoicheiosis astronomike and the Study of Natural Philosophy and Mathematics in Early Palaiologan Byzantium*. Studia Graeca et Latina Gothoburgensia 66. Göteborg, 2003.

Drossaart Lulofs, Hendrik J. *Aristotelis de somno et vigilia liber, adiectis veteribus translationibus et Theodori Metochitae commentario*. Leiden, 1943.

Hult, Karin. *Theodore Metochites on Ancient Authors and Philosophy: Semeioseis gnomikai 1–26 & 71*. Göteborg, 2002.

———. *Theodore Metochites on the Human Condition and the Decline of Rome: Semeioseis gnomikai 27–60*. Göteborg, 2016.

Müller, Christian G., and Theophilus Kiessling. *Theodori Metochitae miscellanea philosophica et historica*. Leipzig, 1821.

Paschos, Emmanuel, and Christos Simelidis. *Introduction to Astronomy by Theodore Metochites* (Stoicheiosis astronomike 1.5–30). Hackensack, N.J., 2017.

Polemis, Ioannis. *Theodori Metochitae carmina*. Corpus Christianorum series Graeca 83. Turnhout, 2015.

Ševčenko, Ihor. "Theodore Metochites, the Chora, and the Intellectual Trends of His Time." In *The Kariye Djami: Studies in the Art of the Kariye Djami and Its Intellectual Background,* edited by Paul A. Underwood, vol. 4, 17–91. London, 1975.

Wahlgren, Staffan. *Theodore Metochites' Sententious Notes: Semeioseis gnomikai 61–70 & 72–81.* Göteborg, 2018.

Relevant Studies

Angelov, Dimiter. "The Moral Pieces by Theodore II Laskaris." *Dumbarton Oaks Papers* 65/66 (2011–2012): 237–69.

Bazzani, Marina. "Theodore Metochites, a Byzantine Humanist." *Byzantion* 76 (2006): 32–52.

Beck, Hans-Georg. *Theodoros Metochites: Die Krise des byzantinischen Weltbildes im 14. Jahrhundert.* Munich, 1952.

Constantinidis, Costas N. *Higher Education in Byzantium in the Thirteenth and Early Fourteenth Centuries, 1204–ca. 1310.* Nicosia, 1982.

Cunningham, Mary, Jeffrey Michael Featherstone, and Sophia Georgiopoulou. "Theodore Metochites's Poem to Nikephorus Kallistus Xanthopoulos." *Harvard Ukrainian Studies* 7 (1983): 100–16.

De Andrés, Gregorio. *Catálogo de los códices griegos desaparecidos de la Real Biblioteca de el Escorial.* Escorial, 1968.

de Vries-van der Velden, Eva. *Théodore Métochite: Une réévaluation.* Amsterdam, 1987.

Featherstone, Jeffrey Michael. "Theodore Metochites's *Semeioseis gnomikai*—Personal Encyclopedism." In *Encyclopedic Trends in Byzantium? Proceedings of the International Conference Held in Leuven, 6–8 May 2009,* edited by Peter Van Deun and Caroline Macé, 333–44. Orientalia Lovaniensia analecta 212. Leuven, 2011.

Förstel, Christian. "Metochites and His Books between the Chora and the Renaissance." In *The Kariye Camii Reconsidered/Kariye Camii Yeniden,* edited by Holger A. Klein, Robert Ousterhout, and Brigitte Pitarakis, 241–66. Istanbul, 2011.

Gaul, Niels. "Performative Reading in the Late Byzantine *Theatron.*" In *Reading in the Byzantine Empire and Beyond,* edited by Teresa Shawcross and Ida Toth, 215–33. Cambridge, 2018.

Hinterberger, Martin. "Studien zu Theodoros Metochites." *Jahrbuch der Österreichischen Byzantinistik* 51 (2001): 285–319.

Hult, Karin. "Theodore Metochites as a Literary Critic." In *Interaction and Isolation in Late Byzantine Culture: Papers Read at a Colloquium Held at the Swedish Research Institute in Istanbul, 1–5 December, 1999*, edited by Jan Olof Rosenqvist, 44–56. Transactions of the Swedish Research Institute in Istanbul 13. Istanbul, London, 2004.

Hunger, Herbert. "Der Ἠθικὸς des Theodoros Metochites." In Πεπραγμένα τοῦ Θ´ Διεθνοῦς Βυζαντινολογικοῦ Συνεδρίου (Θεσσαλονίκη 12–19 Ἀπριλίου 1953), vol. 3, 141–58. Athens, 1958.

———. "Theodoros Metochites als Verläufer des Humanismus in Byzanz." *Byzantinische Zeitschrift* 45 (1952): 4–19.

Kontogiannopoulou, Anastasia. Η εσωτερική πολιτική του Ανδρονίκου Β´ Παλαιολόγου (1282–1328): Διοίκηση, οικονομία. Thessalonike, 2004.

Magdalino, Paul. "Theodore Metochites, the Chora, and Constantinople." In *The Kariye Camii Reconsidered/Kariye Camii Yeniden*, edited by Holger Klein, Robert G. Ousterhout, and Brigitte Pitarakis, 169–87. Istanbul, 2011.

Meletiadis, Chares N. Ἡ ἐκπαίδευση στὴν Κωνσταντινούπολη κατὰ τὸν 16° αἰῶνα. Thessalonike, 2000.

Nicol, Donald M. *The Last Centuries of Byzantium, 1261–1453*. London, 1972.

Polemis, Ioannis. "Ἡ ἡδονὴ τῆς θεωρίας τῶν ὄντων στὸν Θεόδωρο Μετοχίτη: Ἐπιδράσεις τοῦ Φίλωνος τοῦ Ἰουδαίου καὶ τοῦ Συνεσίου τοῦ Κυρηναίου στὸν Ἠθικό." *Hellenika* 49 (1999): 245–75.

———. Θεόδωρος Μετοχίτης: Βυζάντιος ἢ Περὶ τῆς βασιλίδος Μεγαλοπόλεως. Thessaloniki, 2013.

Sathas, Konstantinos N. Βιογραφίαι τῶν ἐν τοῖς γράμμασι διαλαμψάντων Ἑλλήνων ἀπὸ τῆς καταλύσεως τῆς βυζαντινῆς αὐτοκρατορίας μέχρι τῆς ἑλληνικῆς ἐθνεγερσίας (1453–1821). Athens, 1868.

Ševčenko, Ihor. "The Decline of Byzantium Seen through the Eyes of Its Intellectuals." *Dumbarton Oaks Papers* 15 (1961): 169–86.

———. *La vie intellectuelle et politique à Byzance sous les premiers Paléologues: Études sur la polémique entre Théodore Métochite et Nicéphore Choumnos*. Brussels, 1962.

———. "The *Logos* on Gregory of Nazianzus by Theodore Metochites." In *Geschichte und Kultur der Palaiologenzeit: Referate des Internationales Sym-*

posions zu Ehren von Herbert Hunger, edited by Werner Seibt, 221–33. Vienna, 1996.

———. "Palaiologan Learning." In *The Oxford History of Byzantium,* edited by Cyril Mango, 284–93. Oxford, 2002.

———. "The Palaiologan Renaissance." In *Renaissances Before the Renaissance,* edited by Warren Treadgold, 144–71. London, 1984.

———. *Society and Intellectual Life in Late Byzantium.* London, 1981.

———. "Society and Intellectual Life in the Fourteenth Century." In *Actes du XIVe Congrès International des Études Byzantines,* edited by Mihai Berza and Eugen Stănescu, vol. 1, 69–92. Bucharest, 1974. Reprinted in Ihor Ševčenko, *Society and Intellectual Life in Late Byzantium.* London, 1981.

———. "Théodore Métochite, *Logos* 10" and "Théodore Métochite, *Poème* 4." In *La Civiltà bizantina dal XII al XV secolo: Aspetti e problemi,* 138–49 and 150–63. Roma, 1982.

———. "Vita: Theodore Metochites, Literary Statesman." *Harvard Magazine* 81, no. 6 (1979): 1270–332.

Ševčenko, Nancy P. "The Portrait of Theodore Metochites at Chora." In *Donation et donateurs dans le monde byzantin: Actes du colloque international de l'Université de Fribourg (13–15 mars 2008),* edited by Jean-Michel Spieser and Elisabeth Yota, 189–205. Paris, 2012.

Smyrlis, Kostis. "Financial Crisis and the Limits of Taxation under Andronikos II Palaiologos (1282–1321)." In *Power and Subversion in Byzantium: Papers from the Forty-Third Spring Symposium of Byzantine Studies, University of Birmingham, March 2010,* edited by Dimiter Angelov and Michael Saxby, 71–82. Farnham, 2013.

Tinnefeld, Franz. "Neue Formen der Antikerezeption bei den Byzantinern der frühen Palaiologenzeit." *International Journal of the Classical Tradition* 1, no. 3 (1995): 19–28.

Verpeaux, Jean. "Le *cursus honorum* de Théodore Métochite." *Revue des études byzantines* 18 (1960): 195–98.

Voudouri, Alexandra. "Representations of Power in the *Byzantios* Oration of Theodore Metochites: Illusions and Realities." *Parekbolai* 3 (2013): 107–30.

Xenophontos, Sophia. "The Byzantine Plutarch: Self-Identity and Model in Theodore Metochites' Essay 71 of the *Semeioseis gnomikai*." In *The Afterlife of Plutarch,* edited by John North and Peter Mack, 23–39. London, 2018.

Index